Adorno and Neoliberalism

Critical Theory and the Critique of Society Series

In a time marked by crises and the rise of right-wing authoritarian populism, **Critical Theory and the Critique of Society** intends to renew the critical theory of capitalist society exemplified by the Frankfurt School and critical Marxism's critiques of social domination, authoritarianism, and social regression by expounding the development of such a notion of critical theory, from its founding thinkers, through its subterranean and parallel strands of development, to its contemporary formulations.

Series editors: **Werner Bonefield**, University of York, UK, and **Chris O'Kane**, John Jay College of Criminal Justice, City University of New York, USA

Editorial Board

Bev Best, Sociology, Concordia University
John Abromeit, History, SUNY, Buffalo State, USA
Samir Gandesha, Humanities, Simon Fraser University
Christian Lotz, Philosophy, Michigan State University
Patrick Murray, Philosophy, Creighton University
José Antonio Zamora Zaragoza, Philosophy, Spain
Dirk Braunstein, Institute of Social Research, Frankfurt
Matthias Rothe, German, University of Minnesota
Marina Vishmidt, Cultural Studies, Goldsmiths University
Verena Erlenbusch, Philosophy, University of Memphis
Elena Louisa Lange, Japanese Studies/Philology and Philosophy, University of Zurich
Marcel Stoetzler, Sociology, University of Bangor
Moishe Postone, History, University of Chicago
Mathias Nilges, Literature, St Xavier University

Available Titles

Right-wing Culture in Contemporary Capitalism, Mathias Nilges

Adorno and Neoliberalism

The Critique of Exchange Society

Charles A. Prusik

BLOOMSBURY ACADEMIC
LONDON • NEW YORK • OXFORD • NEW DELHI • SYDNEY

BLOOMSBURY ACADEMIC
Bloomsbury Publishing Plc
50 Bedford Square, London, WC1B 3DP, UK
1385 Broadway, New York, NY 10018, USA
29 Earlsfort Terrace, Dublin 2, Ireland

BLOOMSBURY, BLOOMSBURY ACADEMIC and the Diana logo are trademarks of
Bloomsbury Publishing Plc

First published in Great Britain 2020
This paperback edition published in 2022

Copyright © Charles A. Prusik, 2020

Charles A. Prusik has asserted his right under the Copyright, Designs and Patents Act,
1988, to be identified as Author of this work.

For legal purposes the Acknowledgments on p. xi constitute an extension
of this copyright page.

Series design by Ben Anslow

All rights reserved. No part of this publication may be reproduced or transmitted
in any form or by any means, electronic or mechanical, including photocopying,
recording, or any information storage or retrieval system, without prior
permission in writing from the publishers.

Bloomsbury Publishing Plc does not have any control over, or responsibility for, any
third-party websites referred to or in this book. All internet addresses given in this
book were correct at the time of going to press. The author and publisher regret any
inconvenience caused if addresses have changed or sites have ceased to exist,
but can accept no responsibility for any such changes.

A catalogue record for this book is available from the British Library.

Library of Congress Cataloging-in-Publication Data

Names: Prusik, Charles A., author.
Title: Adorno and neoliberalism: the critique of exchange society / Charles A. Prusik.
Description: London; New York: Bloomsbury Academic, 2020. |
Series: Critical theory and the critique of society series |
Includes bibliographical references and index. | Summary: "The first book to investigate the relevance of
Theodor W. Adorno's work for theorizing the age of neoliberal capitalism. Through an engagement
with Adorno's critical theory of society, Charles Prusik advances a novel approach to understanding
the origins and development of neoliberalism. Offering a corrective to critics who define neoliberalism
as an economic or political doctrine, Prusik argues that Adorno's dialectical theory of society can provide
the basis for explaining the illusions and forms of domination that structure contemporary life.
Prusik explains the importance of Marx's critique of commodity fetishism in shaping Adorno's
work and focuses on the related concepts of exchange, ideology, and natural history as powerful tools for
grasping the present. Through an engagement with the ideas of neoliberal economic theory, Adorno and
Neoliberalism criticizes the naturalization of capitalist institutions, social relations, ideology, and
cultural forms. Revealing its origins in the crises of the Fordist period, Prusik develops Adorno's analyses
of class, exploitation, monopoly, and reification to situate neoliberal policies as belonging to
the fundamental antagonisms of capitalist society"– Provided by publisher.
Identifiers: LCCN 2020015229 (print) | LCCN 2020015230 (ebook) |
ISBN 9781350103245 (hardback) | ISBN 9781350103238 (ebook) |
ISBN 9781350103252 (epub)
Subjects: LCSH: Adorno, Theodor W., 1903-1969. | Neoliberalism.
Classification: LCC B3199.A34 P78 2020 (print) | LCC B3199.A34 (ebook) | DDC 148–dc23

LC record available at https://lccn.loc.gov/2020015229
LC ebook record available at https://lccn.loc.gov/2020015230

ISBN: HB: 978-1-3501-0324-5
PB: 978-1-3501-9728-2
ePDF: 978-1-3501-0323-8
eBook: 978-1-3501-0325-2

Series: Critical Theory and the Critique of Society Series

Typeset by Deanta Global Publishing Services, Chennai, India

To find out more about our authors and books visit www.bloomsbury.com
and sign up for our newsletters.

Contents

Foreword *Deborah Cook*   vii
Acknowledgments   xi

Introduction   1
    Why Adorno?   2
    Context and Scope   3

1   Exchange Society   9
    Commodity Fetishism   11
    Real Abstraction   24
    Negative Totality   32

2   Neoliberalism and the Class Antagonism   49
    State Capitalism   53
    The Golden Age of Capitalism   57
    Crisis: The End of the Golden Age   63
    The Neoliberal Revolution   68

3   Natural-History and the Critique of Neoliberal Theory   87
    The Idea of Natural-History   88
    Liberalism: Economy as First Nature   91
    Neoliberal Theory and the Economics of Information   95
    Neoliberalism as Second Nature   103

4   Neoliberal Reason: The Domination of Nature   119
    Dialectic of Enlightenment   120
    Sacrifice: The Entwinement of Myth and Enlightenment   122
    The Organic Composition of Humanity   127
    Neoliberal Reason: Computation, Mechanization, and Mind   129
    The Domination of Nature   133

5   Neoliberal Culture   141
    The Culture Industry: Mass Culture and the Commodity-Form   142
    The Neoliberal Culture Industry   144

>   Flexible Standardization 146
>   Precarity and Crisis 156

Afterword 165

Bibliography 171
Further Sources 174
Index 183

Foreword

Theodor W. Adorno is known for his excoriating critique of late, or monopoly, capitalism. He cogently argued that economic conditions under late capitalism affect not just our life opportunities and life chances but how we interact with others, our self-understanding, psychological states, and even our thought processes. Yet Adorno also recognized, with Karl Marx, that capitalism constantly changes. In fact, it may seem that the only thing that does remain the same under capitalism is ceaseless change. Given the changes in the economy that occurred since Adorno's death in 1969, Charles A. Prusik updates Adorno's critique of late capitalism to make sense of the neoliberal age of austerity. In so doing, however, he reveals that capitalism has only changed in order to remain the same.

Prusik patiently exposes the foundations of capitalism in exchange relations, the commodity-form and commodity fetishism. Indeed, Adorno also followed Marx when he insisted that capitalism depends for its survival on the creation of surplus-value. For Marx, capitalists invariably profit at the expense of the workers they exploit, and Adorno argued that this situation did not change when the liberal (and more highly competitive) phase of capitalism that Marx analyzed was superseded by monopoly conditions. Like liberal capitalism, late capitalist society is a negative totality because it too is based on exploitative and antagonistic class relations. Yet Prusik argues that the neoliberal economic order is itself a negative totality. Under neoliberalism, exploitation only increased owing to globalization and the financialization of economic activity.

Prusik often takes critics of neoliberalism to task for their failure to see that neoliberalism is a variant of monopoly capitalism. Plus ça change, plus c'est la même chose. Although it must constantly overcome crises of its own making, capitalism—even and especially in its neoliberal phase—continues to pit an ever-decreasing number of owners of the means of production against an evergrowing number of workers in order to generate profit. Neoliberal society is riven with the same class relations that plagued its predecessors. Along with his discussion of class antagonisms under neoliberalism, however, Prusik argues that neoliberalism's financialization of activity, and its attempts to discipline workers by obliging them to work in a volatile labor market, represents a response to the crisis of profitability that emerged under the Keynesian-Fordist system. Under neoliberalism, moreover, the state by no means takes a back seat. Allied with the capitalist class, the neoliberal state initiated a ferocious assault on labor that may well end by destroying what it needs to survive.

Capitalism always lurches from one crisis to the next, and Adorno was well aware that late capitalism would itself be overtaken by crisis tendencies. Although the crisis that would lead to the emergence of neoliberalism only occurred toward the end of Adorno's life, Prusik claims that Adorno foresaw certain elements of it, including the inflationary collapse that accompanied the dirigiste regulations of the Keynesian-Fordist system. Furthermore, the breakdown of Bretton Woods added balance of payment deficits to what became a toxic mix. In their unceasing drive to increase profit (which overaccumulation and overproduction under Keynesianism threatened), capitalists began to replace workers with machinery, leading to a diminution in the value of the labor upon which the creation of surplus-value depends. In short, the neoliberal answer to the crisis that was unleashed by Keynesianism effectively undermined the source of profit itself.

Under these perilous conditions, the possibility of a violent backlash by workers had to be eliminated. If the welfare state compromise was, on Adorno's view, one way of containing conflict (especially after the 1929 crash), neoliberalism brought out the big guns. Milton Friedman's monetarist policies (which were subsequently abandoned) amounted to a state assault on unions and workers that was designed to ensure that the balance of power between capitalists and workers would remain on the side of the capitalists. Resistance would be futile; revolt was contained and workers disciplined. Indeed, Prusik also shows why various forms of resistance to the neoliberal project have often fallen far short of their mark.

Far from displacing monopoly capitalism, neoliberalism simply reconstituted it through financialization, the manipulation of market prices, and new tax laws. This also helps to explain why Adorno's account of late capitalism remains relevant. To be sure, the neoliberalism of Friedrich Hayek gave monopoly capitalism a new ideological gloss, but Prusik contends that this gloss can be interpreted through the lens of Adorno's idea of natural history. With Hayek, who borrowed ideas from cybernetics, the economy morphs into an autonomous and self-regulating mechanism—a kind of natural growth with its own "reasons" and its own "laws"—reasons and laws which no individual can know but to which all must submit. Indeed, this conception of the market not only turns the market into a kind of second nature but makes visible one of neoliberalism's major fault lines: its failure to see that value is generated in relations between people, not in relations between things.

Given that the economy now masks itself as a force of nature in its own right, Prusik contends that neoliberalism is not primarily an economic project. Instead, it is political project that "constructs the necessary social blindness in which the economy can appear as fate." This social blindness helps to explain why many cannot even envisage an alterative to capitalism. Citing *Dialectic of Enlightenment* and its idea of a logic of sacrifice, Prusik also reveals the stakes in the neoliberal gambit: neoliberalism is prepared to sacrifice our future by harnessing it to the valorization of capital. Under neoliberalism, moreover, living human labor becomes superfluous. So too does the environment. Borrowing from our future to sustain itself in the present, neoliberalism represents a self-defeating attempt to save capitalism by killing off the source of value. As Adorno was well aware, the price for staying alive under capitalism is death.

Prusik sees neoliberalism as a defensive reaction to capitalism's objective limits. But he also shows how social conditioning and social integration under neoliberalism blind us to the threats that neoliberalism poses to our survival. Making use of Adorno's critique of the culture industry, Prusik believes that this critique too remains relevant because what counts as culture today (in the form of the internet, social media, and the like) remains an important economic sector in its own right. Moreover, digital culture is as incapacitating as the culture industry once was. Under neoliberalism, individuals are socialized as they are integrated into a network of relations, commodity exchanges, and circuits of information. Yet these networks, exchanges, and circuits reflect the very crisis of value to which neoliberalism is failing adequately to respond. Encouraged to adopt an entrepreneurial spirit and to see themselves as human capital, individuals are, as Prusik puts it, socialized to treat their poverty management as entrepreneurial freedom.

This is not a pretty picture: the future of life on this planet is now on sale to the lowest bidder. So what is to be done? Prusik does not evade this question. This book ends with an account of the rise of populism, authoritarianism, and neofascism as responses to the problems—including austerity, debt, unemployment, and underemployment—that neoliberalism has caused. Indeed, Prusik claims that the inability of critics of neoliberalism to understand the economic conditions that sustain it has helped to make effective resistance to neoliberalism problematic. To be sure, possibilities for resistance remain. However, as Adorno constantly emphasized, resistance will only be effective if we understand in detail and in depth just what it is that we are resisting. Prusik makes a valiant effort to underscore the dangers that neoliberalism poses to our future and to the future of this planet even as he gives us tools for resistance by exploring the origins, nature, and trajectory of the neoliberal calamity.

Deborah Cook
The University of Windsor

Acknowledgments

I have accrued too many debts throughout the course of writing this book to possibly repay. Above all, I must thank the generous support and editorial guidance of Werner Bonefeld and Chris O'Kane. I thank them for their assistance and thoughtful consideration. Without their careful review of my work, this book would not have been possible. Many thanks to Jade Grogan, Lucy Russell, Liza Thompson, and all the editors at Bloomsbury who brought this project to completion. Insofar as this manuscript is the result of my dissertation project (as well as countless repudiations of that older text), I must also thank my thesis director, Yannik Thiem, whose supervision of my work made possible my progress as a critical theorist. Additionally, Walter Brogan and Gabriel Rockhill each provided invaluable assistance throughout many stages of this project. I thank my committee for their patience and support.

There are too many friends and colleagues to thank for their thoughtful remarks and pointed disagreements. I must acknowledge all of my colleagues at the Philosophy Department at Villanova University, especially Sarah Vitale and Sean Bray, whose extensive critical feedback significantly contributed to the development of this project. Alexi Kukuljevic similarly has made his mark on this text; I thank him for his discerning capacities and friendship. I also thank Trish Grosse, Dave Mesing, Charlie Strong, Daniel Cunningham, Amanda Holmes, Laura McMahon, Jeff Shusterich, and all friends and colleagues at Villanova who have tolerated my externalizations over the years.

This project has also enjoyed the support of a number of institutional contexts and conferences. In particular, I thank the contributors and organizers of the Ninth International Critical Theory Conference at the John Felice Rome Center of Loyola University Chicago. Additionally, I thank John Holloway and the organizers of the "Critical Theory: 50 Years After Adorno," conference at the Benemérita Universidad Autónoma de Puebla, Mexico, and all participants for responses to my work. Spirited conversations with Fabian Arzuaga, Marcel Stoetzler, and countless other critical theorists of society have all made impressions on me. Additionally, I must thank the generous support and kindness of Deborah Cook, Robert Hullot-Kentor, Martin Jay, Amy Allen, and Philip Mirowski.

Finally, I thank my parents and two sisters for their infinite patience, comraderie, and love. This book was written in the belief that the world can be better. I could not have preserved this conviction without their indelible generosity and strength.

Introduction

> "Mankind is tending more and more to regulate the whole of its social life, although it has never attempted to create a second nature."
> –Karl Mannheim, *Man and Society in an Age of Reconstruction* (1940)

Neoliberalism lives through its crises. In the aftermath of the financial crisis of 2008, the neoliberal order has unfolded as a sequence of political, economic, and social crises without any apparent solution on the horizon. The succeeding years of the "Great Recession" have been characterized by austerity policies, bailouts, and political conflict. Manifesting in inequality, austerity, and sovereign debt crises, the volatility of global capitalism is making itself felt with increasing frequency. The recent shift to authoritarian and fascist politics indexes the antagonistic character of the present. Moreover, the growing threat of ecological collapse signals to the likely displacement of human beings. How can critical theorists make sense of these developments? The interlocking crises of economy, politics, and ecology, I argue, are products of the capitalist form of wealth.

This book is intended as a contribution to the growing literature in critical theory on neoliberalism. I argue that a return to the work of Theodor W. Adorno can illuminate forms of social domination that operate today. As Werner Bonefeld suggests, Adorno's critical theory is a "practice that fights barbarism."[1] In order to comprehend the mediations that connect human relations of exploitation to the impersonal rule of money, we need a theory that can articulate the forms of domination we constitute. Adorno's critical theory conceives of society as process of mediation that is "antagonistic in itself."[2] By identifying domination with specific individuals, institutions, or economic policies, we lose sight of the essential relations of the whole. Adorno's dialectical criticism targets the capitalistically arranged relations of society, which manifest in the abstract form of economic things. His concept of "exchange society" (*Tauschgesellschaft*) can provide the basis for deciphering the impersonal relations of economic domination today that preponderate over life. In what follows I argue that Adorno's theory can be developed as a critical framework for resisting today's global neoliberal order.

Unfortunately, neoliberalism is an elusive object of analysis. The term "neoliberalism" has acquired such a surfeit of meanings in the still-growing literature that skeptics now doubt its existence.[3] Invariably, the term neoliberalism has been used to refer to the globalized capitalism that emerged after the breakdown of the postwar Fordist-Keynesian phase of state-managed capitalism, or to the body of "free market" ideas that have triumphed in recent decades.[4] Alternatively, critical theorists now approach neoliberalism as a political project, or as a form of "political rationality" that has marketized every aspect of life.[5] For critical theorists who have inherited Michel Foucault's analysis in his *Birth of Biopolitics* lectures (1978–79), neoliberalism is defined as a form of "governmentality" that regulates life by market principles.[6] Karl Polanyi's anthropological approach, moreover, has proven to be a productive framework for a number of theorists who engage his notion of "fictitious commodities" and who have analyzed the crises of finance with reference to his understanding of the "double movement" of history.[7] To traditional Marxists, neoliberalism is either regarded as the contrivance of liberal critics of privatization, or reduced to a class project.[8] For many Marxists, neoliberalism represents a distinct "accumulation regime" in the history of capitalism, a global system that has weakened the power of states, shifting to a multinational structure of accumulation.[9]

Why Adorno?

This book tries to overcome a number of limits I see in these approaches. However, given that Adorno developed his work in the context of the Fordist-Keynesian period of capitalism, one might reasonably doubt the relevance of his framework for understanding today's global, neoliberal brand of capitalism. If one submits his work to a quick evaluation, one could only be left with the impression that his critical theory was a sophisticated, but ultimately pessimistic work of cultural criticism.[10] As commentator and translator Robert Hullot-Kentor remarked, Adorno's concepts "now stand mute in sight of the world."[11] Indeed, concepts like "contradiction," "reification," and "totality" seem to have lost their explanatory power. Resigned in the face of the "web of blindness," Adorno's thought appears to be quarantined from any possible practical engagement with today's world.[12] Despite this judgment, however, I maintain that his dialectical criticism continues to be a powerful tool for deciphering forms of domination in the present. There is no shortage of commentaries that have identified the failures of neoliberal economic policy and its injustices, and the limits of neoliberalism's "free market" ideology have been routinely condemned. What is needed, however, is a theory of the social constitution of neoliberalism, of its fundamental relations that manifest in the form of economic abstractions. Rather than identifying neoliberalism as a unique phase of accumulation, I argue that Adorno's dialectical understanding of history as the unity "of continuity and discontinuity" is better suited to theorize the emergence of new forms, insofar as they are manifestations of the essential relations of capitalism.[13] Adorno's critical theory demystifies the appearance of objective and natural economic forms by conceptualizing their origins. His dialectical criticism deciphers the abstractions that rule over us by returning them to their genesis in practice. Negative dialectics is a conceptual practice that resists the naturalized appearance of economic objectivities and the class-divided form of capitalist wealth.

Context and Scope

This book advances the claim that Adorno's critical theory belongs to the tradition of Marx's "critique of political economy."[14] According to many commentators, the critical theory of Max Horkheimer, Theodor Adorno, Friedrich Pollock, Herbert Marcuse--and other contributors to the Institute for Social Research--represents a fundamental rejection of Marx's critique of political economy.[15] This impression is mistaken. As I detail in Chapter 1, Adorno's critical theory is grounded in Marx's critique of political economy, particularly the theory of "commodity fetishism." As Dirk Braunstein has pointed out, Adorno's work was a decisive reference point for the so-called "New Marx Reading" in Germany in the 1960s, which was further developed by Hans-Georg Backhaus, Helmut Reichelt, and later Moishe Postone.[16] The new reading was an important resource for critical theory, freeing the critique of capitalism from orthodox Marxism, shifting analysis to the critique of the *social form* of value.[17] In the following I take up aspects of Adorno's contribution to the new reading, particularly his concept of "exchange society." Adorno engages Marx's analysis of the "commodity-form" to articulate a concept of society that mediates life through the act of commodity exchange. Society, according to Adorno, is a "subjective-objective" process of mediation that "extends nature in a heteronomous manner."[18] In exchange society, social reproduction resembles natural necessity; the abstract and impersonal autonomy of capital appears to us, as Adorno puts it, as a context of "second nature." His critical theory articulates a model of society that mediates individuals through the indirect connections of commodity exchange, integrating them to the universal imperatives of capital accumulation. I argue that this approach to critical theory can be developed to comprehend neoliberalism, because capitalism reproduces itself today through an increasingly abstract, integrated, and impersonal network of commodity exchanges that submits life to the constraints of accumulation.

In Chapter 1, "Exchange Society," I delineate the fundamental concepts and categories of Adorno's critical theory and establish the centrality of Marx's critique of commodity fetishism to his work. In addition to "exchange-value," "fetishism," and "real abstraction," the chapter argues that Adorno's concept of society as a "negative totality" can be mobilized to grasp neoliberalism's abstract and autonomous rule. By detailing Adorno's specific articulation of the Marxist critique of exchange-value, commodity fetishism, and reification, the chapter establishes the necessary conceptual tools for grasping the mediations of the present. The chapter turns to Adorno's engagements with economist Alfred Sohn-Rethel, whose theory of "real abstraction" provided the basis for Adorno's dialectical critique of epistemology, culminating in the notion of the "identity principle." The chapter organizes this constellation of concepts in Adorno's thought to argue that neoliberalism is an "abstractly veiled" totality that mediates disparate moments through the synthetic connections of exchange.

In Chapter 2, "Neoliberalism and the Class Antagonism," I address the problem of the historical periodization of neoliberalism, as well as the question of crisis. Against the view that neoliberalism represents a distinct phase of accumulation, the chapter argues that the origins of neoliberalism can be located in previous contradictions belonging to the Keynesian-Fordist period of state-managed capitalism. By developing Adorno's dialectical framework of "static and dynamic" categories in sociology, I argue that capitalist development is a dual-sided process of transformation and reconstitution. The chapter focuses on Adorno's understanding of the antagonistic class divisions in capitalism, which he identifies as the essential foundation of the totality, an essential disunity that persists through its changes. By extending his analyses and engagements with the "state capitalism debate" in the Institute for Social Research, as well as his theory of monopoly, class integration, and administration, I argue that neoliberalism can be understood in its continuity with the Fordist-Keynesian period, particularly insofar as it has consolidated the concentration of monopoly capital.

In Chapter 3, "Natural-History and the Critique of Neoliberal Theory," I develop Adorno's dialectical framework of natural-history to criticize ideological concepts in neoliberal economics.[19] Adorno's dialectical conceptualization of natural-history targets the production of a context of "second nature," allowing economic ideas and institutions to appear as forms of natural necessity. Tracking developments in political economy, neoclassical economics, and neoliberal theory, the chapter deciphers economic laws as the mystifications of the capitalist object. I argue that Adorno's critique of economics, sociology, and positivism can be used to demystify contemporary economic doctrines. The chapter turns to the development of a neoliberal theory of an "economy of information," particularly in the work of Friedrich von Hayek. Through a critical encounter with an array of free market ideas, I argue that neoliberalism has contributed to the "semblance" of economy as natural necessity, constraining human practices and institutions within an objective logic of fate.

Chapter 4, "Neoliberal Reason," continues the critique of natural-history by adopting Horkheimer and Adorno's anthropological perspective in their *Dialectic of Enlightenment* (1947). The chapter takes up Horkheimer and Adorno's critique of instrumental reason to conceptualize processes of domination in the present, particularly the domination of nature. I address Horkheimer and Adorno's articulation of the concept of reason as a process of civilization, focusing on their category of "sacrifice" as the key to resisting the reduction of thinking to instrumental reason. The chapter returns to this dialectical framework to articulate the instrumentalization of reason by an economic logic, particularly as it relates to the growing crises of ecology. Through engagements with the "computational theory of mind," the chapter relates dominant models of cognition to their social genesis in capitalist relations. By reducing reason to an instrument of economic calculation, I argue, neoliberalism has seriously undermined our ability to counter the imminent threats of climate change. Insofar as the rising threats of ecological collapse are now being submitted to markets, neoliberalism has extended the logic of sacrifice Horkheimer and Adorno identified, extending social domination by reducing life to mere self-preservation.

In Chapter 5, "Neoliberal Culture," I return to Horkheimer and Adorno's concept of the "culture industry" to explain patterns of neoliberal socialization in contemporary culture and work. By interpreting forms of socialization that predominate in the contemporary, digitally mediated world of the internet through the lens of Horkheimer and Adorno's critique of mass culture, the chapter explains the production of subjects. I point to the relevance of Horkheimer and Adorno's concept of the culture industry, emphasizing the persistence of culture's determination by commodity fetishism. By theorizing dominant cultural forms of "networked" mediation in terms of their genesis in capitalist relations, I argue that the constitution of the psychic life of subjects is conditioned by the autonomous and impersonal forms of domination that are immanent to the capitalist totality. The chapter details developments in the 1960s and 1970s that transformed the mediations of work and culture, particularly by regulating labor through new computer and information technologies.

In addition to reproducing the social totality, neoliberal capitalism has significantly damaged the potentials for freedom. The ongoing crises of labor and ecology have generated an age of objective unfreedom for "maimed" individuals, who are increasingly turning to authoritarian movements and leaders. For many critics, resistance to neoliberalism has meant opposing its inequality, or, alternatively, rejecting its market fundamentalism. This approach, I argue, is inadequate for grasping the fundamental forms of domination, which belong to the relations of the capitalist mode of production as a whole. Criticism of neoliberalism, therefore, should not simply reject the unequal distribution of capitalist wealth but, rather, should overcome the form of society that produces wealth through the exploitation of labor. Adorno's work, I hope to show, can help us begin to imagine an alternative future that would not have to sacrifice freedom to economic necessity. His work points to a society of human purposes, of individuals reconciled in their differences. It is a work that asks: What does it mean to resist the closure of the world that is ruled by abstractions?

Notes

1 Werner Bonefeld, *Critical Theory and the Critique of Political Economy: On Subversion and Negative Reason* (London: Bloomsbury, 2014), 2.
2 Theodor W. Adorno, *Negative Dialectics,* trans. E. B. Ashton (London: Routledge, 2004), 214.
3 For example, see Colin Talbot, "The Myth of Neoliberalism," *Public Interest* (August 31, 2016).
4 For an analysis that approaches neoliberalism as a phase of capitalism, see Gérard Duménil and Dominique Lévy's *The Crisis of Neoliberalism* (Oxford: Oxford University Press, 2013). For a critique of neoliberalism that focuses on the dissemination of free market concepts by the Mont Pelerin Society and the neoliberal "thought collective," see Philip Mirowski's *Never Let a Serious Crisis Go to Waste: How Neoliberalism Survived the Financial Meltdown* (London: Verso, 2013).
5 For example, see Jamie Peck's *The Construction of Neoliberal Reason* (Oxford: Oxford University Press, 2010).

6 Michel Foucault, *Birth of Biopolitics: Lectures at the College de France,* trans. Graham Burchell (London: Palgrave Macmillan, 2008). For a recent study that adopts Foucault's approach to neoliberal governance, see Wendy Brown's *Undoing the Demos: Neoliberalism's Stealth Revolution* (New York: Zone Books, 2015).

7 For a Polanyian analysis of neoliberalism, see Nancy Fraser's "A Triple Movement? Parsing the Politics of Crisis After Polanyi," *Beyond Neoliberalism: Approaches to Social Inequality and Difference,* ed. M. Burchardt and G. Kirn (London: Palgrave Macmillan, 2017), 29–43.

8 See for example, David Harvey's *A Brief History of Neoliberalism* (Oxford: Oxford University Press, 2007).

9 See Moishe Postone, "Theorizing the Contemporary World: Robert Brenner, Giovanni Arrighi, David Harvey," in *Political Economy and Global Capitalism: The 21st Century, Present and Future,* ed. Robert Albritton, Bob Jessop, and Richard Westra (London: Anthem Press, 2007), 2.

10 As Frederic Vandenberghe puts it, "Adorno's work was a superb failure." Vandenberghe, *A Philosophical History of German Sociology* (London: Routledge, 2009), 205.

11 Robert Hullot-Kentor, "The Exact Sense in Which the Culture Industry No Longer Exists," *Cultural Critique,* no. 70 (Fall 2008): 137.

12 Adorno, *Negative Dialectics,* 406. Translation modified.

13 Theodor W. Adorno, *History and Freedom: Lectures 1964-1965,* trans. Rodney Livingstone (Cambridge: Polity, 2006), 92.

14 For background and discussion, see Bonefeld, *Critical Theory,* 3.

15 For a reappraisal of this reception, see Chris O'Kane's "Introduction to 'Theodor W. Adorno on Marx and the Basic Concepts of Sociological Theory. From a Seminar Transcript in the Summer Semester of 1962,'" *Historical Materialism,* 24, no. 1 (2018): 1–17.

16 See Dirk Braunstein's detailed analysis of Adorno's Marxism, *Adornos Kritik der politischen Ökonomie* (Bielefeld: Transcript Verlag, 2011).

17 For background and discussion regarding Adorno's role in the "New Marx Reading," consult Riccardo Bellofiore and Tommaso Redolfi Riva, "The New Marx-Lektüre: Putting the Critique of Political Economy Back into the Critique of Society," in *Radical Philosophy,* 189 (January/February 2015): 24–36.

18 Ibid., 25.

19 An earlier version of this chapter was originally published as "Economics as Natural-History: Adorno and the Critique of Neoliberalism," *Architecture and Culture,* 5, no. 2 (July 2017): 165–74, as well as "Neoliberalism: Critical Theory as Natural-History," *The SAGE Handbook of Frankfurt School Critical Theory,* ed. Beverley Best, Werner Bonefeld, and Chris O'Kane, 3 vols. (London: Sage, 2018): 1601–14.

1

Exchange Society

Neoliberalism is unfolding through a contradictory dynamic. This contradiction can be understood as an ongoing process of mediation, characterized by the integration of private individuals into networks of global capitalist markets. Neoliberalism establishes indirect networks of dependency between individuals through financial institutions and speculative capital flows. These networks of dependency are highly sensitive to the volatility of the world market. When an individual in the United States makes a payment on debt, for example, financial institutions speculate on the future value of the interest on an international scale. Financialization has established complex instruments for capital accumulation that has tied seemingly disconnected individuals to the interconnected rule of markets. The financial crisis of 2007–08 revealed the capacity for a systemic crash of the world economy. Despite this global, impersonal form of objective dependency, individuals in neoliberalism experience their membership in society through increasingly atomistic, self-interested modes of identity. As many commentators have indicated, neoliberalism induces individuals to manage every aspect of life according to an entrepreneurial metric of investment, self-discipline, and competition.[1] Today's social relations are mediated and impersonal, and yet individuals experience their mediation through its absence—that is, as isolated individuals. How can critical theory grasp this apparently contradictory logic?

This chapter argues that a return to Adorno's critical theory of society as a "negative totality" can be mobilized to develop a framework for grasping the impersonal, abstract, and contradictory forms of domination in the neoliberal present. Understood as a critical theory of society that develops Marx's critique of political economy and the fetishism of the commodity, Adorno's thought can explain the social constitution of individuals by objective economic imperatives.[2] Specifically, by developing Adorno's critique of commodity fetishism, I argue that the impersonal, mediated, and abstract character of neoliberalism's domination of the individual can be illuminated by conceptualizing society's structuring relations. Moreover, Adorno's Marxist critique of commodity fetishism, exchange, and socialization by the negative totality can provide the basis for an understanding of how subjects are dominated by economic abstractions, and why subjectivity itself functions as a necessary moment in the reproduction of today's neoliberal world. Before I can substantiate this claim I must first situate Adorno's work in relation to Marx's critique of political economy in general, and to Marx's critique of commodity fetishism in particular. I argue that neoliberalism's contradictory logic can begin to be deciphered through a reconstitution of the following concepts: (1) commodity fetishism, (2) real abstraction, (3) society as a negative totality.

Adorno's theory of late capitalism advances a dialectical theory of society as a process of ongoing interdependence between subjects that reproduce itself automatically through commodity exchange. Throughout his work, Adorno invariably refers to late capitalist society as "exchange society" (*Tauschgesellschaft*), "commodity society," or the rule of the "exchange principle."[3] In late capitalism, the institutions of politics, culture, and the forces of industrial production are all mediated by exchange. For Adorno, exchange is "the key to society" because it is the process that makes society a "social entity" by binding together individuals into a network of commodity relations.[4] Adorno thus understands the exchange relation as the "essence of socialization" in capitalism.[5] "The domination of men over men," Adorno insists, "is realized through the reduction of men to agents and bearers of commodity exchange."[6] Exchange, he claims, is not only an economic transaction between individuals but an "all-round mediator" that constitutes society as a universal system.[7]

Society, Adorno insists, is no longer intelligible: "Only the law of its becoming independent is intelligible."[8] This autonomous independence of the social whole is the law of exchange—the universal synthesis that regulates the life of individuals. As Bellofiore and Riva indicate, for Adorno "exchange is the synthetic principle that immanently determines the connection of every social fact," as well as the principle of mediation "that guarantees the reproduction of society through a process of abstraction."[9] In addition to integrating individuals into objective, impersonal economic relations, exchange forms the thinking, behavior, and attitudes of individuals according to the imperatives of capital accumulation. Connecting his theory of exchange society to Marx's theory of the "law of value," Adorno suggests that it is through the process of exchange that "society maintains itself," and "continues to reproduce itself despite all the catastrophes that may eventuate."[10] By expanding Marx's theory of commodity fetishism to the forms of thinking that predominate within late capitalism,

Adorno's critical theory explains how and why individuals constitute the very social relations that dominate them.

Commodity Fetishism

Following Marx's critique of political economy, Adorno's theory of society recovers the human relations and practices that appear in the form of economic things. Adorno's negative dialectics is not an economic theory of society; his critical theory does not purport to uncover the "truth" of society in the form of immutable, economic laws.[11] On the contrary, critical theory targets the "untruth" of society in its reduction to economic objectivities. As Werner Bonefeld suggests, "Negative dialectics is the dialectics of a social world in the form of an economic object, one that is governed by the movement of economic quantities."[12] Thinking against the grain of economic concepts, Adorno's dialectics returns concepts to their sociohistorical genesis. Rejecting the dogmatic scientism of traditional Marxism and its affirmation of economic laws, Adorno's critical theory articulates economic nature as a socially constituted "second nature."[13] The concepts of political economy are thus entirely negative in his thought—negative dialectics is the negation of economic necessity *as* a socially constituted necessity. Society appears natural because of the inevitable character of capitalist relations, which reproduce themselves as an apparently autonomous power over individuals and their needs.

Adorno situates his own work in relation to Marx's critique of political economy as follows: "Marxist critique consists in showing that every conceivable social and economic factor that appears to be a part of nature is in fact something that has evolved historically."[14] Adorno's critical theory deciphers the social practices, institutions, and relations that appear unchangeable. His negative dialectics subverts the objectivity of late capitalist society and its imperatives by recovering the social relations that manifest in the form of abstract laws. Critical theory, according to Adorno, articulates the manner in which human practice reappears to subjects in the form of economic fate.

In *Capital*, Marx developed a critique of classical political economy through an analysis of the "commodity-form." The universal principle of society, he argued, is "the law of value, which capitalism realizes over the heads of men."[15] Above all, the capitalist mode of production is a system of production *for exchange*. Marx's critique presents the fundamental categories of political economy as inversions of social relations in order to grasp the historically specific character of capitalist wealth. Through a detailed analysis of the commodity-form, Marx identified what he called the "dual character of commodities" as a contradictory relation between the "use-value" and "exchange-value" of the commodity.[16]

By unfolding the analysis of the commodity-form as a contradictory unity of use-value and exchange-value, Marx's critique delineates the definite social relations in capitalism that appear in the form of value. Use-value, which refers to the material, physical, or sensuous properties of the commodity, constitutes the "material content of wealth" of society. For Marx, the usefulness of "a thing makes it a use-value."[17] Use-value refers to the domain of social need and is realized in the use or consumption of commodities. In the capitalist mode of production, use-values are the material "bearers" of exchange-value.

Against use-value, Marx identifies exchange-value as the only form in which the value of commodities can be expressed in capitalism. By exchange-value, Marx is referring to the quantitative relation, or proportion, between commodities. Exchange-value is not an intrinsic property of the commodity, but a relation between commodities. In capitalist societies, every commodity is exchangeable with every other commodity. Marx's presentation of the dual character of commodities identifies a fundamental distinction regarding the historically specific character of capitalist wealth. On the one hand, the use-value of commodities "differ above all in quality," while on the other hand, as exchange-values, commodities can only "differ in quantity."[18] As exchange-values, commodities "do not contain an atom of use-value."[19] Exchange-value then, according to Marx, expresses a comparability between commodities that are heterogenous in their physical properties. Because diverse, heterogenous use-values are exchanged, every commodity, insofar as it is an exchange-value, "must be reducible to some third thing," that is, to an equivalence that is commonly shared by all commodities. The comparability in question cannot be attributed to a "geometrical, physical, chemical, or natural property of the commodities."[20] According to Marx, the "third thing" that commodities have in common is that they are all products of labor. Exchange-value then, he concludes, is the bearer of "human labor in the abstract."[21]

Marx's analysis of the dual character of commodities specifies the fundamental contradiction of capitalist society—namely, that the production of material wealth (need) is in no way identical to the production of capitalist wealth (value). For Marx, capitalism can be understood as a definite mode of production that is characterized by the division of labor and the rule of abstract wealth over material wealth—by exchange-value over use-value. Exchange-value represents the necessary mode of expression, or form of appearance, of value.

Marx's *Capital* reveals that the contradictory form of value is grounded in the "dual character of labor" embodied in commodities. On the one hand, Marx refers to the labor process with reference to the production of use-values. As the physical or material products of human activity, use-values are the creation of "concrete labor." On the other hand, as the objectifications of a common labor process, commodities are the products of "abstract labor." According to Marx, the capitalist mode of production is a unique form of social mediation precisely because of this labor abstraction. By abstract labor, Marx is describing a specific dynamic in which the labor process is reduced to a unified principle:

> Let us now look at the residue of the products of labor. There is nothing left of them in each case but the same phantom-like objectivity; they are merely congealed quantities of homogenous labor; i.e., human labor-power expended without regard to the form of its expenditure. All these things now tell us is that human labor-power has been expended to produce them, human labor is accumulated in them. As crystals of this social substance, which is common to them all, they are values—commodity values.[22]

Abstract labor, then, is the substance of value in the capitalist mode of production. As values, commodities are the objectification of human labor power. Understood as the raw expenditure of human energy without regard to the form of its expenditure, labor is a *really existing abstraction*. That is, the abstraction in question is not performed conceptually or mentally prior to the exchange of commodities, but is rather a "real abstraction" that occurs through the dissociation of individual laborers from the social purposes of their labor.

Abstract labor entails the reduction of concrete labors to a common social substance—namely value. In the analysis of the double character of labor, Marx indicates that the labor abstraction "extinguishes" the material properties of the commodity, equalizing the expenditure of human energy into "one homogenous mass" of human labor power.[23] The magnitude of the value objectified in commodities is "socially necessary labor time."[24] By socially necessary labor time, Marx means "the amount of labor-time required to produce any use-value under the conditions of production normal for a given society." The exchange-value of commodities is "definite quantities of congealed labor-time."[25] The magnitude of value is only realized through the act of exchange in markets. In the analysis of the commodity-form, Marx concludes that abstract labor is the substance of value, and exchange is the form in which labor becomes socially valid.

In the capitalist mode of production, the independent private labor of individual producers only becomes social in exchange. Exchange thus functions as a unique process of mediation. Rather than exchanging the value of one commodity directly for another, commodities in markets are compared to the total abstract labor of society. In other words, social labor is not planned, but only realized "*post festum*" through sale.[26] But this act of comparison remains obscure to the exchanging individuals. The abstraction in question occurs "behind the back of individuals" who participate in exchange.[27]

Marx's analysis of commodity fetishism does not target the exaggerated significance of commodities in capitalism, but delineates the impersonal, objective forms of domination that are immanent to the commodity-form. The key to Marx's critique of fetishism lies in grasping why value appears to be an objective, even natural property of commodities, of things. Marx connects fetishism to his analysis of the commodity-form in the following oft-cited passage:

> The mysterious character of the commodity-form consists therefore simply in the fact that the commodity reflects the social characteristics of men's own labour as objective characteristics of the products of labour themselves, as the socio-natural properties of these things. Hence it also reflects the social relation of the producers to the sum total of labour as a social relation between objects, a relation which exists apart from and outside the producers. Through this substitution, the products of labour become commodities, sensuous things which are at the same time supra sensible or social . . . the commodity-form, and the value-relation of the products of labour within which it appears, have absolutely no connection with the physical nature of the commodity and the material [*dinglich*] relations arising out of this. It is nothing but the definite social relation between men themselves which assumes here, for them, the fantastic form of a relation between things.[28]

In the capitalist mode of production, producers do not relate to each other directly—they relate to each other through exchange, through the products of their labor. Value is a definite social relation characterized by the expenditure of abstract labor. The value of commodities is the expression of an indirect, mediated form of social interdependence that appears to individuals—as an objective or natural property of commodities. As Adorno remarks, "Marx developed his analysis of fetishism, which interpreted the concept of value as the reflection of the relationship between human beings as if it were a characteristic of objects."[29] In capitalism, the relations between people become value relations between things. Because of the peculiar social character of labor that produces value, commodities appear to have an autonomous power over subjects; they seem to have a "life of their own." Marx names this social power "the fetishism which attaches itself to the products of labour as soon as they are produced as commodities."[30] Commodity fetishism, then, is not a "mental" or "conscious" error of individuals, but refers to the distorted appearance of the objective relations of capitalist society. "The fetish character of the commodities," Adorno remarks, "is not chalked up to a subjectively mistaken consciousness, but objectively deduced out of the social a priori, the process of exchange."[31]

Commodity fetishism is not merely an illusion—commodity producers really relate to each other indirectly through the mediated exchange of things. Moreover, commodities in capitalism really acquire social properties. As Marx continues, "The social relations between their private labours appear as what they are, i.e. they do not appear as direct social relations between persons in their work, but rather as material relations between persons and social relations between things."[32] Rather than appearing as a definite social relation, value appears as a property of the commodity. The precise connection between labor and value remains obscure to producers because the value of expended labor is only realized in exchange: "Since the producers do not come into social contact until they exchange the products of their labour, the specific social characteristics of their private labours appear only within this exchange."[33] For Marx, the value of commodities is a complex form of interdependence that cannot be directly controlled by the individuals who constitute society. In the capitalist mode of production, individuals are dominated and controlled by things, and the key relations between individuals are not personal, but impersonal and "thing-like." Capitalist society is an impersonal form of mediation in which human beings relate to each other through commodity values: "Their own movement within society has for them the form of a movement made by things, far from being under their control, in fact control them."[34] Marx thus describes the determination of the magnitude of value by labor time: "a secret hidden under the apparent movements in the relative values of commodities."[35] The fetishism that attaches itself to commodities results from the mediated relation between producers, relations that assume the form of appearance of a relation between things, of commodity values.

Adorno's development of the theory of commodity fetishism can be established from the details of his 1962 seminar with Hans-Georg Backhaus, on "Marx and the Basic Concepts of Sociological Theory."[36] In his analysis of Marx's *Capital*, Adorno maintains that what is historically unique about the capitalist mode of production is "the primacy of the apparatus of production over needs."[37] The basic principle of bourgeois society, Adorno insists, is "the abstraction from specific use values, the specific qualities which things develop in themselves and through humans dealing with them, in favour of their universal form of equivalence."[38] The commodity-form is characterized by an abstraction from need. But how is this abstraction possible?

Adorno indicates that Marx's analysis of the commodity-form specifies abstract labor as the key to the exchangeability of commodities: "What makes commodities exchangeable is the unity of socially necessary abstract labour-time [*Arbeitszeit*]. Abstract labour, because through a reduction to unity one abstracts from use-values, from needs."[39] Adorno is establishing a dynamic that is fundamental to his dialectical critique of late capitalist society—namely, that domination is an impersonal form of reproduction in which society maintains itself through an antagonistic abstraction of value from the needs of human beings. In capitalist societies, "The needs of human beings, the satisfaction of human beings, is never more than a sideshow and in great measure no more than ideology."[40]

Because the capitalist mode of production is a system of production for exchange primarily, society is constituted through practices that invert to dominate individuals. As Adorno insists, "The first, objective abstraction takes place, not so much in scientific thought, as in the universal development of the exchange system itself; which happens independently of the qualitative attitudes of producer and consumer, of the mode of production, even of need, which the social mechanism tends to satisfy as a kind of secondary by-product. Profit comes first."[41] Deciphering the connection between abstraction and domination is the key to his dialectical theory of society. Adorno continues in the Marx seminar:

> Through abstract labour-time one abstracts from living opponents. On the face of it, this abstraction makes what is exchanged a thing-in-itself. What is in fact a social relation appears as if [*erscheint als ob*] it were the sum of objective qualities of an object. The concept of commodity-fetishism is nothing but this necessary process of abstraction. By performing the operation of abstraction, the commodity no longer appears as a social relation but it seems as if value were a thing-in-itself.[42]

Commodity fetishism is an objective condition in a capitalist system ruled by private production, where value appears as a natural property of things.[43] This appearance is both real and illusory. The relations of dependency and interconnection between individuals become more objective under capitalism than in precapitalist societies, because social relations become reified value relations. That value appears to be an intrinsic and natural property of things is what Adorno calls "socially necessary illusion." However, the illusions of society are powerful sources of control. Commodity fetishism is an illusion "that is the most real thing of all, the magic formula that has bewitched the world."[44] The act of an equivalent exchange implies, Adorno continues, "the reduction of the products to be exchanged to their equivalents, to something abstract, but by no means—as traditional discussion would maintain—to something material."[45] The social relations of production reproduce themselves in the form of autonomous and seemingly volitional economic things. Exchange-value abstracts from material, and value appears as an immaterial quantity that is independent of its material inscription.

Adorno specifically draws on Marx's critique of political economy and his theory of social labor as foundational to his own critical theory of society:

> In developed societies the exchange takes place . . . through money as the equivalent form. Classical political economy demonstrated, as did Marx in his turn, that the true unit which stands behind money as the equivalent form is the average necessary amount of social labour time, which is modified, of course, in keeping with the specific social relationships governing the exchange. In this exchange in terms of average social labour time the specific forms of the objects to be exchanged are disregarded; instead, they are reduced to a universal unit.[46]

In the attempt to delineate the specifically dominating properties of the exchange abstraction, Adorno insists that exchange "cuts off the qualities, the specific properties, of the goods to be exchanged" as well as the specific qualities "of the producers' specific forms of labour."[47] What is fetishistic about the system of commodity exchange is that value, which is a relation between persons, must disappear in its form of appearance as a thing:

> It is characteristic of the commodity economy [*Warenwirtschaft*] that what characterizes exchange—i.e. that it is a relation between human beings—disappears and presents itself as if it were a quality of the things themselves that are to be exchanged. It is not the exchange that is fetishized, but the commodity.[48]

Adorno's theory of fetishism specifies the activity, or practice of abstraction, that binds individuals and things to universal imperatives that rule over them. In the money form, social relations appear as "a metal, a stone, as a purely physical, external thing."[49] The structuring relations between individuals appear as they are—namely, as material relations between persons and social relations between things. As Christian Lotz puts it, "Commodity fetishism is the necessary way social relations appear in capitalism as 'thinglike' formations... their social genesis becomes invisible on the surface of commodity exchange."[50] The sociohistorical processes that are generative of the categories of political economy (e.g., value, labor, profit) are extinguished in their results as commodity values.

But if society reproduces itself through the exchange of commodities of equivalent value, how does capital ever accumulate? The contradiction in the concept of capitalist society lies in the appearance of an equivalent exchange of value that is profitable. As Adorno remarks, "Exchange is the rational form of mythical ever-sameness. In the like-for-like of every act of exchange, the one act revokes the other; the balance of accounts is null."[51] In other words, if capitalist society is characterized by the equivalent exchange of value, how does value ever return as more value in the form of profit? "The illusion," according to Adorno, "is not the exchange, because exchange really takes place." The mysterious character of an equivalent exchange of money for more money lies "in the concept of surplus-value."[52]

Continuing in his seminar, Adorno analyzes Marx's concept of surplus-value as the foundation of profit. Surplus-value is already produced prior to the circulation of commodities. The unequal exchange of equivalent value is founded upon the transformation of the commodity, labor power, into surplus-value producing labor. To further delineate the concept of surplus-value, Adorno specifies Marx's categories of necessary and surplus labor time: "In order to understand the concept of surplus-value, two time-spans have to be compared: the time which is necessary for the production of labour-power and the time the worker gives in labour."[53] The unequal exchange of equivalents is possible through the exchange of labor time for an equivalent in the form of the wage. However, the time expended in labor and the time needed for the reproduction of labor power are not equivalent. Adorno continues:

> On the one hand, exchange takes place in the form of equivalents: the worker gives his labour-time and receives what is required for the reproduction of his labour-power in return. Here lies the source of surplus-value without having to consider the commodity produced. One exchanges the same for the same [*Gleiches mit Gleichem*] and simultaneously the same for the not-same [*Gleiches mit Nicht-Gleichem*].[54]

The appearance of an equivalent exchange of money for more money is founded upon the extraction of surplus-value. What appears as an equivalent exchange is premised on the "difference between the labour-time expended by the worker and that needed for the reproduction of his life." Adorno thus agrees entirely with Marx's theory of exploitation—of the relation between wage-labor and capital that "involves the exchange of living labour against the wage."⁵⁵ The laborer who sells the commodity, labor power, is compensated through the wage in order to reproduce his or her means of subsistence. Surplus-value is produced during the surplus labor time that exceeds necessary labor time. Bonefeld explains: "As Adorno saw it, the mysterious appearance [*Schein*] of value equivalence lies in surplus value. What appears in the form of equivalent exchange between two unequal values is surplus value in the form of profit."⁵⁶ The capitalist exchange relations, then, reproduce society through the mysterious form of an equivalent exchange of unequal values. Surplus labor time is the foundation of capitalist wealth; profit is produced through the materialization of unpaid labor. "In the sphere of circulation," Adorno insists, "entrepreneurs scramble for surplus-value, which is, however, already produced."⁵⁷ The mysterious character of an equivalent exchange of money for more money is only possible on the basis of the transformation of the commodity labor power into surplus-value-producing labor.

Surplus-value, therefore, does not simply occur within the act of exchange. The illusion of equivalence in exchange presupposes the commodification of labor power, and with it the wage relation of capitalist societies in general. Adorno continues the analysis of surplus-value by suggesting that behind the production of surplus-value lies "the entirety of class relations."⁵⁸ The categories of political economy presuppose the class antagonism. "The exchange-relation," Adorno indicates, is, "in reality, preformed by class relations: that there is an unequal control of the means of production: that is the heart of the theory."⁵⁹ Behind the appearance of fair, equivalent exchange lies the class antagonism—the intrinsically hostile relationship between the owners of the means of production and the sellers of labor power:

> The decisive exchange act, namely the act of exchanging live labour for wages, in fact presupposes the class system; and it is decisively modified and modelled by this class system in such a way that the semblance of freedom for all parties which is created by the legal contract of the wage agreement is, in reality nothing but that: a semblance.⁶⁰

The semblance of free and equivalent exchange "veils" the antagonism between capital and wage-labor. By antagonistic, Adorno is not simply referring to the unequal distribution of capitalist wealth between classes, but rather to the constitutive force that is immanent to the production of surplus-value. Adorno thus asserts that the sale of labor power presupposes coercion as the foundation of its sale. Without the prior dispossession of the class of laborers from their means of subsistence, there cannot be any capital accumulation. Economic competition is only a "derivative" of the class antagonism: "The former conflicts are really the ones which take place after the central conflict, over control of the means of production has already been decided, so that competition is carried on within the sphere of an already appropriated surplus value."[61]

Adorno thus identifies the class antagonism between the owners of production and the sellers of labor power as the foundation of the capitalist form of wealth. But this coercive social relationship vanishes in the appearance of an equivalent exchange of commodity values in markets. As he insists in *Negative Dialectics*, "The class relationship makes up the objective motor of the production process which the life of all men hangs by, and the primacy of which has its vanishing point in the death of all."[62] Rejecting the explanations of subjective economics for the behavior of individuals in markets, Adorno's theory of society follows Marx's conception of the capitalist totality as a universally constituting process regulated by the law of value. As Adorno insists, the law of value is "the real objectivity to which all individuals are subjected."[63]

Adorno's understanding of class antagonism suggests that all social actors are reduced, following Marx, to "character masks"—to functions of capital.[64] Individuals (regardless of their subjective motivations) are dominated by the objective imperatives of their class role. In their functionalization by the antagonism, individuals act as mere "personifications" of economic categories. Society "preserves itself not in spite of its antagonism but through it," because the production of surplus-value presupposes the separation of the class of wage-laborers from their means of subsistence.[65] Both the capitalist and the wage-laborer are personifications of capitalist categories; society reproduces itself through the wage relation, through the antagonistic relations that disappear in their appearance as commodity values. "The abstraction of exchange value," Adorno suggests, "is a priori allied with the domination of the general over the particular, of society over its captive membership."[66] Capitalists and wage-laborers alike thus exist as "mere partners in social wealth and social struggle," each under the "compulsion of the universal" that degrades individuals to functions of society.

Adorno's understanding of social domination is thus characterized by its *impersonal* form. His critique targets the form of wealth that reproduces itself through mediated relations as a power independent over all social classes. The liberal, bourgeois ideal of free and equal exchange within the relations of private property both conceals--and requires--the exploitation of living labor:

> The assertion of equivalence of what is exchanged, the basis of all exchange, is repudiated by its consequences. As the principle of exchange, by the virtue of its immanent dynamics, extends to the living labours of human beings it changes

compulsively into objective inequality, namely that of social classes. Forcibly stated, the contradiction is that exchange takes place justly and unjustly.[67]

The central contradiction of capitalist society is the class antagonism, the social relations of production that disappear in the appearance of the free and equal exchange between buyers and sellers. The appearance of equivalence (of free and voluntary exchange in markets) is simultaneously true and a social semblance. Capitalist social relations assume the form of reified economic abstractions; exchange becomes an autonomous principle, dissociated from human needs. "Exchange value," Adorno insists, "dominates human needs and replaces them; illusion replaces reality."[68] Society is thus "antagonistic from the outset," because the production of capitalist wealth requires the equal exchange of equivalence as inequivalence, of an exchange of the "same for the same and simultaneously the same for the not-same." Capitalist society, then, "does not simply survive despite conflict, but because of it."[69] The exchange of equivalents conceals the class antagonism—and by extension—the domination of people by people.

The historical origins of exchange as the general social mediator lie in the coercive separation of labor from the means of production. According to Adorno, the emergence of exchange-value as a universal form of dependency entailed the forcible deracination of individuals from traditional, precapitalist forms of life. Adorno explicitly refers to Marx's treatment of the origins of exchange-value in the *Grundrisse*:

> The dissolution of all products and activities into exchange-values presupposes the dissolution of all solidified personal (historical) relationships of dependency in production, as much as the all-round dependency of the producers on each other. The production of every individual is dependent on the production of all others; as much as (also) the transformation of one's products into food has become dependent on the consumption of all others. . . . This reciprocal dependency is expressed in the constant necessity of exchange and exchange-value as an all-round mediator.[70]

The historical expansion of exchange liquidates precapitalist forms of life. The exchange abstraction positions individuals in value relations of impersonal dependency, establishing dynamic and supra-individual networks that reproduce society behind their backs. In developed bourgeois society, all life is dominated by the principle of exchange, and by the necessity of securing for the individual the greatest share of the social product. Human beings are socialized in—and through—the supra-individual relations of exchange, relations that remain external to them.

Social domination then, in Adorno's understanding, is immanent to the class-divided relations of production and to the extraction of surplus-value from living labor. Late capitalist society (despite its capacity to contain its conflicts) only perpetuates itself through its conflicts. A reconciled society would be free from the class antagonism: "For the absolutization of labor is that of the class relationship: a humankind free of labor would be free of domination."[71] But through the vanishing of the antagonistic social relations in exchange, value appears to individuals as a fated, natural necessity. Society, as an antagonistic totality, survives through the unity of functions individuals must fulfill for survival. Adorno's critique of fetishism targets the autonomization of the exchange principle in its appearance as second nature: "Humans no longer recognise themselves in what is seemingly inflicted upon them by a secret ruling and are therefore ready to accept that fate."[72] But this fate ultimately "refers back to humans, human society, and could be turned around by humans."[73]

However, due to the totalizing form of exchange and its fetish character, society appears unchangeable. In their functionalization as members of classes, individuals are captive to the processes of domination they constitute. In order to survive, individuals must adapt to the law of exchange: "The concrete form of the total system requires everyone to respect the law of exchange if he does not wish to be destroyed, irrespective of whether profit is his subjective motivation or not."[74] Society reproduces itself through the exchange principle, the socially synthesizing practice that integrates individuals to the whole that lives through them. The "universal extension of the market system," Adorno insists, "is not something that takes place beyond the specific social conflicts and antagonisms, or in spite of them. It works through those antagonisms themselves," even as it threatens to tear society apart.[75]

But as a result of the fetishistic form of society's reproduction, individuals imagine themselves as agential subjects rather than the objects of economic compulsion. Although the law of exchange "provides the objectively valid model for all essential social events," individuals treat commodity values as the autonomous property of things.[76] For Adorno, the subject of late capitalist society undergoes a necessary process of objectification. The domination of individuals by society is itself an abstractly mediated process. In its objectification, the individual becomes a "subjectless subject."[77] Subjectivity exists in the form of objectification. The exchange principle negates subjectivity from the outset: "The universal domination of exchange-value over human beings, which a priori does not permit subjects to be subjects, degrades subjectivity itself to a mere object, relegating that principle of universality, which asserts that it would establish the predominance of the subject, to untruth."[78] Subjects are leveled by the abstract universal, the exchange principle that compels the spontaneity of subjects to internalize the objective determinacy of the whole that lives through them.[79]

Because commodities are really exchanged as equivalents in markets, individuals do not experience the exploitation of living labor in the form of market prices. "Exchange has," Adorno suggests, "as something which occurs," that is, a "real objectivity" which is "nevertheless objectively untrue." Exchange "violates its own principle, that of equality; that is why it necessarily creates false consciousness, the idol of the market."[80] False consciousness is determined by the fetishism of the commodity. Reflecting the inverted form of the fetish character of commodities, false consciousness is "a necessary form of objective process that holds society together."[81] To the individuals who must adapt and conform to exchange, the social totality assumes the appearance of a natural necessity. As individuals become increasingly interchangeable in their mediation by the exchange abstraction, individuality is seized upon defensively—that is, as self-preserving individualism.

Adorno thus suggests that commodity fetishism has a subjective correlative, and names this position the "spell" [Bann] of late capitalist society. In their subordination to a social process that has primacy over them, individuals "stand under a spell," as atomized fragments of a totality that is indifferent to their unique purposes.[82] According to Adorno, the spell is "the equivalent of the fetish-character of the commodity" in human experience.[83] Under the spell of society, subjects determine themselves without reference to the social relations and institutions that condition their behavior. Capitalist socialization unfolds as a contradictory process in which subjects become increasingly functionalized by exchange, but subjects nevertheless posit themselves as self-determining, autonomous subjects. By becoming agents of value through the universal, the law of value and exchange, subjects are in truth the objects of capitalist society and its antagonistic relations.

Under the spell of capitalist social relations and the fetishistic properties of the commodity, the subject internalizes objectification as a naturally imposed necessity. Commodity fetishism is a semblance, and yet this semblance is an "ultimate reality" because the categories of illusion are "in truth categories of reality."[84] The domination of people by impersonal relations "degrades subjectivity to a mere object" and "makes an untruth of the general principle that claims to establish the subject's predominance."[85] However, this domination is not a naturally imposed necessity, but remains a form of human practice. The laws of capitalist society and exchange appear natural because of their mediated and anonymous form. Deciphering the spell of the subject's rule by abstractions is the critical intent of Adorno's negative dialectics, and the key to this practice consists in recovering the social genesis of economic concepts in the mediated relations that form them.

Real Abstraction

Adorno's theory of society focuses the Marxist critique of fetishism on the production of the subjective forms of knowledge in late capitalism. But if the reification of consciousness is really as total as Adorno suggests, such a theory seems to preempt its own capacity to conceptualize the society it purports to comprehend. In order to specify the relation between the critique of political economy and Adorno's theory of society in terms of the subjective experience of late capitalist society, I will clarify the role the concept of "real abstraction" plays in his work.[86] In addition to Marx's critique of the categories of political economy, Adorno's critical theory develops a parallel theory of the fetishistic constitution of subjectivity. The key to this parallelism lies in the concept of real abstraction, which Adorno developed through his lifelong engagement with epistemology. As stated previously, Adorno's critical theory of society thinks against the inverted appearance of social relations in the form of economic things. Although this form of social constitution is a supra-individual process of domination that occurs "behind the backs" of individuals, Adorno's theory holds that this process generates profound epistemic consequences for living subjects. Beyond the claim that social relations are reified, Adorno's theory indicates that the commodity-form is the structuring precondition of the socially valid forms of cognition in late capitalist society.

As indicated in his critique of commodity fetishism, Adorno identifies the socially synthetic practice of exchange as the binding, universal nexus of material relations that return in the form of social relations between things. But what does it mean to say that this practice is *really abstract*? Adorno's thought was crucially influenced by the economist Alfred Sohn-Rethel, who was the first to introduce the concept of real abstraction into Marxist theory.[87] Developed in the context of the neo-Kantian attempt to naturalize epistemology, Sohn-Rethel's work unearths the material genesis of cognition and science through an extensive historical exposition of the relation between abstract thought and commodity exchange. For Sohn-Rethel, the key dilemma of the materialist theory of knowledge consisted in the apparent inescapability of "the concept" as the medium of thought. If "consciousness is determined by life" as the Marxist adage demands, then how can theory become reflexive of its own material genesis if reflection is conceptually mediated? The primacy of the concept appears as the inescapable medium for materialist theories of knowledge. Sohn-Rethel approaches the problem by positing the concept of a "really existing abstraction" as the link between practice and cognition. By deriving forms of abstract thought from the objectively abstract constituents of commodity exchange, Sohn-Rethel conceptualized the latter as a material practice that is generative of an epistemic framework.

Retaining Marx's analysis of the commodity-form and its categories, Sohn-Rethel derives the categories of epistemology and modern science from exchange in his study, *Intellectual and Manual Labor: A Critique of Epistemology*. As he indicates in the following passage, the concept of a real abstraction is not metaphorical—commodity exchange is a real abstraction imposed by social forms:

> The essence of the commodity abstraction, however, is that it is not thought-induced; it does not originate in men's minds but in their actions. And yet this does not give "abstraction" a merely metaphorical meaning. It is abstraction in its precise, literal sense. The economic concept of value resulting from it is characterised by a complete absence of quality, a differentiation purely by quantity and by applicability to every kind of commodity which can occur on the market.[88]

Real abstraction, then, is not a mental abstraction, but occurs prior to consciousness in practice. By exchanging commodities through the equivalent form (money), exchange *abstracts from* the concrete properties of the thing. Commodity exchange is an abstraction from material. Such an abstraction, according to Sohn-Rethel, is characterized by the socially imposed inversion of quality and quantity. The act of exchange occasions an abstraction in reality insofar as qualitatively specific, concrete, and heterogenous objects are treated "as if" they were purely differentiated by quantity.

For Sohn-Rethel, real abstraction occurs in commodity exchange and is realized as the social synthesis that conditions the cognition of nature. Insofar as individuals exchange their commodities for equivalent values, they unconsciously treat qualitatively different things as quantitative values. Commodity exchange treats nonidentical objects as identical, as representations of value. The quantitative equalization that occurs in the exchange of commodities is not the result of the private evaluations of individuals but arises from the commodity-form itself. The unconscious enactment of the exchange abstraction, however, is constitutive of corresponding forms of thought. The validity of scientific knowledge derives from the purity generated by the exchange abstraction. In the abstraction from material nature and use-value, the abstraction of exchange gives rise to the abstractions of thought. Theoretical consciousness, with its capacity for formalization, is ultimately rooted in exchange, because the act of exchange establishes an equivalence by eliminating the "entire empirical reality of facts," by treating use-values as exchange-values.[89] The genesis of science and epistemology is the socially synthetic act of commodity exchange, which, for Sohn-Rethel, culminates in epistemology in the figure of the Kantian transcendental subject.[90]

The practice of commodity exchange is the real condition of possibility for subjective knowledge with objective validity. Sohn-Rethel's claim is that the transcendental subject is the blind expression of the real identity constituted by exchange. His recovery of the social genesis of Kantian epistemology provides the basis for Adorno's critique of idealism, and is fundamental to his wider critique of the economic rationalization of thought in late capitalist society. To develop this connection further, Sohn-Rethel describes exchange as an objective formalization of the constituent properties of material things; by equating use-values to pure quantity, to value, exchange imposes an abstract spatiotemporal framework on concrete things: "Exchange empties time and space of their material contents and gives them contents of purely human significance connected with the social status of people and things." Commodity values are exchanged within a form that constitutes society as an abstractly interconnected synthesis. As commodity exchange generalizes throughout the whole of society, space and time become reflexively abstract for the general intellect. Abstract time is defined, according to Sohn-Rethel, by "homogeneity, continuity, and emptiness of all natural or material content, visible or invisible."[91] The quantitative homogeneity and purity of empirical reality that originate in exchange generate a correlative purity in knowledge. Time assumes the character of "absolute historical timelessness and universality" that mark the exchange abstraction as a whole.[92] The production of reified time (which emerges as a historically necessary component of the expansion of the world market) is borne in the exchange abstraction.

Sohn-Rethel distinguishes the social genesis in exchange from the validity of knowledge by indicating that what begins as an unconscious practice unfolds as an increasingly private mode of consciousness that remains cutoff from its social genesis:

> As commodity production develops and becomes the typical form of production, man's imagination grows more and more separate from his actions and becomes

increasingly individualized, eventually assuming the dimensions of private consciousness. This is a phenomenon deriving its origin, not from the private sphere of use, but precisely from the public one of the market.[93]

The possibility of theoretical knowledge arises from the conceptual reflection of the exchange abstraction. While the real act of commodity exchange generates a practical social synthesis, the individual mind undergoes a theoretical, mental synthesis. This socially synthetic act in class-divided societies, then, not only atomizes individuals as bearers of value but also determines socially valid thought as private—that is, as a form of "practical solipsism" in individuals.[94] The abstraction in question belongs to the relation between the exchanging agents and not the agents themselves; the form and content of thought is preeminently social, but appears to individuals to be the result of their own private spontaneities, of their individual evaluations of commodities and prices.

Sohn-Rethel's analysis of real abstraction, then, posits the identity of thought and society. He identifies the paradigmatic philosophical expression of the false inversion of practice and thought in Kant's transcendental idealism. In particular, Sohn-Rethel returns the *apriority* of the Kantian transcendental subject to its genesis in exchange; establishing the conditions of possibility of scientific knowledge in the *a priori* categories of the subject, Kant's transcendentalism reflects an already achieved social *apriorism*. For Sohn-Rethel, the key to the Kantian transcendental subject lies in the empirically synthetic unity of exchange society: "Kant was right," he insists, "in his belief that the basic constituents of our form of cognition are preformed and issue from a prior cognition, but he was wrong in attributing this preformation to the mind itself engaged in the phantasmagorical performance of 'transcendental synthesis,' locatable neither in time nor in place."[95] The apriority of the Kantian subject reflects the fetish character of the commodity; the constitution of the private, bourgeois "thought form" is grounded in the commodity-form.

Marx's analysis of the commodity-form converges with the Kantian transcendental subject in the concept of universal necessity. For Marx, the commodity-form is the universally necessary social form of the product, while in Kant the transcendental subject is the universally necessary form of objective experience. As Sohn-Rethel insists, "I define the Kantian 'transcendental subject' as the fetish concept of the capital function of money."[96] The Kantian appearance of an *a priori* capacity for universal reason arises from this fetish character—that is, from the subject's blindness to its real development in historical forms of life.

Although Adorno never entirely adopted Sohn-Rethel's method of genetic reconstruction, his critical theory of society is clearly informed by the latter's recovery of the social constitution of epistemology. As Sohn-Rethel once put it, historical materialism is the "anamnesis of genesis."[97] Inspired by the attempt to locate the social genesis of thought in the commodity-form, Adorno's negative dialectics similarly gives Kant's Copernican revolution an "axial turn," by negating the universality of epistemology through an analysis of its fetishistic constitution. As Adorno indicates in *Negative Dialectics*: "Sohn-Rethel was the first to point out that hidden in this principle, in the general and necessary activity of the mind, lies work of an inalienably social nature."[98] Breaking from the orthodoxy of traditional Marxism (which deduces the contents of experience from labor, technology, and the productive forces), Adorno's theory unearths the mediated form of cognition as a fetishized moment of the social whole. Throughout his mature work, he continues to describe the exchange abstraction in terms that closely resemble Sohn-Rethel's: "Exchange itself is a process of abstraction. Whether human beings know it or not, by entering a relationship of exchange and reducing different use-values to labour-value they actualise a real conceptual operation socially."[99] Appearing as an immediacy in prices, the mediated form of the exchange abstraction relieves subjects of the need to reflect on the social genesis of value. Defining abstraction as a form of practical reduction, where difference is reduced to sameness, Adorno shows that exchange creates an "objective conceptuality" in reality itself.[100]

While the concept of real abstraction is a decisive reference point in his critique of subjectivity, Adorno's development of the concept breaks from Sohn-Rethel's affirmative understanding of scientific progress, to develop a critique of the progressive instrumentalization of reason by modern science and technology. For Adorno, the fetishistic constitution of thought by the exchange abstraction requires a critical confrontation with the concepts and categories of late capitalist society. Developing the critique of the exchange abstraction into a wide-ranging analysis of epistemology, science, and the instrumentalization of reason, Adorno's mature work increasingly refers to "identity thinking" as the paradigmatic form of cognition in late capitalism. By identity thinking, Adorno means that in order for the subject to comprehend an object in thought, the object must be subsumed under a concept. Identity thinking refers to the relation between universal and particular; by identifying particulars with reference to their generalizable predicates, concepts abstract from sensuous particularity. Identity thinking relates the phenomena of experience to unity, to a conceptualized reference point. In the identifying judgment, objects of experience are comprehended by subsuming their predicates under a universal concept or law. But this act of subsumption necessarily represses other elements that are not represented by the concept. Adorno's dialectical critique of identity thus refers to a "contradiction *in* the concept," as opposed to contradiction between concepts.[101] The contradiction in the concept refers to the inadequacy of identity—that is, to the fact that the concept "does not exhaust the thing conceived."[102] In cognizing objects through judgments, concepts preempt the experience of sensuous particularity. But every concept is simultaneously more and less than the object it unifies. Identity, then, is necessarily "untrue" because judgments of identity only indicate what things exemplify or represent, rather than what they are in themselves.[103]

Identity thinking is subsumptive and dominating; it reduces objects to the cognitive forms of the subject. To the extent that identity thinking is an act of mastery over nature, Adorno invariably refers to the act as an "identity compulsion."[104] The Kantian transcendental subject is paradigmatic in this regard. The concepts of the Kantian subject constitutively define objects via their likeness to the categories of the subject. Adorno thus describes Kant's epistemology as the subjective expression of the objectively inverted social world. By attributing necessity and universality to the concept of lawfulness, the Kantian subject reflects the "societal world the living collide with."[105] The doctrine of the transcendental subject unconsciously exemplifies the form of a society modeled on the exchange abstraction.

Adorno's critique of transcendental idealism is thus mobilized as a part of his larger effort to emancipate cognition from its instrumental function in exchange society. The process of abstraction, which idealist philosophy mistakenly attributes to cognition, is only possible on the basis of the objective abstraction of exchange. Decoding the transcendental subject as the "conceptual reflex" of exchange society, Adorno's dialectical criticism exposes the ideological content of the Kantian unity of consciousness. The possibility of the subject's constitution of objects, Adorno suggests, is modeled on the real objectivity of the "total, seamless amalgamation of the acts of production in society," by which the "objectivity of commodities" is formed in the first place.[106] What appears as the stability and impenetrability of the "I" is only a defensive reaction formation to reified social relations. The transcendental subject, then, can be interpreted as a philosophical disavowal of the subject's real impotence: "In the intellectual supremacy of the subject, its real powerlessness has its echo."[107] The transcendental subject's spontaneity is, in truth, passivity, a reaction to the reification of the world. Adorno describes this contradiction as the "essential antinomy of bourgeois society in general."[108]

Against identity thinking, Adorno's negative dialectics states that "objects do not go into concepts without leaving a remainder, that they come to contradict the traditional norm of adequacy."[109] The untruth of identity consists in the irreducibility of particulars. Negative dialectics, against identity thinking, is "the consistent sense of non-identity."[110] By nonidentity, Adorno is referring to the incapacity of things to be grasped by concepts; the nonidentical is the moment of the object that cannot be subsumed under identity. Negative dialectics gains its leverage against identity thinking through the limits of the concept. For Adorno, that concepts do not cover their objects is the key to breaking the spell of identity. "Concepts," he argues, "are moments of the reality that requires their formation."[111] His dialectical criticism negates the false identity of concept and object. Without intending to revoke the validity of synthetic judgments tout court, Adorno's critique targets the "fallacy of constitutive subjectivity" by opening "the non-conceptual with the aid of the concept, without reducing it to the concept."[112] Negative dialectics brings concepts into critical reflection by revealing their nonconceptual moment; by exposing nonidentity as the secret "telos" of identity, negative dialectics subverts identity thinking in its function as a moment of the totality.[113] Negative dialectics, as Adorno indicates, is aimed at "breaking through the appearance of total identity" in order to subvert the "coercion" of identification through the experience of the concept's immanent limit.[114]

While Adorno's negative dialectics appears to criticize identity thinking for failing to adequately grasp objects on epistemological grounds, his critique is primarily deployed as a strategy in articulating the objective "untruth" of the society that mediates thinking. As Brian O'Connor suggests, abstract rationality and identity thinking are, for Adorno, "isomorphic to the economic structure of society."[115] Identity thinking asserts the coincidence of concept and reality. Negative dialectics, however, interprets forms of thought as reflections of an objectively untrue world. According to Adorno, the exchange and identity principles are logically similar: identification, he suggests, is "schooled in exchange."[116] The subjective moment of his dialectical criticism thinks against the contradictory relation between concepts and things, while the objective moment thinks against the "topsy-turvy" appearance of economic nature as a socially constituted second nature.

As indicated in his critique of commodity fetishism, Adorno's theory of late capitalism suggests that individuals are mediated by the social totality. By virtue of the inverted form of appearance of society, the class-divided relations disappear in the appearance of commodities. This mediated form of interdependence vanishes in the immediacy of market prices. Because individuals are functionalized as agents of value in exchange, as atomistic units, they are compelled to identify themselves with what they are not—to functions of the social object. Adorno thus locates the constitution of identity thinking in exchange:

> The exchange principle, the reduction of human labor to an abstract general concept of average labor-time, is fundamentally related to the identification principle. It has its social model in exchange, and it would not be without the latter, through which non-identical particular essences and achievements become commensurable, identical. The spread of the principle constrains the entire world to the identical, to totality.[117]

The exchange principle, by reducing the particular to a function of the universal, expresses the concordance of thought with capital. Identity thinking is classificatory thinking—it is instrumental and economizing. In commodity exchange, individuals treat their products as equivalents, as exchange-values. The act of exchange renders qualitatively different labors identical as abstract labor. Identity thinking, too, renders different objects equivalent insofar as thinking asserts the identity of concept and object. Developing as the correspondingly subjective model of capitalist society, identity thinking draws the subject into an instrumental, manipulative relation to objects. Intolerant of anything outside itself, the individual masters reality by reducing it to its "circle of identification."[118] If society dominates subjects through the exchange principle, subjects dominate objects by reducing them to the forms of the subject. In addition to the fetishism of the commodity and the reification of social relations, Adorno's critical theory indicates that the exchange abstraction is internalized by subjects as identity thinking. The abstractness of the dominant, socially valid forms of thinking (e.g., in science and technology) refers back to the commodity-form, to the objective abstraction of the exchange principle, and Adorno thus names his critical theory "the phenomenology of the anti-mind."[119]

Negative dialectics confronts concepts with the social reality they purport to represent. What social relations disappear in the concepts of "wage-labor," "exchange-value," and "profit"? What practices and historical contents vanish in the movements of financial markets? As Adorno's critical theory has indicated, capitalist society is an objective conceptuality; the real abstraction of commodity exchange entails the reproduction of antagonistic social relations in the form of money. The critique of identity is also a critique of the coercive force of the objective abstractions of a society dominated by the law of value.

Bonefeld connects Adorno's critique of identity thinking to the critique of political economy: "For example, the conceptuality of the wage-labourer as a personification of variable capital in the concept of wage-labour entails what it denies."[120] The concept of variable capital entails the denial of its human content—that is, purposeful human practice. In its subsumption under capital, labor becomes commodified as labor power. Spontaneous, purposeful human practice is denied in the concept, variable capital, which reduces individuals to commensurable variants of exchange. The concept of exchange too, which posits the equal exchange of equivalents, subsists through its denial—namely, through the class antagonism and the extraction of surplus-value from living labor. Negative dialectics is linked to the critique of political economy as the attempt to break the spell of the social world in its appearance as a natural, economic object. As a practice of dialectical criticism, it focuses upon the inverted concepts and categories of political economy, of money, price, and profit to decipher the vanished social relations in the abstract rule of value.

Through the progressive spread of the exchange principle in the global expansion of capitalist markets, identity thinking assumes hegemonic status. As a consequence, thought and consciousness become functions of the economy, and rationality becomes instrumentalized by subjects in their atomistic fragmentation. As Lotz puts it, "Consciousness and its mental apparatus becomes subjected to the logic of investment, capital, and processing money."[121] In its mediation by exchange, consciousness experiences the inverted constitution of society in the fetishism of commodities. Borne in the objective exchange abstraction, subjectivity objectifies itself in things and things obtain subjectively autonomous properties. In order to further clarify how Adorno's critique of subjectivity connects with the specificity of "late capitalist" society, I must clarify his critical concept of society as a "negative totality." Such a concept, I argue, can be mobilized for the wider purpose of solving the problem with which I began—namely, why do individuals in neoliberalism experience their increasingly mediated, integration into globalized capitalism atomistically, as self-interested individuals who are cut off from their social relations and institutional dependencies?

Negative Totality

The exchange principle unites society as a negative totality. In addition to synthesizing individuals and empirical facts, exchange reifies social relations. Suffusing the institutions of law, administration, and the culture industry, the exchange principle mediates individuals as an abstract universal—an objectively necessary tendency that lives through the individuals who constitute it. The primacy of exchange means that "individuals are subsumed under social production, which exists as a doom outside of them."[122] In their roles as character masks of capital, individuals are compelled to identify with, and live through, the social totality that subsists through them. As Adorno insists, the "law which determines how the fatality of mankind unfolds is the law of exchange."[123] Returning to Hegel's dialectical conception of totality, Adorno subverts the concept to reveal the immanent violence of a social whole that rules through its particular moments: "Society is a system in the sense of a synthesis of an atomized plurality, in the sense of a real yet abstract assemblage of what is in no way immediately or 'organically' united."[124] The negative totality is the inescapable condition of universal social domination. Through the pervasive expansion of the universal (the law of exchange), individuals must conform to estranged social forms that arise through the antagonisms of the whole.

Through a dialectical inversion of the Hegelian concept of totality and its figures of reconciliation, Adorno's concept of negative totality delineates the unreconciled position of subjects to the society that forms them. As he insists in his well-known reformulation of the Hegelian doctrine, "The whole is the false."[125] In their mediation by exchange and the total subsumption of human beings under capital, individuals live through social purposes that remain external to them. The systematic integration of life and consciousness betrays society as a disunited unity: "The unity of the system derives from unreconcilable violence."[126] Adorno's dialectical criticism thinks in and against the Hegelian concept of totality, which he describes as the "all-penetrating ether of society."[127]

But capitalist society is an antagonistic disunity that appears in the form of unity; the unjust exploitation of labor power appears in markets as a just exchange of equivalence. The socially synthesizing law of exchange integrates subjects into relations of objective dependency, compelling individuals to adapt to collective imperatives: "The economic process, which reduces individual interests to the common denominator of a totality, which remains negative, because it distances itself by means of its constitutive abstraction from the individual interests, out of which it is nevertheless simultaneously composed."[128] The universal law of exchange reduces individuals to fungible moments of the whole; the violence of the negative totality reduces the particular to its function in the reproduction of the universal. The abstract identity of the universal and the particular is coercively established through the primacy of capitalist relations. As Adorno writes,

> Even where individuals think they have escaped the primacy of the economy, all the way down to their psychology, the *maison tolérée*, of what is unknowably individual, they react under the compulsion of the generality; the more identical they are with it, the more un-identical they are with it in turn as defenseless followers. What is expressed in the individuals themselves, is that the whole preserves itself along them only by and through the antagonism.[129]

Individuals are blindly subjected to the universal. The identity of subject and object is coercive, the result of unreconcilable violence. It is not individuals who consciously form their social purposes but the blind, unconscious law of value which conditions them.

The negative totality is an entirely critical concept in Adorno's thought. The "private interest," which liberal economists praise as the ground of the general interest, is only the result of the socially determined wage relation, and the class antagonism that maintains the priority of the totality over the life of individuals.[130] As he insists, "The thesis that individuality and individuals alone are the true reality" is entirely "incompatible with Marx's . . . theory of the law of value."[131] In their reduction to character masks, individuals on both sides of the class-relation must fulfill the supra-individual ends of capital. This antagonistic socialization entails a constant struggle for positions of relative advantage. Consequently, subjectivity is overwhelmingly "maimed" in its submission to the valorization process. This psychological maiming, which will be detailed in subsequent chapters, frequently unfolds as the production of "coldness," "narcissism" and "paranoid projection" in the face of growing economic insecurity. Self-preservation, Adorno indicates, compels individuals to liquidate individuality by "blurring the boundary between itself and its surroundings, and sacrificing most of its independence and autonomy."[132]

Adorno's dialectical critique of the negative totality conceptualizes the constitution of subjects as a process of subject-object mediation. Insofar as the subject is determined by the class-relation and the administrative apparatus of late capitalism, the subject exists through a process of objectification. Subjects, in other words, are transformed into objects. And yet, society remains subjective because it "refers back to individuals who form it."[133] The objective relations of society can only be reproduced through practice, through individuals and their activity. However, due to society's inverted form of appearance, society as subject remains opaque to individuals. The socially necessary illusion of capitalist society is that its reproduction appears in the fetishistic form of the commodity, and the blind law of value appears as an autonomous power over life.

In order to survive the antagonisms of the totality, individuals must adapt and conform to their roles as fragments of the whole. Individual's dependence on society for their means of subsistence conditions the inescapability of capitalist relations, as well as the comparative evaluation of individuals to one another in the competitive struggle over the social product. Deborah Cook summarizes this aspect of Adorno's account of socialization by exchange: "One effect of this process is that individuals begin to measure their self-worth equally abstractly in terms of the value of the goods they possess and the positions they occupy in the economic system."[134] In a society dominated by exchange, subjects are compelled to adapt to the objectivity of capitalist relations for survival. The self-preservation of subjects is only secured through an act of "mimesis."[135] By imitating the determinacy of the negative totality, subjects preserve themselves from the antagonisms of the social object through an act of self-objectification. "Reification," as Adorno insists, "is a function of subjectivization. . . . The more subjectivization there is, the more reification there is."[136] By imitating the social world *in its reified objectivity*, the subject negates subjectivity as a self-preserving reflex against an external, irrational context of economic objectivity.

In order to further detail the integration of subjects and their consciousness into society, Adorno splits the negative totality into two contradictory moments: "essence" [*Wesen*] and "appearance" [*Erscheinung*]. The essence of society refers to the antagonism, the class-divided relations, and their mediation by exchange. By appearance, Adorno refers to the surface manifestation of social relations in things, to the fetish character of the commodity. The essence of society is not an ontological, pure "being-in-itself," existing separately from its appearance. The essence of society is immanent to its inverted form of appearance. Echoing Hegel, Adorno insists that the essence of society *must* appear.[137] The appearance of social relations in things is not an illusion—it is the real movement of an "untrue" totality. Adorno suggests that the essence is "downright mischief-making [*Unwesen*], the arrangement of the world which degrades human beings into the means of their *sese conservare* [self-preservation], curtailing and threatening their life, by reproducing it and deceiving them that things are so, in order to satisfy their needs."[138] The antagonistic essence of society disappears in its appearance in real abstractions.

Through the blind, autonomous reproduction of the totality, the essence of capitalist society "passes over" into its fetishized appearances—what is mediated appears as an immediacy, as commodity-value. As a result of the mediated, indirect manifestation of society, all facts and phenomena of society are predistorted by the falsity of the social object. What appear as self-evident, empirical facts that refer to social reality (e.g., in economics, sociology, or opinion polls) are indirect fragments of the whole.[139] The fetishistic disappearance of social relations in exchange obstructs consciousness from the experience of society's essence, even as consciousness finds itself identifying with a social essence hostile to its ends.

In addition to criticizing the general antagonisms of capitalist society, Adorno's critical theory targets the specific relations and institutions of "late capitalism," in particular. Through the development of late capitalism and the totalizing integration of individuals into exchange, society obtains a systematic character, which Adorno calls the "total administration" of the world. The semblance of liberal autonomy and freedom that had characterized the bourgeois individual gradually dissolves through the total administration of the world by the industrial, state-managed systems of late capitalism. The totalizing integration of individuals compels them to identify "in their innermost behavior patterns with their fate in modern society."[140] The seamless, systematic network of exchange realizes the primacy of the whole over its parts, functionalizing individuals as powerless executors of the system. The integration of individuals into the exchange abstraction entails a "process of increasing rationalisation," within the extension of the world market system.[141]

The exchange abstraction, in subsuming difference under identity, reduces individuals to the irrational purposes of capital. However, because of the fetish character of commodity exchange, the social totality remains abstractly veiled. The primacy of the whole remains invisible to the individuals who constitute it. What remains a socially mediated relation appears as an immediacy in market prices. As Adorno insists, "The totality of the process of mediation, which amounts in reality to the principle of exchange, has a produced a second, deceptive immediacy. This enables people to ignore the evidence of their own eyes and forget difference and conflict or repress it from consciousness." All social phenomena are so completely mediated by the whole that mediation vanishes: "Everything is now one."[142]

Although Adorno suggests that society contains "non-capitalist enclaves" that continue to exist, the total administration of the world by capitalism is quickly encompassing all remaining forms of life.[143] Extending beyond the economic sphere, the exchange abstraction provides the model for the total administration of cultural consumption, law, politics, and the state on a planetary scale: "The power of this abstraction over human beings is more palpable than the power of any other single institution that has been tacitly constructed on the basis of this principle, which is thus drummed into people."[144] Coercively organizing life through the leveling power of identity, the exchange principle reduces the particular to the universal, to the irrational social system that rationalizes social purposes according to instrumental ends. But just as identity thinking fails to exhaust objects in their "cover concepts," the totality similarly fails to completely subsume the individual under the universal. As Adorno insists, "The name of dialectics says no more, to begin with, than that objects do not go into their concepts without leaving a remainder, that they come to contradict the traditional norm of adequacy."[145] The possibility of negative dialectics turns on the incapacity of the capitalist system to reproduce itself without systemic crises. Contradiction indicates the "untruth of identity." However much society autonomizes itself from living subjects it remains a form of human practice, and alternative forms of practice can disrupt the "course of the world."

To summarize Adorno's critical theory briefly, in a capitalist system of private production, all social relations are mediated by exchange—the universal principle that connects individuals as relations of value. Because capitalist production is coordinated by market signals, production takes place for exchange primarily, leading to the separation of social relations from traditional values, customs, and forms of life. Society autonomizes itself from individuals through the exchange principle. The fetishism of the commodity results from the form of social mediation that belongs to capitalism, whereby material relations between persons appear as social relations between things. Adorno's critique of the totalizing reproduction of exchange society revealed the class antagonism to be the constitutive premise of the semblance of fair and equal exchange. The exploitation of living labor through the class-divided relations of society is the antagonistic essence of capitalism. By virtue of its antagonisms, society's unity is not a reconciled unity, but an immanently negative disunity.

However, this disunity subsists in the inverted form of a unity—of a totality that remains hostile to individuals who must internalize its dynamics. By splitting the totality into essence and appearance, Adorno's dialectical critique portrays the process of negative socialization that characterizes late capitalism. Due to the fetishistic constitution of society by exchange, the antagonistic essence of society disappears in apparently objective and quasi-natural things. As Bonefeld suggests, Adorno's negative dialectics "comprehends essence in its appearance, that is, as a disappeared essence."[146] The negative primacy of exchange subsumes individuals under production, compelling them to adapt and conform to their predetermined roles. The objective tendency of capitalism requires individuals to self-identify with their function as character masks; governed by the impersonal abstractions of capital that coordinate their behavior, individuals do not perceive their individualism as a socially constituted result of the totality. Reified human relationships "damn human beings to powerlessness and apathy" within the objective untruth of the totality.[147] Just as exchange reduces the particular to the abstract universal, consciousness is similarly leveled by the total administration of the world.

Adorno's critique of society as a negative totality extends the analysis of exchange to its function in a number of dominant institutions of late capitalism. In addition to the previously discussed class antagonism, Adorno's postwar work turns to analyses of the "Keynesian-Fordist welfare state," "rationalization and standardization," "bureaucracy," "the culture industry," and "monopoly capital" to further develop a theory of the total administration of individuals in mass society. While the details of his theory of late capitalism must be modified in order to comprehend the emergence of neoliberalism in its historical specificity, this study contends that Adorno's critical theory can be mobilized to illuminate forms of social domination within today's neoliberal world. In particular, the critique of commodity fetishism, exchange, and negative totality can provide the basis for grasping the contradictory logic of neoliberalism, because the forms of domination belonging to finance capital are indirect, mediated, and abstractly veiled.

As will be detailed in the chapters to follow, one key development in neoliberalism is the growing abstractness of exchange. Historically, money has assumed the form of a commodity, such as gold, or paper money issued by states. Since the breakdown of the Bretton Woods System, however, the virtualization of fiat money has conferred extraordinary power on financial institutions, the private banking system, and national central banks.[148] Adorno's extension of the concept of commodity fetishism can be used to unveil the objective social relations that appear in neoliberalism to individuals in the form of abstract, monetary values. Grounded in the negative, contradictory unity of the totality, the concept of commodity fetishism reflects the essential, antagonistic structure of society in its inverted manifestations.

As previously mentioned, this social logic can be defined in terms of two countervailing tendencies. On the one hand, neoliberalism integrates subjects into increasingly mediated, indirect networks of globalized capital. The financialization of the industrial economies in the OECD north requires the expansion of world markets, as well as accumulation through speculation and debt. To this end, individuals in neoliberalism are governed by the rule of abstraction. On the other hand, despite neoliberalism's mediated, indirect, and global structure, individuals are compelled to adopt an increasingly individualistic, competitive mode of conduct in a world of rising economic precarity and austerity. This atomistic individualism, however, is only possible on the basis of society's disappearance. As Lotz puts it, "The effect of the appearance of the social totality as a thinglike configuration . . . produces a paradoxical effect. Society itself appears to its members as something that exists only *for them*, for their interests." This self-interest is objectively contradicted, however, by the "objective dependency of all individuals and institutions on earth on all other individuals and institutions."[149] Today's neoliberal order is an abstract conceptuality, a totality where everything can be exchanged for everything. "It occurs to nobody," Adorno laments, "that there might be services that are not expressible in terms of exchange value."[150] The process of neoliberal rationalization, of the extension of markets on a planetary scale (e.g., in biotechnology, intellectual property rights, and the privatization of the environment), indexes the total subsumption of life under the commodity-form.

But the socially constituted relations of the current neoliberal order are abstractly veiled. What appear to individuals in the form of contingent price fluctuations in markets are, in fact, monetized social relations that remain obscure in their global distribution. Financialization entails the integration of individuals into capital's abstract universality. As Bonefeld indicates, the concept of capital entails "not only the complete independence of the individuals from one another but also their complete dependence on the seemingly impersonal relations of the world market."[151] The more the negative totality constrains the world to abstract identity, the more the totality disappears behind the backs of private individuals. As a socially constituted "second nature," society appears as an inescapable context of economic fate. Neoliberal individualism is the subject's defense mechanism against an antagonistic system that disempowers subjects in a world of crisis.

The financial crisis of 2007–08 demonstrated the objective irrationality and instability of today's global capitalist world. This study contends that Adorno's theory of society remains a powerful tool for deciphering the social constitution of subjects in neoliberalism, as well as its fetishized appearances in finance, subjectivity, economic theory, and culture. The continued relevance of Adorno's dialectical criticism lies in the persistence of society's contradictory relations. This contradiction can be comprehended in terms of the antagonistic relations of capitalism, as well as the coercive severance of abstract wealth from human needs. Exchange-value expresses the contradictory development of neoliberalism's social logic—namely, as simultaneous dependency and independency. Such antagonisms, however, remain abstractly veiled because of neoliberalism's impersonal mediations. Those in the Global North who use personal computers, for example, are removed from the exploitation of labor and the extraction of resources in the periphery. The fetishistic constitution of neoliberal society cuts off individuals from their relations, and the world market appears to have autonomized itself entirely from the will and intentions of individuals, institutions, and even states.

In order to comprehend the historical specificity of neoliberalism and its forms of social domination, this analysis will detail key transformations to the structure of capitalism that unfolded after the breakdown of the Keynesian-Fordist system in the 1970s and 1980s. Insofar as neoliberalism has been understood as an ideological assault by finance capital against the Keynesian welfare state, and is characterized by flexible accumulation, rising class inequality, unemployment, and debt, the details of Adorno's political-economic analysis seem historically obsolete. Indeed, Adorno's specific analyses of the postwar welfare state in the industrial West must be revised for a critical theory of the succeeding neoliberal order. However, as Chapter 2 will show, Adorno's understanding of the dynamic of capitalism as a contradictory object can be developed to conceptualize neoliberalism's fundamental antagonisms. In particular, Adorno's dialectical understanding of the historical development of capitalism (as a dialectic of "continuity and discontinuity") can position critical theory with important resources for understanding neoliberalism as a system that perpetuates the fundamental antagonisms of capital through modified forms of appearance. Through a reevaluation of his political and economic writings on the state, rationalization and standardization, monopoly, and crisis, I will show why Adorno's work can provide the basis for delimiting neoliberalism in its developmental response to the crises of the Fordist-Keynesian system. In particular, Adorno's dialectical understanding of the unfolding of capitalist society as a contradictory unity between "static" and "dynamic" processes can establish the framework for theorizing the perpetuation of society's essential antagonisms in neoliberalism. The basis for deploying Adorno's critical theory of society for an analysis of neoliberalism consists in the latter's abstractly mediated forms of domination. The persistence of society's antagonisms continues in today's neoliberal world as the domination of individuals by the rule of abstractions. Chapter 2 asks: How can dialectical criticism grasp the automatic reproduction of neoliberalism as a system that lives in and through crisis? If individuals experience their mediated domination as atomistic, self-interested individuals, how does neoliberal society continue to reproduce itself despite the overt crises and forms of political and economic inequality that have emerged in recent years?

Notes

1. For example, see Brown, *Undoing the Demos* and Mirowski, *Never Let a Serious Crisis Go to Waste*.
2. As has been widely noted, Adorno's critical theory is grounded in Marx's analysis of "commodity fetishism," as well as Georg Lukács's concept of reification. For accounts of the influence Lukács's concept of reification on Adorno, see Gillian Rose, *The Melancholy Science: An Introduction to the Thought of Theodor W. Adorno* (London: Verso, 2014), 35–66. See also Chris O'Kane, "Fetishism and Social Domination in Marx, Lukács, Adorno, and Lefebvre" (PhD diss., University of Sussex, 2013).
3. For an account of Adorno's sociology of exchange society, see Matthias Benzer, *The Sociology of Theodor Adorno* (Cambridge: Cambridge University Press, 2011) and Stefan Breuer, "Adorno's Anthropology," *Telos*, 64, no. 64 (1965): 15–31.
4. Adorno, "Marx and the Basic Concepts of Sociological Theory: From a Seminar Transcript of the Summer Semester 1962," trans. Verena Erlenbusch-Anderson and Chris O'Kane. *Historical Materialism*, 26, no. 1 (2008): 7. Adorno, *Introduction to Sociology*, trans. Edmund Jephcott (Stanford: Stanford University Press, 2000), 31.
5. Adorno, *Introduction to Sociology*, 32.
6. Adorno, "Marx and the Basic Concepts," 14.
7. Adorno, *Negative Dialectics*, 328.
8. Theodor W. Adorno, "Introduction," in *The Positivist Dispute in German Sociology*, trans. Glyn Adey (London: Heinemann Educational Books, 1977), 15.
9. Riccardo Bellofiore and Riva, "The Neue Marx-Lektüre," 25.
10. Adorno, *History and Freedom*, 50.
11. For an account of Adorno's understanding of Marx, see Braunstein's *Adornos Kritik der politischen Ökonomie*.
12. Werner Bonefeld, *Critical Theory and the Critique of Political Economy: On Subversion and Negative Reason* (London: Bloomsbury, 2014), 5.
13. Traditional Marxism—for example, in the orthodox tradition of "dialectical materialism"—posits dialectics as the science of the general laws of economic nature. Adorno frequently criticizes the official Marxist doctrines of the USSR: "Only such an inversion of the Marxist motives as that of Diamat, which prolongs the realm of necessity with the assertion that it would be that of freedom, could degenerate into falsifying the polemical Marxist concept of natural lawfulness from a construction of natural history into a scientific doctrine of invariants." *Negative Dialectics*, 355.
14. Adorno, *History and Freedom*, 135–36.
15. Adorno, *Negative Dialectics*, 199.

16 Karl Marx, *Capital Volume I: A Critique of Political Economy*, trans. Ben Fowkes (London: Penguin Books, 1990), 125–26.
17 Ibid.
18 Ibid., 128.
19 Ibid.
20 Ibid., 127.
21 Ibid., 128.
22 Marx, *Capital*, 128.
23 Ibid., 129.
24 Ibid.
25 Ibid., 130.
26 Ibid., 168.
27 Ibid., 135.
28 Ibid., 164–65.
29 Adorno, "Marx and the Basic Concepts," 62.
30 Marx, *Capital*, 165.
31 Adorno, *Negative Dialectics*, 190. Translation modified.
32 Ibid., 166.
33 Ibid., 165.
34 Ibid., 167–68.
35 Ibid., 168.
36 For background and context on Adorno's contributions to the Backhaus seminar, as well as his wider influence on the formation of the "New German Reading of Marx" in the 1960s, see Chris O'Kane, "Introduction," 1–17.
37 Adorno, "Marx and the Basic Concepts," 6.
38 Theodor W. Adorno, "Ist Soziologie eine Wissenschaft vom Menschen? Ein Streitgespräch," in *Adornos Philosophie in Grundbegriffen. Auflösung einiger Deutungsprobleme*, ed. F. Grenz (Frankfurt: Suhrkamp, 1965), 236.
39 Ibid.
40 Adorno, *History and Freedom*, 51.
41 Theodor W. Adorno, "Society," trans. F. R. Jameson, *Salmagundi*, 10–11 (1969): 148.
42 Adorno, "Marx and the Basic Concepts," 6.
43 While Adorno's critique of fetishism refers to the disappearance of objective social relations in the realization of commodity exchange primarily, his cultural criticism also deploys fetishism to indicate the preponderance of exchange-value over use-value in cultural commodities, a phenomenon which he links to the reification of consciousness: "The aspect of the commodities that is enjoyed now itself constitutes their utility value—their fetish character, one might say. And if one speaks of a reified consciousness, I would say that one of the central aspects of this reification of consciousness is that it attaches itself to the fetish character of commodities, to what things represent on the market, instead of attaching itself to what these things

actually mean for people." See Theodor W. Adorno, *Philosophical Elements of a Theory of Society*, trans. Wieland Hoban (Cambridge: Polity Press, 2019), 45.
44 Theodor W. Adorno, "Sociology and Empirical Research," in *The Positivist Dispute*, 80.
45 Adorno, "Introduction," 13.
46 Adorno, *Introduction to Sociology*, 32. To the extent that Adorno neglects Marx's analysis of the "money-form" in *Capital* his thought has been criticized for failing to adequately theorize valorization and the circulation of capital. For criticisms of this significant lacuna in his work, see Christian Lotz, *The Capitalist Schema: Time, Money, and the Culture of Abstraction* (Lanham: Lexington Books, 2014), 20–25, and Frank Engster, *Das Geld als Mass, Mittel, und Methode: Das Rechnen mit der Identität der Zeit* (Berlin: Neofelis Verlag, 2013), 321–503.
47 Adorno, "Ist Soziologie?" 236.
48 Adorno, "Marx and the Basic Concepts," 7.
49 Karl Marx, *Grundrisse*, trans. Martin Nicolaus (London: Penguin Books, 1973), 239.
50 Lotz, *The Capitalist Schema*, 102.
51 Theodor W. Adorno, "Progress," in *Critical Models: Interventions and Catchwords*, trans. Henry W. Pickford (New York: Columbia University Press, 2005), 159.
52 Adorno, "Marx and the Basic Concepts," 7.
53 Ibid., 9.
54 Ibid.
55 Adorno., *Philosophical Elements*, 97.
56 Bonefeld, *Critical Theory*, 43.
57 Adorno, "Marx and the Basic Concepts," 8.
58 Ibid., 9.
59 Ibid., 5.
60 Adorno, *Philosophical Elements*, 58.
61 Adorno, *Introduction to Sociology*, 67.
62 Adorno, *Negative Dialectics*, 320.
63 Ibid., 300.
64 Adorno, "Marx and the Basic Concepts," 8.
65 Adorno, *Negative Dialectics*, 313–15.
66 Adorno, "Introduction," 14.
67 Ibid., 25.
68 Adorno, "Sociology and Empirical Research," 80.
69 Adorno, *History and Freedom*, 50.
70 Adorno, *Negative Dialectics*, 328.
71 Theodor W. Adorno, *Hegel: Three Studies*, trans. Shierry Weber Nicholsen (Cambridge: The MIT Press, 1999), 26.
72 Theodor W. Adorno, "Individuum und Organisation," *Soziologische Schriften I*. Gesammelte Schriften, Band 8 (Frankfurt: Suhrkamp, 2018), 448.

73　Ibid., 452.
74　Adorno, "Introduction," 14.
75　Adorno, "Society," 149.
76　Adorno, "Sociology and Empirical Research," 80.
77　Theodor W. Adorno, "Graeculus. Notizen zu Philosophie und Gesellschaft," in *Frankfurter Adorno Blätter VIII*, ed. Rolf Tiedemann (Frankfurt: Edition Text und Kritik, 2003), 9–41, esp. 23.
78　Adorno, *Negative Dialectics*, 180.
79　A number of commentators of Adorno's psychoanalytic interpretation of ego formation indicate the manner in which his theory breaks with Freud's understanding of internalization, primarily as a result of the dissolution of family authority in late capitalism. For an example of this interpretation, see Jessica Benjamin's "The End of Internalization: Adorno's Social Psychology," *Telos*, 32 (Summer 1977): 42–64. For a critique of this interpretation, see Benjamin Y. Fong's *Death and Mastery: Psychoanalytic Drive Theory and the Subject of Late Capitalism* (New York: Columbia University Press, 2016), 86–108.
80　Ibid., 190.
81　Adorno, "Marx and the Basic Concepts," 7.
82　Adorno, *Negative Dialectics*, 337.
83　Ibid.
84　Adorno, "Marx and the Basic Concept," 7
85　Adorno, *Negative Dialectics*, 178.
86　Note that the term "real abstraction" was first used by Georg Simmel. While Marx does not use the term "real abstraction," he frequently refers to the abstractions of capital in the *Grundrisse*. Sohn-Rethel's concept of real abstraction has been criticized for neglecting Marx's understanding of abstraction as a "labor abstraction." For an analysis of the limits of Sohn-Rethel, as well as discussion of his relation to Adorno's thought, see Frank Engster and Oliver Schlaudt, "Alfred Sohn-Rethel: Real Abstraction and the Unity of Commodity-Form and Thought Form," trans. Jacob Blumenfeld, *The SAGE Handbook of Frankfurt School Critical Theory*, vol. 2 (2018): 284–301.
87　For details regarding Sohn-Rethel's influence on Adorno's critique of epistemology, see Stefan Müller-Doohm, *Adorno: A Biography*, trans. Rodney Livingstone (Cambridge: Polity Press, 2005), 219–22.
88　Alfred Sohn-Rethel, *Intellectual and Manual Labour: A Critique of Epistemology*, trans. Martin Sohn-Rethel (Atlantic Highlands: Humanities Press, 1978), 20.
89　Ibid., 48.
90　Note that for Sohn-Rethel, the emergence of coinage in Greek antiquity is the key to the division of intellectual and manual labor, as well as the formation of the abstract intellect. Horkheimer would criticize Sohn-Rethel in his correspondence with Adorno, particularly for his transhistorical analysis of human practice, as well

as his positivistic treatment of economic categories. Adorno's assessment of Sohn-Rethel's work, however, was ambivalent. See Adorno-Horkheimer, *Briefwechsel Band 1* (Frankfurt: Suhrkamp, 2003), 225–27.
91 Ibid.
92 Ibid., 49.
93 Ibid., 26.
94 Ibid., 64.
95 Ibid., 7.
96 Ibid., 77.
97 Alfred Sohn-Rethel, *Warenform und Denkform* (Frankfurt: Suhrkamp, 1978), 139.
98 Adorno, *Negative Dialectics*, 178.
99 Adorno, "Marx and the Basic Concepts," 2–3.
100 Adorno, "Sociology and Empirical Research," 80.
101 Theodor W. Adorno, *Lectures on Negative Dialectics*, trans. Rodney Livingstone (Cambridge: Polity Press, 2008), 7 (emphasis in the original).
102 Adorno, *Negative Dialectics*, 5
103 Note that Adorno's critique of the Kantian subject is not an absolute repudiation of transcendental idealism. In many places Adorno will affirm the Kantian "thing-in-itself" against the absolute idealism of Hegel and Fichte. See Theodor W. Adorno, *Kant's Critique of Pure Reason*, trans. Rodney Livingstone (Stanford: Stanford University Press, 2001), 18.
104 Ibid., 151–61.
105 Adorno, "Subject and Object," in *Critical Models*, 254.
106 Adorno, *Negative Dialectics*, 181.
107 Ibid.
108 Ibid.
109 Ibid., 5.
110 Ibid.
111 Ibid., 11.
112 Adorno, *Lectures on Negative Dialectics*, 65.
113 Adorno, *Negative Dialectics*, 152.
114 Ibid., 146.
115 Brian O'Connor, *Adorno's Negative Dialectic* (Cambridge: The MIT Press, 2004), 3.
116 Theodor W. Adorno, *The Jargon of Authenticity*, trans. Knut Tarnowski and Frederic Will (Evanston: Northwestern University Press, 1973), 107.
117 Adorno, *Negative Dialectics*, 149,
118 Ibid., 172.
119 Ibid., 356.
120 Werner Bonefeld, "Negative Dialectics in Miserable Times: Notes on Adorno and Social Praxis," *Journal of Classical Sociology*, 12 (2012): 130.
121 Lotz, *The Capitalist Schema*, 81.

122 Adorno, *Negative Dialectics*, 330.
123 Adorno, "Sociology and Empirical Research," 80.
124 Adorno, "Introduction," 37.
125 Adorno, *Minima Moralia*, trans. E. F. N. Jephcott (London: Verso, 2005), 50.
126 Adorno, *Hegel: Three Studies*, 27.
127 Theodor W. Adorno, "Late Capitalism or Industrial Society?" *Can One Live After Auschwitz?* trans. Rodney Livingstone (Stanford: Stanford University Press, 2003), 120.
128 Adorno, *Negative Dialectics*, 305.
129 Ibid.
130 Ibid., 328.
131 Ibid., 199.
132 Adorno connects the psychological maiming of subjects to the formation of a "weak ego," and the latent capacity for an authoritarian personality. See *Current of Music*, ed. Robert Hullot-Kentor (Cambridge: Polity Press, 2009), 462.
133 Adorno, "Introduction," 43.
134 Deborah Cook, *Adorno, Foucault, and the Critique of the West* (London: Verso, 2018), 71.
135 Note that the concept of mimesis plays a highly ambivalent, though significant, part in Adorno's critical theory. Developed as an element in his psychoanalytic account of the development of the ego in the *Dialectic of Enlightenment*, Adorno argues that "mimesis of death" is a necessary stage in self-preservation. For a differential account of the use of the concept in Adorno's work, see Own Hulatt's "Reason, Mimesis, and Self-Preservation in Adorno," *Journal of the History of Philosophy*, 54, no. 1 (2016): 135–51.
136 Adorno, *Kant's Critique of Pure Reason*, 114.
137 Adorno, *Philosophical Elements*, 50.
138 Adorno, *Negative Dialectics*, 169.
139 Adorno thus criticizes the methodology of empirical sociology for failing to conceptualize society as a contradictory object: "That society does not allow itself to be nailed down as a fact actually only testifies to the existence of mediation. This implies that the facts are neither final nor impenetrable, even though the prevailing sociology regards them as such in accordance with the model of sense data found in earlier epistemology." "Introduction," 11.
140 Adorno, "Society," 152.
141 Ibid., 149.
142 Adorno, "Late Capitalism or Industrial Society?," 124.
143 Theodor W. Adorno, "On the Logic of the Social Sciences," in *The Positivist Dispute*, 107.
144 Ibid., 120.

145 Adorno, *Negative Dialectics*, 5.
146 Bonefeld, *Critical Theory*, 65.
147 Adorno, *Negative Dialectics*, 190.
148 See Georgios Daremas, "The Social Constitution of Fetishism," in *The Unfinished System of Karl Marx: Critically Reading Capital as a Challenge for Our Times*, ed. Judith Dellheim and Frieder Otto Wolf (New York: Palgrave Macmillan, 2018): 219–49.
149 Lotz, *The Capitalist Schema*, xix.
150 Adorno, *Minima Moralia*, 222.
151 Bonefeld, *Critical Theory*, 152.

2

Neoliberalism and the Class Antagonism

It is often said that neoliberalism has corrupted liberal, democratic societies. By allowing private markets to control previously non-marketized areas of public life, many critics understand neoliberalism as a form of economic control that has undermined the political organization of liberal societies. But in denouncing neoliberal policies on the basis of the economic inequality and political injustice of financialization, critics have fallen prey to a number of misconceptions that obscure neoliberalism's logic. In claiming that the crises of neoliberalism are crises *of* finance and unregulated markets, such an approach fails to grasp the extent to which neoliberalism is an expression of the fundamental contradictions of the capitalist whole. By separating the phenomena of privatization, financialization, and globalization from their historical development, critical theory cuts off neoliberalism from the relations of capitalist society. Neoliberalism, however, can more adequately be understood with reference to the immanent logic of the capitalist system. Rather than specifying neoliberalism as a corruption of liberal, democratic societies by finance, this chapter aims to conceptualize the origins of neoliberalism with reference to its function in the capitalist totality. By returning to Adorno's analyses of the preceding, Fordist-Keynesian phase of capitalism, I argue that neoliberalism is the expression of antagonistic relations of the capitalist totality—specifically, the capital-labor relation.

In failing to grasp the emergence of neoliberalism with reference to the contradictory development of the capitalist totality, critics often resort to an undialectical formulation of its trajectory. This approach posits a set of false dualisms that obscure the mediated relations of society. Such a critique of neoliberalism perceives, for example, an opposition between "markets," on the one hand, and "states," on the other. Moreover, critics often frame the process of neoliberalization as being a problem of the "overextension" of markets in previously state-managed sectors. By doing so, the critique of neoliberalism fails to perceive the extent to which marketization is a state-facilitated process.[1] Further, the critics who oppose neoliberalism as a corruption of society similarly posit a one-sided opposition within the economy—namely, between "finance" and the "real economy." This analysis tends to depict neoliberalism as an economic project, usually characterized by such notions as "neoliberal reason," or "neoliberal governmentality" that undermines democracy.[2] But by criticizing speculative financial markets from the standpoint that affirms a purportedly "real" or "useful" sector of production, critics remain imprisoned in the fetishistic form of capitalistically arranged relations. The critique of neoliberal, financialized global capitalism that affirms the previous era of state-managed, national capital presupposes that individuals were reconciled to society in the Keynesian-Fordist system. In focusing upon financialization, privatization, and the rising inequality of wealth, the critique of neoliberalism fails to grasp the degree to which neoliberalism emerged from the crises of the Keynesian-Fordist system. By denouncing the inequality and insecurity of finance in the name of defending national economic growth, critics unwittingly affirm the false immediacy of what is mediated—that is, the total system of production for the sake of profit. As Adorno remarked in his critique of the bourgeois ideal of authentic existence in *Minima Moralia*,

> The fraud of genuineness goes back to bourgeois blindness to the exchange process. Genuine things are those to which commodities and other means of exchange can be reduced, particularly gold. But like gold, genuineness, abstracted as the proportion of fine metal, becomes a fetish. Both are treated as if they were the foundation, which in reality is a social relation, while gold and genuineness precisely express only the fungibility, the comparability of things; it is they that are not in-themselves, but for-others. The ungenuineness of the genuine stems from its need to claim, in a society dominated by exchange, to be what it stands for yet is never able to be. The apostles of genuineness, in the service of the power that now masters circulation, dignify the demise of the latter with the dance of the money veils.[3]

By opposing neoliberalism through the political attempt to restore the economy to its "foundations" through a return to national growth, regulation, and the redistribution of wealth, critics implicitly affirm liberal democratic societies without grasping the exploitative foundations of capital. Moreover, the one-sided critique of multinational, globalized capitalism runs the risk of affirming a right-wing, authoritarian defense of national economies.[4]

But the financialization of economic activity that has characterized the neoliberal period since the 1970s, I argue, is not a historical aberration, but belongs to the system and its antagonistic form of socialization. Against the critique of neoliberalism that targets the putative "newness" of finance capital, this chapter mobilizes Adorno's dialectical framework for conceptualizing how neoliberalism has reconstituted the fundamental relations of capital. In particular, I argue neoliberalism has reconsolidated the concentration of monopoly capital through financialization. The basis of comparing the succeeding periods of capitalism consists in the continuity of the objective relations of production. Adorno's dialectical concept of society as the simultaneous "subject" and "object" illuminates the historical "unity of continuity and discontinuity."[5] In alighting on what is claimed to be discontinuous with the past in the contemporary period, critics fail to grasp how capitalism reconstitutes its continuous moment within its transformations. A dialectical critique of neoliberalism exposes the transformation of capitalist institutions and relations within the reproduction of the law of value.

In losing sight of what persists within the changes of globalized, neoliberal capitalism, critical theory neglects the fundamental, twofold compulsion of the negative totality. This compulsion is grounded in the commodity-form itself—that is, in the need to reproduce and expand capital. Adorno's "static" and "dynamic" categories in sociology can illuminate how neoliberalization has reconstituted the power of monopoly capital in the extension of financial markets. As Adorno suggests, "The new does not add itself to the old but remains the old in distress, in its hour of need, as it becomes topical as an immanent contradiction through its act of reflection, its indispensable confrontation with the universal in the old."[6] The capitalist system, in revolutionizing the techno-scientific forces of production in its need to produce profit, only expands in order to preserve what is the same. The capitalist totality is a self-referential circle that must constantly adapt to reproduce itself. The dynamism of financial markets preserves and maintains society's static moment: the class antagonism.

As argued in Chapter 1, Adorno's work reveals exchange as the universal principle of socialization. The analysis of exchange-value, commodity fetishism, and real abstraction exposed the constitution of subjects by the totality. By expanding Marx's critique of commodity fetishism, Adorno's theory focused upon the reification of consciousness, revealing the reduction of cognition to "identity thinking" as a key development in late capitalist society. The critique of commodity fetishism revealed the mediated form of capitalist wealth, which entails the social relations between persons that appear as relations between things. The mysterious character of exchange, however, does not originate in circulation. The illusion of an equivalent exchange of unequal values—that is, of money that is exchanged for more money (M . . . M')—is only possible through the concept of surplus-value. The equivalence of unequal exchange is thus founded upon the class difference, of the hostile conflict between capitalists and laborers. The coercive separation of laborers from the means of production is the foundation of profit. The illusion of society lies in the disappearance of the objective relations of production in the quantitative relations between commodity values. "The profit-motive," Adorno argues, "and thereby the class relationship, are objectively the motor of the process of production on which everyone's life depends and whose primacy has the vanishing-point in the death of all."[7] The essence of capitalist society, that is, the antagonistic relation between the class of capitalists and the class of laborers, appears in fetishistic form as a relation between commodities. By illuminating the coercive, exploitative relations that are veiled within the appearances of finance, I argue that neoliberalism can be understood as the expression of crisis tendencies of the antagonistic totality.

In focusing upon circulation, inequality, and financial markets, critics of neoliberalism neglect to conceptualize the social genesis of finance in the objective relations of society. Indeed, since the breakdown of the Bretton Woods system in the 1970s, the capitalist system has undergone large-scale transformations, characterized by the rising prominence of financial speculation and credit-sustained accumulation. In the face of a rising crisis of profitability, neoliberals enacted far-reaching transformations to the state-managed economies of the OECD north through the deregulation of financial relations. Finance, or what Marx referred to as the "mystification of capital in its most flagrant form," operates as a speculative gamble on the future exploitation of labor power.[8] Appearing in abstraction from the social relations of production, credit-sustained accumulation defers declines in the rate of profit as money searches after more money without regard to the limits of capital. But the dynamic self-expansion of speculative accumulation only expands to preserve the static foundations of the system. Credit-sustained accumulation is a real abstraction from the exploitation of labor power. Neoliberalism extends the network of exchange relations on a planetary scale as a speculative deferral of exploitation onto the future. Finance names what Adorno calls the "taboo" of the commodity, namely the "commandment that the traces of the human in the product be erased, that the product itself exist purely in itself."[9] The fetish character of credit money consists in the disappearance of social labor—of the absent human relations that appear as relations between monetary commodities. That neoliberalism appears as an immaterial, virtual, and speculative phase of accumulation does not abrogate the critique of political economy and the law of value, but only confirms the fetishistic constitution of its forms of appearance.

By regulating the accumulation of capital through the state's administrative interventions in the economy, the Keynesian-Fordist system set in motion key crisis tendencies. This chapter derives the origins of the neoliberal offensive from the overaccumulation and uneven development of capitalism, which culminated as a crisis of profitability in industrial economies. By returning to Adorno's analyses of the postwar system, I argue that theorizing the transition to neoliberalism can be delimited according to the inner-logic of the totality. Specifically, Adorno's interventions in debates regarding the transition from the liberal market system to the phase of monopoly capital can help us theorize the succeeding transition from the Keynesian-Fordist system to neoliberalism. I argue that the immanent logic of neoliberalization entails the survival of previous conflicts that are immanent to the antagonistic relations of the capitalist totality. To develop this claim, I turn to the following concepts in Adorno's work: (1) state capitalism, (2) class integration, (3) monopoly capital. Adorno's dialectical theory focuses on the "structural laws that govern the facts" of society, laws that "manifest themselves in them, and are modified by them." Against empirical analyses regarding the unequal distribution of capitalist wealth, Adorno's conceptualization of the immanent "tendencies" of the capitalist system can illuminate the origins of the neoliberal order.[10] By turning to the details of his collaborations with Max Horkheimer, Friedrich Pollock, and other theorists at the Institute of Social Research, this chapter will establish Adorno's critique of one-sided approaches to theorizing the historical development of capitalism as the key to grasping how neoliberalism perpetuates old forms of domination in new institutional arrangements.

State Capitalism

The political-economic orientation of the Institute of Social Research was informed, among other developments, by the emergence of fascism in Europe. In addition to the right-wing, authoritarian regimes in Germany, Italy, and Spain, the rising importance of the state was also apparent in the Soviet Union and the United States. In order to theorize this large-scale transformation, Friedrich Pollock of the Institute of Social Research produced a number of studies that would shape the development of Adorno and Horkheimer's critical theory.[11] Breaking from the classical Marxists within the institute, Pollock adopted a Weberian framework for grasping the increasing importance of state regulation in advanced industrial economies. Pollock argued that "state capitalism" had replaced the system of market competition of the liberal period. Through empirical studies of transformations in the economy in the Soviet Union, Germany, and the United States, Pollock published a series of articles detailing the end of the market system. Analyzing several modes of state intervention, Pollock concluded that the capitalist mode of production was compatible with state planning; states could be planned either through monopolistic "cartels," which interfere with markets, or alternatively through state ownership of production such as the Soviet model.[12] State capitalism, Pollock argued, had replaced the system of market exploitation with a more direct form of political appropriation of surpluses by the state.

In order to prevent the global crises of the Great Depression, Pollock suggested that national capitals had found institutional mechanisms for regulating production and distribution. But far from being a socialist economy, Pollock maintained that state capitalism intervened in the economy in order to preserve capitalism. The category names the following tendencies: "That state capitalism is the successor of private capitalism, that the state assumes important functions of the private capitalist, that profit interests still play a significant role, and that it is not socialism."[13] State planning and direct intervention in the economy had emerged as the dominant means of securing accumulation. For Pollock, the crises of capital were caused by the "anarchy" of unplanned markets; by regulating market competition, state capitalism had abolished the crisis tendencies of the system.[14] Because of the large-scale development of the industrial productive forces, Pollock argued that state capitalism would permanently replace the classical, laissez-faire system: "The medium-sized private enterprise and free trade, the basis for the gigantic development of men's productive forces in the 19th century, are being gradually destroyed by the offspring of liberalism, private monopolies and government interference."[15] As a result of the rising concentration of capital in monopolies and cartels, as well as the government's control of the credit system and trade, the international system had been eclipsed by state capitalism: "Freedom of trade," Pollock continues, "enterprise and labor are subject to governmental interference of such a degree that they are practically abolished."[16] Against the classical Marxists who continued to forecast the inevitable breakdown of capitalism, Pollock stressed the new capacity of capitalist states to contain the laws of crisis. In the hybrid, "mixed economies" of the industrial West, Keynesian policies of deficit spending, demand management, full employment, and price fixing replaced the market system with a general economic plan. As Pollock insisted in his famous formulation, state capitalism replaced the "profit motive" with the "power motive."[17] Rather than being defined as a system of private producers coordinated by market signals, state capitalism would be characterized by political conflicts for control of the state.

In both formally democratic societies and totalitarian systems, Pollock suggested that the primacy of the state over the economy meant that Marx's critique of political economy had reached its limits. Pollock stressed the centrality of the state and the power of ruling cliques within society as the key agent of social domination rather than the impersonal law of value Marx described: "Government control of production and distribution furnishes the means for eliminating the economic causes of depressions, cumulative destructive processes and unemployment of capital and labor. We can even say that under state capitalism economics as a social science has lost its object."[18]

In breaking from the Marxist method of immanent critique, Pollock's approach to theorizing the development of industrial capitalism generated a split within the Institute of Social Research. While Pollock's formulations regarding the importance of politics, state administration, and monopoly clearly influenced Adorno and Horkheimer's postwar analyses of fascism, authoritarianism, and the totally administered society, the extent to which they adopted Pollock's framework as their own remains a point of some contention.[19] On the one hand, Pollock's category of state capitalism informed Adorno's articulations of the welfare state. On the other hand, Adorno's dialectical conceptualization of society is not entirely compatible with Pollock's Weberian, ideal-typical methodology. Although Pollock's conclusions regarding state capitalism are often interpreted as the decisive influence on Adorno and Horkheimer's methodological break from traditional Marxism, Adorno's critical theory differs from Pollock's approach in several ways.

Adorno rejected Pollock's contention that the state's management of the economy had resolved the immanent contradictions and crises of capitalism. While Pollock argued that economic interventionism had effectively resolved Marx's laws of crisis, Adorno criticized his "undialectical assumption that a non-antagonistic economy is possible in an antagonistic society."[20] Adorno's critical theory of society, I have shown, is grounded in Marx's critique of political economy and its categories. Although Adorno's sociological critique of the Fordist system points to new institutional arrangements that "integrate" the working class into mass society, the fundamental antagonism of society persists despite its altered, surface manifestations. In the capitalist mode of production, class position is determined objectively, as relation to the means of production. For Adorno, the state's downward redistribution of capitalist wealth does not resolve the contradictory relations of production: "Society remains class struggle."[21] Despite the capacity of the administered structure of state capitalism to contain its conflicts, society is a disunited, negative totality that sets in motion crises that are immanent to its contradictory reproduction. "The fact is," Adorno insists, "that the model according to which capitalism operated was never as pure as liberal apologias supposed."[22] According to Adorno, in Marx, the model took the form of an "ideological critique"—that is, the critique of fair and equal exchange only had to show "how little the conception that bourgeois society had of itself corresponded to reality."[23] The compact between capital and labor that was established in the aftermath of depression and war succeeded, temporarily, in containing the conflicts of capital through rising economic equality, but could not resolve the fundamental antagonisms of the totality. "The disappearance of classes," Adorno writes, "is mere illusion, epiphenomenon."[24]

Against Pollock's Weberian framework that periodizes capitalism according to distinct phases, Adorno's dialectical theory stresses the continuity of society's relations as the key to grasping the emergence of transformation. Douglas Kellner captures this point: "The problem with Weberian ideal types is that they tend to provide a static model of society rather than a more dynamic Marxian model which would root social trends within existing social relations and struggles."[25] As opposed to differentiating the development of capitalism according to distinct phases, dialectics conceptualizes transformation as one side of the double-sided progression of the totality. Capitalist society, Adorno argues, is not only a process of dynamic growth and transformation. The reproduction of the totality requires the reproduction of its static moment. Marcel Stoezler summarizes this dialectic well: "Capitalism expands to stay the same."[26] The dynamism of the capitalist totality, Adorno argues, "is only one side of dialectics," because "constant change is the best way to conceal the old untruth."[27]

Adorno's intervention in the question of state capitalism can provide the basis for conceptualizing the transition from Fordism to the succeeding period, as his dialectical framework accounts for historical transformation within the invariant categories of capitalist society. Rather than breaking from Marx's immanent critique of political economy, Adorno's postwar writings account for wide-scale, institutional transformations within the fundamental categories of capitalist society. Just as the concept of "state capitalism" cut off the origins of new phenomena from the history of capitalist development, the contemporary critique of neoliberalism similarly reifies its logic. Moreover, in suggesting that neoliberalism has returned capitalism to the classical, laissez-faire system by dismantling the power of the welfare state, critics fail to acknowledge the extent to which the neoliberal revolution entailed an aggressive assault on labor by the state. As Bonefeld has argued, "Competition entails therefore the power of the state to secure the fundamental sociability of the unsocial interests."[28] Just as the conception of the liberal, bourgeois market system failed to represent its reality, the "market fundamentalism" of today's neoliberal economics similarly veils the fact of exploitation in the semblance of "market competition." By turning to the details of Adorno's analysis of the Keynesian-Fordist system, we can begin to understand how, and why, neoliberalism emerged as a political project that restored the concentration of capital.

The Golden Age of Capitalism

Adorno's analysis of the Keynesian-Fordist system can be reconstructed from his essay "Reflections on Class Theory" (1942), as well as his address to the 16th Congress of the German Sociological Association, "Late Capitalism or Industrial Society?" (1968). Adorno's first analysis of class appears to follow Pollock's assessment regarding the fragmentation of the market system. In the aftermath of the Great Depression, advanced industrial nations applied forms of state intervention and public subsidy to prevent future crises. Through Keynesian policies of full employment, welfare provision, and more progressive tax laws, the industrial economies departed from the liberal principles of free market competition. "All these institutions," Adorno suggests, "are naturally breaches of the pure competition principle inherent in the liberal model and no longer permit any explanation of the totality of social life, and the reproduction of the life of society, with the traditional terms of liberal exchange society."[29] Adorno's category of "monopoly capital" identifies the breakdown of the laissez-faire system. Among other distinguishing elements of monopoly capitalism, Adorno specifies the "integration" of the proletariat into the relations of society as the fundamental development of late capitalism. Describing traditional Marxism as class "theory," Adorno argues that the revolutionary position of the proletariat had been undermined in monopoly capitalism. The central doctrine of theory, he continues, is the category of "pauperization," according to which their shared "poverty turns proletarians into a class."[30] Rejecting the predictions of class theory, Adorno argues that the "relative immiseration of the proletariat" had been counteracted in the twentieth century by redistributing greater proportions of capitalist wealth to the workers in order to incorporate them into "mass society."

In addition to improved wages and living standards, the availability of credit fueled the consumption of automobiles, electronic goods, and housing during the "long boom." Within the fields of industrial relations and management, the working classes could be more easily integrated into consumer society. Protected from the most extreme forms of poverty, the working class loses its former unity as a revolutionary class. According to Adorno, "The overwhelming majority of mankind are unable to experience themselves as a class."[31] Managed by the state's functions, the proletariat loses its negative position vis-à-vis capital, regressing in consciousness in the United States, or functionalized as an "administered proletariat" by the "state-machineries" in the command economies of the Soviet bloc.[32]

For a time, the Keynesian system successfully regulated the antagonistic relation between labor and capital. In exchange for higher wages, job security, and the availability of cheaper consumer goods, the working class enjoyed greater economic security as industrial nations entered a phase of unprecedented growth.[33] Marx's predictions regarding the rising immiseration of the proletariat, Adorno argues, could not have foreseen labor's integration in industrial society. "The relations of production," he suggests, "have proved to be more flexible than Marx expected."[34] Characterizing late capitalism as a system of totalizing reification, Adorno's sociological observations describe a pacified, conformist working class managed by the products of the culture industry. Because of the state's Keynesian management of demand, as well as the heightened bargaining power of trade unions, the working class received a greater share of the social product than in the market system: "Shorter working hours; better food, housing, and clothing; protection for family members and for the worker in old age; an average increase in life expectancy—all these things have come to the workers with the development of the technical forces of production."[35]

Often referred to as the "Golden Age" of capitalism, the postwar system brought forth unprecedented productivity growth, wealth, and technological progress. In both the United States and Soviet Union, developments in industry and technology fueled production.[36] The postwar "long boom" in the United States was characterized by the rising consumer power of the masses and the system of industrial relations which reduced class conflict.[37] The US government's arms expenditures (i.e., "military Keynesianism") fueled productivity growth and subsidized crucial branches of production.[38] For the majority of US manufacturing workers, career employment for one company was expected. In counteracting the tendency of the price of labor power to fall, the Fordist system managed labor by integrating workers into an increasingly homogenous mass class.[39] In addition to the government's management of the corporate and manufacturing sectors in the industrial North, the economies of the Global South were submitted to large-scale planning by the world's administrative institutions such as the International Monetary Fund and the World Bank. The so-called third world nations were quickly integrated into the "development model," which compelled heterogeneous and diverse economic modes of production to industrialize according to the plans of economists and state managers.[40]

Against the Marxist predictions regarding immiseration, crisis, and the formation of the proletariat as the universal social subject, Adorno's category of mass society suggests that capitalism could manage its conflicts:

> The predictions of class theory, such as pauperization and the collapse of capitalism, have been insufficiently realized for their meaning not to be distorted beyond recognition. To speak of "relative pauperization" is ludicrous. Even if Marx's by no means unambiguous law of the falling rate of profit had turned out to be true, we would have to concede that capitalism has discovered resources within itself that have postponed its collapse until the Greek Calends.[41]

The proletariat, rather than realizing itself as the subject of history, appeared to more closely resemble the capitalist class that ruled over it. "The trade unions," Adorno insists, "become monopolies," that "call for blind obedience from those permitted to become members."[42] In their total administration by the welfare state, the working class is "objectively blocked" from consciousness of its class position. The objective antagonism between workers and capitalists, however, has not been overcome, but only fails to appear within the administered relations of mass society. Through the downward redistribution of profits from capitalists to the working class, the antagonistic relations of society vanish in the joint administration of production, distribution, and consumption. "No proletarian," Adorno insists, "knows that he is one anymore."[43]

While it might seem that his analyses regarding the reification of classes in late capitalism suggest the end of class conflict, Adorno's theory conceptualizes the objective survival of the antagonistic relations of society despite their subjective disappearance: "The latest phase of class society," he writes, "is dominated by monopolies; it tends towards fascism, the form of political organization worthy of it."[44] In spite of the relative amelioration of conflict, the disappearance of class consciousness only reinforces the domination of the class tied to labor. Social domination persists in late capitalism through the anonymous rule of the capitalist class that exercises its control over the masses outside of the market system. The Keynesian policies were not an act of charity or goodwill, but rather, as Adorno suggests, "the rationale of such progress is the system's consciousness of the conditions that enable it to be perpetuated." By absorbing the workers into the unity of the system and its mediations, exploitation can continue without resistance. For white, male employees in the United States, the hostile relations between worker and manager seemed to recede as wages and benefits rose. The "ruling class is so well fed by alien labor that it resolutely adopts as its own cause the idea that its fate is to feed the workers and to 'secure for the slaves their existence within slavery' in order to consolidate its own."[45] The associated rise of "corporatist management" in the 1950s further consolidated the ideology of classless society, as the working class and managers seemed to possess a unity of interests with national economic growth.[46] Class differences, Adorno remarks, are "far less in evidence now than in the decades following the industrial revolution."[47] The predictions of traditional class theory, far from being realized in the unity of the working class, appeared obsolete in the postwar compact between labor and capital.

However, despite the prosperity of the Keynesian-Fordist system, Adorno maintained the centrality of class antagonism as the essential, static foundation of late capitalism. While specific sectors of the economy continued to function according to market principles, other sectors were increasingly regulated and manipulated by private monopolies that were allowed to administer prices. Protected by the "permanent arms economy" in the United States, which succeeded in stimulating growth, the rising corporate classes could reproduce their control from outside of the market process: "The ruling class disappears behind the concentration of capital."[48] Ruling immanently through the system, the power of the capitalist class depends on its political influence outside of the economy. Monopolists and oligopolists protect the accumulation of capital by obstructing possible competitors from entering the market:

> For exploitation does not just occur through the process of exchange but is rather produced through the system as such. Equal rights and equal opportunities among the competing parties is largely a fiction. Their success depends on the power of their capital outside the competitive process, a power they already possess on entering the marketplace. It depends further on the political and social power they represent, on old and new conquistador spoils, on their affiliation with feudal property that a competitive economy has never entirely liquidated, and on their relations with the direct governing apparatus of the military.[49]

In monopoly capitalism, the ruling class secures accumulation by ruling anonymously through the system. Disappearing behind the formal, legal equality of exchange and its reflexes in the political system, national capitals manage the economy in favor of the capitalist class. The state now acts as the "general capitalist," insofar as it facilitates the accumulation of domestic productive capital by investing in specific sectors and protecting monopolists from market principles.[50] Through welfare spending and benefits, as well as the attending rationalization of the labor process within manufacturing, the invisibility of classes sustains the objective reality of the class antagonism.

To further delineate Adorno's analysis of monopoly capitalism, it is helpful to attend to an internal differentiation specified within the ruling class. In addition to the integration of the working class into mass society, Adorno claims that the ruling class itself undergoes a transformation. Splitting into a capital-owning class of monopolists, on the one hand, and a salaried managerial class, on the other, the ruling class of the Fordist system forms a conflicted disunity. The former bourgeoisie of the liberal system, now reduced to a managerial class, is now subjected to the economic and political "command of large capitalists," as well as the same "threat of police" as the workers.[51] By rearranging the balance of power in favor of concentrated sectors of corporate owners, monopoly capitalists appear as expressions of the general interest: "By virtue of its omnipotence the particular is able to usurp the totality."[52] For Adorno, capitalist competition no longer occurs between individual entrepreneurs, but is rather structured by "asymmetries in power, position, resources, and advantages."[53] Class society remains a hostile, antagonistic whole; membership in a class by no means "translates into equality of interests in action," because class society is a contradictory object.

In establishing the altered institutional arrangements of late capitalism, Adorno's analysis of the postwar compact between capital and labor expresses processes of historical transformation without losing sight of how the period of state-managed capitalism reconstituted the fundamental relations of society. The essence of capitalism remains the class antagonism. Despite the downward redistribution of wealth to the masses, the capitalist mode of production is founded upon the production of surplus-value. The administration of labor by the welfare state merely counteracts the crisis tendencies of the totality. But the division of society "into exploiters and exploited," Adorno insists, "not only continues unabated but is increasing in coercion and solidity."[54] The reduction of individuals to bearers of exchange-value "remains true despite all the difficulties now confronting some categories of the critique of political economy."[55] Through all of its modifications, the essence of society can only reproduce itself through the unequal relations of production. By fighting to receive a greater share of the national product, the workers did not overcome the commodity-form, but were "integrated all the more deeply" into the totality.[56] According to Adorno, "Keynesianism, that is, strengthening the public sector to prevent crises, is rational because it counteracts the explosive tendency of crises. Nonetheless, nothing is changed in the structure of control over the means of production." While the rationality of fair and equal exchange continues in the Keynesian system, "the overall structure is so determined by the interest of self-perpetuation among ruling cliques" that the irrationality of the whole is even greater.[57]

In refusing to accept the positivist methodology in sociology and its rigid adherence to observable "facts," Adorno's critical theory is better able to conceptualize the persistence of class exploitation within its transformations. In falling under the "spell" of a classless society, empirical sociology and economic theory remain fixated on the surface appearances of society, thereby succumbing to the fetishized form of appearance of capitalist relations. Positioning his own approach against "subjective" economics and sociology, Adorno's dialectical theory targets the inverted manifestation of society's facts: "The laws of the market, in whose system it remains in an unreflected manner, remain a façade. Even if a survey provided the statistically overwhelming evidence that workers no longer consider themselves to be workers and deny that there still exists such a thing as the proletariat, the non-existence of the proletariat would in no way have been proved."[58] Empirical sociology cannot conceptualize the mediated relations of exchange society. The subjective findings of sociology—which suggest the end of class conflict—would have to be compared with the objective relations of production, of the worker's "lack of control over the means of production" in late capitalism.[59]

By disappearing behind the concentration of capital, class rule consolidates its position in an anonymous and impersonal form. However, if the ruling class must secure the conditions of accumulation by counteracting the system's crises, Marx's prognosis regarding pauperization finds itself "verified in an unsuspected way."[60] Far from eliminating the contradictions of the totality, the dirigiste methods of regulation only set in motion structural tendencies that would undermine profits. The objective need by the capitalist class to preempt crisis betrays the instability of the system. The Keynesian-Fordist system had secured productivity growth, but in managing capital accumulation, the capitalist class, according to Adorno, enacted "the law of crisis against their will."[61] In spite of the advanced development of the productive forces and prosperity in the postwar boom, the capitalist totality remained a contradictory object, subject to the blind law of value: "Production takes place today, as then, for the sake of profit."[62] Human needs are satisfied indirectly as a by-product of exchange-value. Although the prosperity and new availability of consumer goods had temporarily contained class conflict, the development of the capitalist system had become independent of "even of those in control."[63]

In temporarily solving the problem of distribution, Adorno suggests, late capitalism had only exacerbated social domination. Suffusing throughout the society and its regulatory institutions, the exchange principle binds subjects to the irrationality of the whole: "Human beings continue to be subject to domination by the economic process. Its objects have long since ceased to be just the masses; they now include those in charge and their agents."[64] In defending itself against the anarchy of market competition, the dirigiste methods had secured the conditions of productivity growth, but in doing so had produced the conditions for the overaccumulation of capital. The resilience of the postwar system confirms the resilience of capitalism, but also implicitly confirms "the theory of its collapse."[65] If Marx's theory of pauperization was not realized "a la lettre," the objective irrationality of the whole only confirms humanity's dependence "upon an apparatus that has escaped the control of those who use it."[66] In refusing to affirm the progress of late capitalism and its semblance of freedom and equality, Adorno's critical theory points to structural tendencies that rule immanently within the system: "Its model would be Marx's law of crisis—even if it has become so obscured as to be unrecognizable—which was deduced from the tendency of the rate of profit to fall."[67] According to Adorno, the crisis tendencies are immanent to the capitalist mode of production and its antagonistic relations. Far from overcoming the law of crisis, the postwar Keynesian-Fordist system only postponed it.

Crisis: The End of the Golden Age

Even if the Keynesian-Fordist arrangement succeeded in counteracting the crises of capitalism, the system remained vulnerable. "Social integration," Adorno argues, "grows in tandem with social contradictions, with social antagonisms."[68] Ruled by the law of value, the capitalist totality is a contradictory object. While the processes of integration and rationalization temporarily secured the reproduction of the relations of production, such processes later functioned as barriers to profit. In the 1960s, a number of signs of crisis appeared. The crises of late capitalism are immanent to the antagonistic relation between capital and labor. In its total mediation by the exchange principle, late capitalist society continues to reproduce the antagonistic relations of production, as well as the domination of subjects by the social whole. Despite the dynamism of the postwar compact, the totality can only reproduce itself as a negative universal. The efforts to "ward off or postpone the system immanent tendency," such as the law of crisis, "are already prescribed within the system."[69]

Adorno's work draws from elements of Marx's theory of crisis by conceptualizing society as both "subject" and "object."[70] As subject, late capitalist society defended itself from the threat of collapse through the state's management of distribution. But as object, society remains blind to its contradictions. In spite of the success of the postwar system, Adorno remarks, "the writing on the wall suggests a slow inflationary collapse."[71] While holding an equivocal position regarding the technical details of Marx's disputed, "law of the tendency of the rate of profit to fall," Adorno's analysis clearly points to the possibility of a long-term crisis: "Models of the process of the general and particular are the development tendencies within society, such as those leading to concentration, over-accumulation and crisis."[72] Society as object can only reproduce itself through the antagonistic relations of production. This objective antagonism, however, is not directly grasped by the state managers of the economy. Because it is a contradictory object, society cannot "perceive its own subjectivity, because it does not possess a total subject and through its organization it thwarts the installation of such a subject."[73]

Capitalists are compelled to find new markets and to reduce the costs of production by investing in labor-saving machinery and technology. The need for new markets and development of the productive forces underlies the formation of the world market and the corresponding extension of the exchange principle across the globe. According to Clarke, the "tendency to develop the productive forces without regard to the limit of the market also underlies the tendency to the global overaccumulation and uneven development of capital, as the development of social production confronts the limits of its capitalist form as production for profit."[74] The pressure of global, capitalist competition leads to not only the overaccumulation and overproduction of capital but also the displacement of living labor. The tendencies of overaccumulation and crisis are not accidental limits belonging to the anarchy of unregulated markets—such tendencies are immanent to the capitalist totality and its contradictory reproduction. Ruled by the blind law of value, capitalists do not produce commodities to fulfill human needs, but to realize exchange-value. The ceaseless need to produce surplus-value compels capitalists, in their role as "character masks," to intensify the labor process through investments in machinery. But in increasing the mass of commodities in production, the price of commodities declines in markets. The dynamism of capitalist growth thus compels the overaccumulation of capital, bringing about declines in the value objectified in commodities.

The crises of Fordism can be understood as a failure of state regulation to resolve the contradictory tendencies of accumulation. As Adorno suggests, the capitalists "are forced to try to accumulate surplus-value." By investing in machinery, they "create a dynamic which turns against themselves; more and more labor is set free, thereby creating the conditions of crisis and the continuously increasing threat to the system itself."[75] Capitalists are obligated to reduce the length of necessary labor time to extract surplus-value. But in reducing necessary labor time they reduce the value of labor power. The reproduction of the capitalist totality thus sets in motion an "internally contradictory historical dynamic," where investments in productive technology diminishes the value-creating substance—that is, abstract labor.[76]

The advances in technology and production within the Fordist system also corresponded, because of the irrational basis of the system, on a "corresponding growth in social poverty." As Adorno remarked, "The industrial reserve army, overpopulation, and pauperism grow in proportion to 'functioning capital.'"[77] Even as a greater share of the social product is redistributed to workers through the administrations of the welfare system, the production of surplus-value for capitalists necessitates investment in labor-saving technology. Alongside the advances in production and material wealth, Adorno also signaled to the rising "superfluity" of living labor.[78] The rationality of the welfare system, which had succeeded in managing the volatility of the liberal market system, was unsuccessful in overcoming the irrationality of system organized for the production of profit.

According to Adorno, the dirigiste methods of economic planning contained the problem of immiseration, but failed to counteract the tendency of overproduction. The overproduction of commodities follows from the advanced state of the productive forces in industrial economies, leading to long-term crises of profitability: "Overproduction, which ensnares and replaces seemingly subjective needs, gushes from a technical apparatus that has made itself so autonomous that below a certain level of production, it becomes irrational, in other words, unprofitable."[79] The crises of overproduction and overaccumulation derive from the relations of production—that is, from an objectively contradictory social object. The devaluation of commodities in markets coincides with the progressive accumulation of capital. The crisis of profitability of the dirigiste model was not a result of a declining rate of exploitation, but rather a crisis of the overaccumulation of capital in relation to its possible outlets for profitable employment.[80] Notwithstanding the welfare system's downward redistribution of wealth to the working class, the postwar system remained capitalist in its social relations; the production of surplus-value can only occur through the antagonism, the unequal control of the means of production, and the materialization of unpaid labor. The strengthening of the public sector and domestic national capitals, Adorno argues, did not fundamentally alter the capital-labor relation, but only mitigated its antagonistic form through inflationary spending. "That is why we have," he continues, "latent inflation as a constant, controlled inflation as a constant. Because inflation relates to the veil of money, it is generally something that necessarily reinforces the power of the industrial production apparatus."[81] But despite the controlled inflationary spending, "nothing is changed in the structure of the control over the means of production."[82]

By postponing the tendencies of crisis through Keynesian interventions, the postwar system faced long-term problems of profitability by 1968–69. Keynesian policies accommodated the overaccumulation and uneven development of capital through inflationary deficit spending, as well as the expansion of domestic and international credit.[83] But the long-term, secular crises of the postwar system first appeared in the 1970s in the form of a crisis of money, as inflation and balance of payments deficits emerged as significant barriers to capital.[84] Moreover, the OPEC oil embargo of 1973 destabilized economic relations, and supplied the banking system new surpluses through the "recycling" of petrodollars.[85] The flooding of petrodollars into the Eurodollar markets established a new level of influence of financial institutions, and contributed to the rising volatility in the world monetary system. According to Mandel, "Accelerated dollar inflation meant an aggravation of the US balance of payments deficit and a growing threat to gold-dollar parity at a fixed rate of exchange."[86] Faced with rising inflation, declining rates of profit, and balance of payments deficits, the United States terminated the convertibility of the dollar into gold, thus ending the foundation of the postwar, Bretton Woods monetary system. Shifting to a system of "floating" exchange rates, the world's monetary system left the determination of exchange rates to the markets, thereby bringing about a new wave of speculation in currency trading.[87] But rather than stabilize inflation, the floating "non-system" only exacerbated market volatility in the form of increasing balance of payments deficits. The system of floating exchange rates quickly undermined the expansionary policies of governments, as inflationary spending could lead to speculation against national currencies.[88] To manage the risks of speculation, financiers soon devised new techniques and instruments (e.g., securities and derivatives), to "hedge" against currency fluctuations. Profits could now be made by betting on price differences in unstable markets.[89]

The breakdown of the Bretton Woods system and associated crises of money signaled the termination of the Keynesian-Fordist order, which for decades had stabilized capitalism and produced unprecedented growth. While the postwar boom had contained the antagonisms of society through its technologically advanced, industrial forces of production and system of demand management, such an arrangement could not prevent the overaccumulation of capital, and the corresponding crises of profitability. While credit-sustained accumulation briefly deferred the effects of crisis after the abandonment of the gold standard, the return of economic recession in 1974 led to a wave of bankruptcies and defaults in the financial sector—a clear indication that the postwar system had reached its limits.[90]

As will be detailed in the following section, the neoliberal efforts to revive profitability can be understood as "modifications" of the capitalist system. Considered as a defense of the "system immanent tendency" of the totality, neoliberalism can rightly be defined as an expression of the essential antagonisms of capitalist society. "In order to avoid destruction, every form of society unconsciously works towards its destruction and with it also that of the whole that lives on in the form of any society."[91] The neoliberal efforts to ward off its crises include processes of financialization—the real abstractions of the exchange principle that reproduce the capitalistic relations of society. On the one hand, neoliberalization is a dynamic process of transformation and expansion: the financialization of industrial economies has radically dissolved the system of welfare support which had stabilized the capital-labor relation. On the other hand, the neoliberal offensive also reconstituted the regulatory institutions of a totally administered world; the multinational corporation and planetary, financial bureaucracies such as the IMF and World Bank have established new regulatory structures for market-oriented development in the periphery.[92] Rather than breaking from the form of social domination that is fundamental to the capitalist mode of production, neoliberalism reconstitutes the static reproduction of society's relations. Far from unfolding as an attack on economic interventionism, neoliberalism is a mode of interventionism. In focusing upon the transformations to the postwar order that unfolded throughout the 1970s and 1980s, the following section aims to delineate how neoliberalism has reproduced the antagonistic relations of society through new forms.

The Neoliberal Revolution

The neoliberal revolution largely succeeded in dismantling the Keynesian-Fordist system through a sequence of confrontations with labor. In addition to deindustrialization, financialization, and cuts to welfare spending, the neoliberal revolution introduced "monetarist" policies to reduce inflation. As McNally suggests, the transition from Keynesianism to neoliberalism indexed the "turn to a more virulent form of capitalism, which would result in a new wave of expansion—albeit with a growth pattern based on soaring social inequality, rising global poverty, and increased human insecurity."[93] In addition to these developments, neoliberalism has been characterized by the increasing importance of financialization, privatization, and debt for securing accumulation. To specify the contours of neoliberalism's dismantlement of the welfare system, it is useful to recall the following developments.

In the United States, the crises of inflation and unemployment persisted throughout the 1970s, despite the shifts in fiscal and monetary policy. In response, the US Federal Reserve chairman Paul Volker decided to raise interest rates by fiat—marking a dramatic effort by the government to control inflation.[94] Now famously referred to as the "Volker Shock," the Fed's efforts to control inflation led to an alarming downturn in economic activity as tight credit and high interest rates sharply reduced productive investment.[95] In addition to declines in manufacturing output and reduced consumer spending, workers also faced the political rule of the "New Right," in the United States and the United Kingdom. The appointments of Ronald Reagan and Margaret Thatcher introduced bitter attacks on the strength of labor throughout the 1980s, as both governments submitted the power of labor to disciplinary control through outsourcing, cuts to welfare spending, and direct confrontations with public union strikes to restore corporate profits.[96]

As the Fordist mode of production shifted to a "post-Fordist" model of lean production, the replacement of living labor in the manufacturing sectors laid the basis for new waves of unemployment within the industrial North. Faced with competitive pressure from international firms (especially Japan), US manufactures struggled to maintain profitability. Due to the advances of the "third technological revolution," which was defined by innovations in the application of computer and microchip technologies in production, manufacturing plants rationalized further segments of the workforce out of existence.[97] As firms shifted to outsourcing labor in the periphery and "flexible" production methods within the core, the corporatist structure of management that had promised rising wages and job security had clearly reached an end. In addition to offshoring and redundancy, neoliberalism contained the strength of labor by cutting welfare provisions and privatizing public assets. The disciplining of labor in the core coincided with a form of "peripheral Fordism" in developing economies, as well as new waves of primitive accumulation in Asia.[98]

Neoliberalism financialized manufacturing firms and deregulated the banking system. Throughout the 1970s, the quantity of financial transactions outpaced the movement of commodities in trade as speculation in money proved more remunerative for manufacturing firms.[99] Financial speculation can be understood as a gamble on the future exploitation of labor. Faced with declines in the rate of profit, finance capital abstracts from accumulation by borrowing from the future.[100] But by postponing declines in profitability through credit, capitals "maintain solvency on an ever-more fictitious basis."[101] The need by capital to contain the strength of labor becomes all the more urgent as changes to the relations of production can function as barriers to the future production of surplus-value. The expansion of credit-sustained accumulation introduced a significant vulnerability to the system, as the wave of speculation in the 1970s quickly eroded the guarantee of money by central bank reserves.[102] In an effort to regain control of the money supply, policy makers turned to Milton Friedman's "monetarism" to replace Keynesian deficit spending, and blamed the crisis on excessive wages and state expenditures. Monetarism adheres to a deflationary policy of monetary tightening and rejects the Keynesian commitment to full employment, favoring the submission of labor to market discipline. The monetarist offensive thus established the economic framework for the political offensive of the New Right. As Bonefeld argues, "During the 1970s, the monetarism of the New Right developed as a response to the dissociation between money and exploitation."[103]

Far more than a narrow economic policy, monetarism represented a large-scale, statist offensive which subordinated the power of labor to money capital. The monetarist doctrines regarding market fundamentalism provided the institutional basis for the state's assault on union power, as cuts to welfare spending and the rising threat of offshoring laid the basis for a new period of labor flexibility. According to Aronowitz and DiFazio, "The ensuing decade witnessed rapid deterioration in union power and *therefore* a decline in real wages."[104] The increasing need for credit to maintain previous levels of consumption further eroded the bargaining power of labor, as an indebted working class found itself more vulnerable to market discipline. Monetarism thus greatly contributed to the fragmentation of labor in the 1980s, which was further exacerbated by the "anti-government" politics of the Reagan-Thatcher administrations. Criticizing the excessive power of trade unions and the inflationary effects of welfare spending, the New Right articulated a critique of government bureaucracy—the attending dismantlement of the welfare state could thus be legitimated on the basis of "free market" ideology. (Liberal society, monetarists argued, should defend the rights of individual entrepreneurs from the excessive interference of governments.) But in criticizing the government's excessively bureaucratic interference in the economy and private sector, monetarists failed to acknowledge the bureaucratic structure of financialization. As Adorno puts it, "The bureaucracy is the scape goat of the administered world."[105]

Despite the "free market" rhetoric, neoliberalism unfolded as a statist project that reconsolidated the capital-labor relation. Through direct assaults on union strikes and a regressive restructuring of tax laws, the neoliberal revolution further entrenched the power of the state to secure the future exploitation of labor. Privatization coincided with further mechanisms for administrative control. As Clarke argues, "Cuts in public expenditure were associated with the development of more rigorous systems of financial and bureaucratic control of public services."[106] Rather than freeing liberal, competitive markets from excessive bureaucracy, monetarism subordinated the public sector to centralized financial institutions and unaccountable policy experts. As the New Right was waging its confrontation with the welfare system on the basis of anti-government defense of the private sector, state expenditures in fact increased in the United States in the 1980s, both absolutely and as a proportion of GNP.[107] The Reagan administration ran an extraordinary deficit during this period, particularly through massive armaments buildup.[108] Neoliberalism therefore—during its initial appearance—is not a return to the classical liberal market system, but is better understood as a statist, class project, characterized by a restrictive monetary policy and an expansive fiscal policy. In spite of the ideology of "market fundamentalism" and "sound money," the monetarist revolution coincided with increases to the deficit throughout the 1980s, as the United States turned from the world's largest creditor into the largest borrower.[109]

Throughout the neoliberal revolution, economic activity would be punctuated by a series of debt crises. Although consensus had emerged among policy experts and state managers regarding monetarism as the most adequate strategy for reducing inflation, the policies of monetary tightening reached their limits in 1982 as the need for credit by governments threated the international monetary system. After a brief revival of profits, the limits of credit-sustained accumulation appeared in the form of a scarcity of credit. Bonefeld writes: "In the face of looming collapse of international credit relations, monetarism as an economic policy was dropped and replaced by a policy of fiscal redistribution and credit expansion, containing labour through a renewed speculative deferral of overaccumulation and crisis."[110] The failure to overcome the deeper crises of overaccumulation recoiled on the New Right with the return of economic recession in 1981–82, as governments were forced to return to Keynesian demand management policies.[111]

In addition to the crises of inflation and unemployment in the core, the crises of capital revealed itself in the form of the "Third World debt crisis," as governments in the developing South were soon unable to repay increasing interest rates. According to McNally, "Between 1968 and 1980, total Third World external debt went up twelve times, from $47.5 billion to more than $560 billion."[112] As banks faced the threat of default, states forgave them of their "bad debt" through tax relief, thereby redistributing private debt by selling it to public institutions.[113] Monetarism, therefore, did not simply reverse Keynesian policies, but reversed the redistributive function of deficit spending. Moreover, credit-sustained accumulation functions as a mechanism of disciplining labor; as welfare provisions are dismantled and wages decrease, the buying power of workers depends all the more crucially on the availability of credit. The origins of neoliberalism, then, did not consist in a discontinuous break from the preceding phase of state-managed capital, but rather reintegrated labor through the market-facilitating institutions of the state. As Susan Strange argues, "The end of 'monetarist' policy may easily turn out to be the exact opposite of its ideological intentions. Instead of freeing the private sector and the market economy from the toils of state intervention, it may actually end, in involving the state more extensively and more permanently in industry and business than it had ever been before."[114] In addition to direct confrontations with union strikes, the neoliberal project betrayed its statist colors in the form of economic and political support for Pinochet's fascist regime in Chile.[115] As Bonefeld maintains, neoliberalism "recognises the free economy and the strong state as interdependent categories."[116] In perpetuating the nonmarket element of exchange—that is, the element "grafted" on from outside—neoliberalism reproduces the class antagonism through the institutional defense of elements of society that are protected from market competition.

While the postwar social compact had committed to the downward redistribution of wealth, the neoliberal revolution did not fundamentally transform the interventionist function of the state, but rather pursued expansionary fiscal policies, while simultaneously imposing policies of public austerity. Cuts to wages and rising levels of private debt significantly damaged the bargaining power of labor throughout the 1980s, as the working class was increasingly ill-equipped for collective struggles against austerity. Despite a number of significant confrontations with the neoliberal offensive, struggles against capital were increasingly fragmented as the rising threat of unemployment contributed to declines in union membership.[117] Although it failed to permanently revive the rate of profit, neoliberalism succeeded in transferring wealth from labor to capital by managing class conflict through credit-sustained accumulation and policies of economic austerity.

The origins of neoliberalism are immanent to the development of the capitalist system. Far from representing a "corruption" of the purportedly "real" economy, financialization is a manifestation of an untrue social whole. While contemporary criticism of neoliberalism denounces its unequal distribution of wealth, while tacitly affirming the relative "equality" of the preceding Keynesian system, such an analysis fails to grasp the form of capitalist wealth.[118] And if neoliberalism does represent a new phase of capital, it cannot be new because it has replaced the equality of democratic society with the inequality of competitive markets. Neoliberalism cannot replace what has always been socially necessary illusion. In focusing on the forms of credit-sustained accumulation that have assumed greater roles in economic activity, critics of neoliberalism cut off its development from its mediated relations. Just as Pollock's category of "state capitalism" isolated the emergence of new institutional arrangements from the contradictory relations of society as a whole, the attempts to define the neoliberal period similarly reify its logic in a one-sided, undialectical fashion. Such approaches, in failing to criticize how neoliberalism reproduces the fundamental categories of capital, remain imprisoned in the fetish character of capitalist wealth.

A dialectical analysis of neoliberalism, however, illuminates the perpetuation of the "old untruth" in the new. The moment of continuity that persists throughout the development of capital is the capitalistic relations of a society that appear in mystified form as a relation between things. As revealed in Adorno's critique of late capitalism, the production of profit is founded upon the unequal control over the means of production. But the reproduction of fair and equal exchange is never simply the result of market competition, but depends on the coercive power of the capitalist class to rule through the system: "Economic intervention is not, as the older liberal school believed, an alien element grafted on from outside, but an intrinsic part of the system, the epitome of self-defense."[119] Just as the free market system depended on nonmarket forces to dispossess the "doubly free laborer" from the means of production, neoliberalism too enlists the interventionist power of the state to facilitate markets. Far from developing as a "retreat" of the state against the rising influence of finance capital, neoliberalism unfolded as a statist assault against labor.[120]

Adorno's analysis of the reification of class relations enables us to see how neoliberalism rearranged the balance of power between labor and capital. It is useful to recall Adorno's analysis of the reification of class relations within Fordism, because the neoliberal revolution depended on several prior conditions. The fragmentation of labor under the New Right's offensive could not have been possible without the processes of integration of the working class into society. Adorno's analyses of reification, integration, and standardization describe processes of socialization that preempt the formation of a universal, revolutionary social subject. Ruled by the exchange abstraction and the fetish character of the commodity, subjects live under the "spell" of capitalist relations. In facing a hostile, negative social whole that remains abstractly veiled, subjectivity remains blinded to the anonymous character of social domination. Although Adorno's critical theory was perhaps ill-equipped to predict the waves of resistance to society in 1968–69, his assessment of such movements nevertheless points to significant limits that would be exploited by the neoliberal project. The student-led resistance movements of the 1960s, according to Adorno, primarily assumed the form of a social critique of alienation, standardization, and hierarchy: "Only in more recent times have traces of a countervailing trend become visible among various sections of the younger generation: resistance to blind conformism, the freedom to choose rational goals, revulsion form the world's deceptions and illusions, the recollection of the possibility of change."[121]

Despite the far-reaching critiques of alienation, administration, and social inequality, the resistance movements did not primarily emerge as a critique of the capitalist totality. And while the emerging forms of opposition to society succeeded in expanding the postwar compact to previously excluded groups, resistance to capital also provided the basis for the fragmentation of the labor movement. As Clarke puts it, "The outcome of the crisis was not a growing class polarisation, and a revolutionary confrontation of the working class with the capitalist state. Rather it was an intensification of the divisions within the working class institutionalised within the social democratic state form."[122] The working class did not oppose the totality as a unity, but rather, as Benanav and Clegg put it, as a "unity-in-separation."[123] Rather than unifying labor, the succeeding period of offshoring and deindustrialization only continued the fragmentation within the labor movement itself.

By opposing society on the basis of its forms of alienation and standardization, the critique of late capitalism was also vulnerable to assimilation by the New Right's critique of government bureaucracy. In addition to the civil rights, anti-war, women's, and gay liberation movements, the 1960s critique of society was equally a critique of hierarchy, bureaucracy, and unfreedom.[124] According to Clarke, "The emerging forces of the New Right, on the other hand, were able to tap growing popular resentment at the alienated forms of capitalist state power, which came to a head over the issues of inflation and taxation, which the monetarism of the New Right articulated in terms of the relationship between money and the state."[125] While the New Left's critique of alienation was—in part—assimilable by the neoliberal critique of government bureaucracy (and moreover as a critique of welfare spending), the labor movement's critique of capitalism was reduced to a limited critique of "crony-capitalism."[126] But in focusing upon the behavior of individual financiers and rent-seeking capitalists (i.e., "personifications" of capital), while at the same time affirming the "real" sector of national production, labor was susceptible to the right-wing, populist critique of globalized capital. Social domination, however, is not the direct result of individuals in their roles as functions, nor is it the result of the "parasitic" character of finance: "The powerlessness of the workers is not merely the ruse of the rulers but the logical consequence of industrial society."[127] In attributing the effects of crisis, unemployment, or debt to the short-sidedness and greed of financial speculators, the critique of neoliberalism finds itself allied with the authoritarian defense of the national economy against its purported enemies.

In failing to conceptualize neoliberalism as the expression of the capitalist whole, critics who counterpoise finance against a "real economy" of production also fail to grasp the dynamics of market competition within the former. Replacing an economy of "exchange" with the "inequality" of competition, critics often suggest that neoliberalism is an economic form of governance, characterized by private entrepreneurship, deregulation, and decentralization.[128] While it is true that the neoliberal offensive "deregulated" the world monetary system to facilitate the increasing role of credit-sustained accumulation, the characterization of neoliberalism as a competitive market system fails to grasp its contradictory logic in several respects.

As argued in Chapter 1, Adorno's theory of exchange society targets the domination of subjects by an objective, negative totality. The coercive separation of the class of laborers from the means of production was revealed as the hidden premise of equal exchange. The concept of surplus-value resolves the "mysterious character" of an equivalent exchange of unequal values, the social basis of which is the wage relation. The accumulation of capital depends on the materialization of unpaid labor time in production, and moreover on the class separation of capitalist society. The inequality of wealth is reproduced through the form of equality of wages. But how can neoliberalism have replaced the equality of exchange with the inequality of competition if such an equality was already an illusion? Just as the alleged phase of "state capitalism" was not an absolute break from the laissez-faire liberal system (owing to the nonmarket, coercive mechanisms of the state within classical liberalism), neoliberalism too has not replaced fair and just exchange with competitive markets.

Moreover, by opposing neoliberalism on the basis of its competitive, unequal, and unregulated markets, critics fail to apprehend the extent to which neoliberalism has reconstituted monopoly capital.[129] The financialization of the corporation—which required decisive interventions by the state—enabled monopoly capitals to manage competitive markets. By replacing the "corporatist" structure of management that had legally separated the class of owners from managers throughout the postwar boom, US corporations enacted a fundamental reorganization within the structure of corporate governance in favor of narrow sectors of concentrated capital. Ideologically named "shareholder primacy" such a rearrangement defined corporate success in terms of share price, thus directly tying managers to the interests of owners. The shareholder primacy arrangement established the basis for a wave of financial manipulation and asset-price inflationism. According to William Lazonick, "With superior corporate performance defined as meeting Wall Street's expectations for quarterly earnings per share, companies turned to massive stock repurchases to 'manage' their own corporation's stock prices."[130] The rise of shareholder orthodoxy in the United States further incentivized financial speculation, as the manipulation of stock prices often proved more remunerative than investing in wages or research and development.

Financialization, then, should not be understood as an overextension of competitive markets, but rather as a monopolistic manipulation of the value of assets outside of the competitive process. Through stock "buybacks," mergers and acquisitions, corporate raiding, managers can inflate the price of stock to pay out dividends to boards of directors.[131] The expansion of finance did not index the retreat of the state from the economy; by undoing the former tax laws that had "double taxed" dividends in the postwar system to incentivize investment in production, wages, and research, the neoliberal state intervened to protect corporate owners for investments in money capital.[132] In addition to the rising global competition that transformed the competitive relations between corporations in the United States (widening the gap between large and small firms), the shift to shareholder interests lent concentrated segments of the asset-owning class more extensive managerial control over society. Monopoly capital persists in neoliberalism as the institutional power of the corporation to undermine market competition through the manipulation of stock prices.

The rising inequality of wealth that has developed under neoliberalism, then, is not the result of the overextension of "market society," but in fact reflects the power of monopoly capital to secure profitability by undermining competition. So-called policies of deregulation largely exacerbated and facilitated the concentration of monopoly capital, as financial managers and corporate executives were further rewarded with stock repurchases and layoffs.[133] By removing the regulations on stock buybacks, the neoliberal state lent executives and shareholders a new dimension of control over the coordination of production. In addition to downsizing the labor force, lifetime employment in single firms was largely abandoned in the name of issuing stock options to employees. This consolidated the ideology of market fundamentalism—by exchanging security and pensions for stock options, the appearance of a unity of interests between owners and workers can be preserved despite declines in wages.

But given that neoliberalism has largely restored the OECD countries to "Gilded-Age" levels of economic inequality, Adorno's analysis of class integration might reasonably be accused of irrelevance for evaluating the present. As neoliberalism has succeeded in reducing wages in the core, while introducing extensive waves of primitive accumulation in the periphery, Marx's prediction regarding the immiseration of the world's proletariat is no longer as "ridiculous" as it once seemed.[134] Although he could not have foreseen the scale and extent of the neoliberal assault against the welfare state under the Reagan-Thatcher governments, Adorno's dialectical theory of exchange society can help illuminate the fetishistic constitution of society in its domination by finance capital. Despite the inequality of wealth between workers and owners, social domination in neoliberalism does not appear as a direct relation between exploiter and exploited, but is mediated by the exchange abstraction and its fetishistic properties. The anonymous, supra-individual form of domination in exchange society perpetuates class rule through the fetishistic character of world money. What Adorno calls "the universal extension of the market system" did not liberalize developing economies as much as it expanded the administration of the world by capital. The relations of credit and debt that circulate today sustain human relations in the form of abstract, value relations. The exploitative content of market exchange is concealed by its form of appearance in money. But money, as Adorno remarks, is "only a symbol of congealed labour and not a thing in itself."[135] Money is the form in which capitalist relations manifest as things; it is the semblance of exchange-value as a "thing-in-itself" that culminates in the abbreviated form of (M . . . M')—of money that returns as more money.[136] But through the ever-increasing dissociation of monetary accumulation from exploitation, the totality threatens to disintegrate as the speculative deferrals of credit stretch into a future abstracted from the production of surplus-value.

By abstracting credit-accumulation from exploitation, speculative capital defers the long-term crises of reproduction by betting on the future. In the face of stagnating and declining wages, US consumption was fueled by borrowing and mortgages; failing to restore accumulation, the development of neoliberalism was thus punctuated by a sequence of speculative bubbles and busts.[137] But as the chains of credit stretched into the future on an entirely fictitious basis, the limits of this compensatory mechanism appeared with the implosion of financial markets in 2008. Facing free fall, the US Federal Reserve and treasuries infused the collapsing financial institutions with trillions of dollars to remove the toxic assets from their books.[138] The state's intervention in the crisis reveals its centrality in neoliberalism—the succeeding years were characterized by, as Altvater describes it, "a kind of financial socialism" that socializes losses and "guarantees toxic debt," while securing private gains.[139]

But as the state intervened to manage the crisis and sluggish recovery, resistance to austerity has been fractured by economic precarity, sovereign debt crises, and reactionary populist movements. The global crises of neoliberalism have not restored the proletariat to its position as the universal social subject as predicted by class theory. In the face of uncertainty regarding labor flexibility and the rising threat of automation, workers in the core do not positively identify with specific functions in the production process. For many of the precariously employed, the neoliberal techniques of "self-management" are internalized at the expense of collective bargaining rights. But the ideological character of so-called market freedom only veils the objective domination of subjects by the abstract rule of exchange. The image of a "classless society" persists in the semblance of market neutrality, but the relations of credit and debt sustain the class antagonism as the exploitation of living labor "disappears" in the form of money that returns as more money.[140]

In the absence of any long-term economic recovery in the wake of the financial crisis, resistance to neoliberal austerity has divided into progressive, social democratic struggles for a return to the Keynesian welfare state, and a right-wing, populist, and racist defense of national economic security.[141] Appeals to a mythologized, pre-financial phase of national economic growth underwrite today's reactionary critique of globalized capitalism. As a consequence of the abstract, mediated forms of domination today, resistance to austerity has focused on tangible, concrete "enemies" of the population, as well as the alleged "parasites" of productivity growth.[142] The resurgence of right-wing fascist and authoritarian movements (e.g., the UKIP, AfD, National Front, and Golden Dawn) expresses the powerlessness of populations living under the threat of rising economic uncertainty. The authoritarian, racist critique of capital targets "personifications" of capitalist categories—that is, financiers, state managers, and perceived "enemies" of the people.[143] To the authoritarian critic, individual financiers and rent-seeking capitalists appear as plenipotentiaries of the totality. As Horkheimer and Adorno argue, the critique of circulation leaves production intact, falling prey to the anti-Semitic anti-capitalism that targets individuals, "Bourgeois anti-Semitism has a specific economic purpose: to conceal domination in production."[144] Rather than criticizing the capitalistically organized relations of society, and the reduction of individuals to functions of capital, the false critique targets the behavior of individuals. The fetishistic critique of neoliberalism similarly attributes the abstract and impersonal imperatives of the totality to the phenomena of finance, speculation, and greed. Adorno's analysis of class reveals that the rulers "can survive only as long" as the ruled "turn what they yearn for into an object of hate."[145] So long as workers labor under the spell of an inverted world, the conditions of poverty and crisis will be identified with tangible, concrete enemies. For Adorno, the right society would entail neither a return to the welfare system nor a more just and equitable distribution of wealth. Freedom from domination would entail the historical overcoming of the dialectic of static and dynamic categories—that is of the twofold compulsion that subordinates life to the reproduction of capital, as well as the exploitation of living labor which sustains it.

Notes

1 For an analysis of the centrality of the state in both neoliberal and ordoliberal thought, see Werner Bonefeld, *The Strong State and the Free Economy* (London: Rowman & Littlefield, 2017).

2 See, for example, Michel Foucault's *Birth of Biopolitics* lectures, which depict neoliberalism as an economic mode of "governmentality." Foucault, *The Birth of Biopolitics: Lectures at the College de France*, trans. Graham Burchell (New York:

Palgrave Macmillan, 2008). For an example that develops Foucault's genealogy to argue that neoliberalism is, above all, a normative order of economic reason, see Brown's *Undoing the Demos*. For an example of a critique of neoliberalism that counterpoises the capitalism of production against finance, see Elmar Altvater, "Postneoliberalism or Postcapitalism? The Failure of Neoliberalism in the Financial Market Crisis," *Development Dialogue*, 51 (January 2009): 73–86. For a prominent example of a moral philosopher who criticizes the corrosive effects of market overreach, see Michael Sandel's *What Money Can't Buy: The Moral Limits of Markets* (New York: Farrar, Straus and Giroux, 2012).
3 Adorno, *Minima Moralia*, 155.
4 See, for example, John Abromeit's analysis of contemporary, right-wing populism through the lens of Adorno and Horkheimer's critique of authoritarianism. John Abromeit, "Frankfurt School Critical Theory and the Persistence of Right-Wing Populism," in *Critical Theory and Authoritarian Populism*, ed. Jeremiah Morelock (London: University of Westminster Press, 2018), 3–27.
5 Adorno, *Negative Dialectics*, 320.
6 Theodor W. Adorno, "Reflections on Class Theory," in *Can One Live After Auschwitz? A Philosophical Reader*, ed. Rolf Tiedemann and trans. Rodney Livingstone (Stanford: Stanford University Press, 2003), 95.
7 Adorno, *Negative Dialectics*, 320.
8 Marx, *Capital, vol. III*, 267.
9 Adorno, *Hegel: Three Studies*, 26.
10 Adorno, "Introduction," 37.
11 Rolf Wiggershaus, *The Frankfurt School: Its History, Theories, and Political Significance*, trans. Michael Robertson (Cambridge: Polity Press, 2007), 282. For perhaps the most important of Pollock's essays on this question, see "State Capitalism: Its Possibilities and Limitations," in *The Essential Frankfurt School Reader*, ed. Andrew Arato and Eike Gebhardt (New York: Continuum, 1985), 71–94.
12 See Douglas Kellner, *Critical Theory, Marxism and Modernity* (Baltimore: The Johns Hopkins University Press, 1992), 56.
13 Cited in ibid., 59.
14 See Wiggershaus, *The Frankfurt School*, 283.
15 Pollock, "State Capitalism," 73.
16 Ibid., 73.
17 Ibid., 81.
18 Ibid., 87.
19 For details regarding the extent of Pollock's influence on Horkheimer and Adorno, as well as the wider debate regarding the political economy of National Socialism in the work of Franz Neumann and Otto Kirchheimer, see David Held, *Introduction to Critical Theory: Horkheimer to Habermas* (Oxford: Polity Press, 2004), 64, and

Deborah Cook, "Adorno on Late Capitalism," *Radical Philosophy*, 89 (May/June 1998): 16–26, and Helmut Dubiel, *Theory and Politics: Studies in the Development of Critical Theory,* trans. Benjamin Gregg (Cambridge: MIT Press, 1985).

20 Adorno and Horkheimer, *Briefwechsel*, vol. II, 139.
21 Adorno, "Society," 149.
22 Adorno, "Late Capitalism or Industrial Society," 123.
23 Ibid.
24 Adorno, "Society," 150.
25 Kellner, *Critical Theory, Marxism*, 62.
26 Marcel Stoetzler, "Needless Necessity: Sameness and Dynamic in Capitalist Society," *Fast Capitalism*, vol. 12 (2015): 51.
27 Adorno, "Reflections on Class Theory," 94.
28 Bonefeld, "Authoritarian Liberalism, Class and Rackets," *Logos*, vol. 16, no. 1–2 (2017).
29 Adorno, *Philosophical Elements of a Theory of Society*, 29.
30 Adorno, "Reflections on Class," 103.
31 Ibid., 97.
32 Adorno, *Negative Dialectics*, 204.
33 For a well-known account of the Golden Age, see Herman Van der Wee, *Prosperity and Upheaval: The World Economy 1945-1980* (Harmondsworth, 1987).
34 Adorno, "Late Capitalism," 112.
35 Ibid.
36 According to Adorno, to the extent that both the United States and Soviet Union were systems coordinated by statist processes of administration, the postwar period indexed a structural convergence between the competing systems. See *Negative Dialectics*, 152.
37 For detailed history regarding the role of consumer spending in the postwar boom, see Lizabeth Cohen's *A Consumer's Republic*: "A thriving mass consumption economy was more than the panacea of postwar planners. For the next quarter century consumer spending indeed helped secure an historic reign of prosperity, longer lasting and more universally enjoyed than ever before in American history. National output of goods and services doubled between 1946 and 1956, and would double again by 1970, with private consumption expenditures holding steady at two-thirds of gross national product . . . over the era." Lizabeth Cohen, *A Consumer's Republic: The Politics of Mass Consumption in Postwar America* (New York: Vintage Books, 2003), 121.
38 For the most well-known Marxist articulation of "military Keynesianism," see Ernest Mandel, *Late Capitalism,* trans. Joris De Bres (London: Verso, 1999). See Adorno's analysis in *Philosophical Elements of a Theory of Society*: "The existence of blocs, of armaments: the world reproduces itself economically only through the establishment of the armament apparatus, in the East and West, an apparatus

that guarantees prosperity while devouring the national product and threatening humanity with annihilation," 126.

39 Adorno, *The Authoritarian Personality*, lxiii. In addition to the concentration of capital in a narrower, monopoly class, Adorno specifies the integration of labor into monopolistic unions as central to the reproduction of the welfare system: "Because the workers have joined to form gigantic professional organizations—just think of the huge organizations of the complete workforce that have existed in America since the merger of the AFL and the CIO—which have their own bargaining power, as one calls in America, the power to negotiate the most favourable possible terms with the great economic monopolies, the share of the national product received by each worker can no longer simply be expressed according to the law of supply and demand." Adorno, *Philosophical Elements*, 30.

40 According to Susan George, the postwar development model was a key factor leading to the debt crisis of the developing world. See George, *A Fate Worse than Debt: The World Financial Crisis and the World Poor* (New York: Grove Weidenfeld, 1990), 14–15.

41 Adorno, "Late Capitalism," 112.

42 Adorno, "Reflections on Class," 100.

43 Theodor W. Adorno and Siegfried Kracauer, *Der Riß der Welt geht auch durch mich . . . , Briefwechsel 1923-1966*, vol. 7 (Frankfurt am Main: Suhrkamp, 2008), 602.

44 Adorno, "Reflections on Class," 96.

45 Ibid., 105.

46 For the most well-known analysis of corporatism in the context of the US postwar boom, consult John Kenneth Galbraith's *The Affluent Society* (Boston: Houghton Mifflin Company, 1971). Also see Adolf A. Berle and Gardiner C. Means, *The Modern Corporation and Private Property* (London: Routledge, 1991).

47 Adorno, "Late Capitalism," 111.

48 Adorno, "Reflections on Class," 99.

49 Ibid., 98.

50 "For all its protestations to the contrary, for all its dynamism and its growth in production, contemporary society displays certain static tendencies. These belong to the relations of production. Those have ceased to be just property relations; they now also include relations ranging from those of the administration on up to those of the state, which functions now as an all-inclusive capitalist organization." Adorno, "Late Capitalism," 119.

51 Ibid., 99.

52 Adorno, "Reflections on Class," 99.

53 See Tom Houseman, "Social Constitution and Class," in *The SAGE Handbook of Frankfurt School Critical Theory*, 704.

54 Adorno, "Reflections on Class," 97.

55 Adorno, *Introduction to Sociology*, 33.

56 Adorno, *Philosophical Elements*, 53.

57 Ibid., 128–29.
58 Adorno, "Introduction," 84.
59 Ibid.
60 Adorno, "Reflections on Class," 105.
61 Adorno, "Introduction," 32.
62 Adorno, "Late Capitalism," 117.
63 Ibid., 124.
64 Ibid., 116.
65 Ibid., 123.
66 Ibid., 116.
67 Adorno, "Introduction," 37.
68 Adorno, *Philosophical Elements*, 65.
69 Adorno, "Introduction," 37.
70 See Chris O'Kane: "The exchange abstraction is central to Adorno's subjective-objective account of reproduction in the negative totality of late capitalist society, encompassing the economy, the state, and culture. Moreover, Adorno does not claim that capitalism's crisis tendencies have been overcome. Rather, by reading his account of industrial society in light of his comments in *The Positivist Dispute*, we can see these developments as modifications that derived from the crisis-prone process of accumulation as counteracting tendencies that prevented an internal contradiction in the historical trajectory of capital accumulation between unprecedented technological development, immiseration, the falling rate of profit, and crisis." O'Kane, "'Society Maintains Itself Despite All the Catastrophes That May Eventuate': Critical Theory, Negative Totality, Crisis," *Constellations*, 25 (2018): 293.
71 Ibid., 37.
72 Ibid., 40.
73 Ibid., 33.
74 Simon Clarke, "The Global Accumulation of Capital and the Periodisation of the Capitalist State Form," in *Open Marxism*, ed. Werner Bonefeld, Richard Gunn, and Kosmas Psychopedis, vol. 1 (London: Pluto Press, 1992), 135.
75 Adorno, "Marx and the Basic Concepts," 8.
76 O'Kane, "Critical Theory," 290.
77 Adorno, "Reflections on Class," 103–04.
78 Adorno, *Philosophical Elements*, 124.
79 Adorno, "Late Capitalism," 122.
80 See Simon Clarke, *Keynesianism, Monetarism, and the Crisis of the State* (Aldershot: Edward Elgar Publishing, 1988), 7.
81 Adorno, *Philosophical Elements*, 129.
82 Ibid.
83 Clarke, "Global Accumulation," 145.
84 Clarke, *Keynesianism, Monetarism*, 343–45.

85 See Susan Strange, *Casino Capitalism* (Manchester: Manchester University Press, 1997), 15–17.
86 Mandel, *Late Capitalism*, 464.
87 See David McNally, *Global Slump: The Economics and Politics of Crisis and Resistance* (Oakland: PM Press, 2011), 94–96. See also Edward LiPuma and Benjamin Lee, *Financial Derivates and the Globalization of Risk* (Durham: Duke University Press, 2004).
88 Clarke, *Keynesianism, Monetarism*, 344.
89 McNally, *Global Slump*, 97.
90 See Werner Bonefeld, "Monetarism and Crisis," in *Global Capital, National State, and the Politics of Money*, ed. Werner Bonefeld and John Holloway (London: Macmillan Press, 1996), 40.
91 Adorno, "Static and 'Dynamic' as Sociological Categories," trans. H. Kaal, *Diogenes*, 9, no. 28 (1961): 44.
92 See Silvia Federici, *Revolution at Point Zero: Housework, Reproduction, and Feminist Struggle* (Oakland: PM Press, 2012), 76–111.
93 McNally, *Global Slump*, 26.
94 See Harvey, *A Brief History*, 23–24.
95 See McNally, *Global Slump*, 35.
96 The Reagan-Thatcher opposition to labor can be seen—perhaps most decisively—in Reagan's disruption of the national air-traffic controllers strike in 1981. See McNally, *Global Slump*, 35.
97 According to Stanley Aronowitz and William DiFazio "For example, employment in the steel industry declined from 600,000 production and maintenance workers in 1960 to fewer than 200,000 by 1992; most of the reduction occurred in the 1980s." Aronowitz and DiFazio, *The Jobless Future* (Minneapolis: University of Minnesota Press, 2010), 48. For the most well-known analysis of the effects of the third industrial revolution, see Mandel's *Late Capitalism*, 175–79, 190–93.
98 See McNally, *Global Slump*, 133–35. For an analysis of "peripheral Fordism," see Harvey's *The Condition of Postmodernity* (Cambridge: Blackwell Publishers, 1990), 141–73.
99 Werner Bonefeld and John Holloway, "Introduction: The Politics of Money," *Global Capital*, 1.
100 John Holloway, "The Abyss Opens: The Rise and Fall of Keynesianism," *Global Capital*, 17.
101 Bonefeld, "Monetarism and Crisis," 44.
102 Ibid., 43.
103 Ibid., 45.
104 Aronowitz and DiFazio, *The Jobless Future*, 23.
105 Adorno, "Individuum und Organisation," 446.
106 Clarke, *Keynesianism, Monetarism*, 317.

107 Ibid., 337.
108 See Eric Hobsbawm, *The Age of Extremes: A History of the World, 1914-1991* (New York: Vintage Books, 1996), 412.
109 Ibid., 51.
110 Bonefeld, "Monetarism and Crisis," 50.
111 Ibid.
112 According to Harvey, "These debt crises were orchestrated, managed, and controlled both to rationalize the system and to redistribute assets. Since 1980, it has been calculated, 'over fifty Marshall Plans (over $4.6 trillion) have been spent by the peoples at the Periphery to their creditors in the Center.'" Harvey, *A Brief History of Neoliberalism*, 162.
113 Bonefeld, "Monetarism and Crisis," 51.
114 Strange, *Casino Capitalism*, 49.
115 For details regarding neoliberal support of the Pinochet dictatorship, as well as its institutional support from the Chicago school, see Karin Fischer, "The Influence of Neoliberals in Chile Before, During, and After Pinochet," in *The Road from Mont Pelerin*, ed. Philip Mirowski and Dieter Plehwe (Cambridge: Harvard University Press, 2009), 305–46.
116 Bonefeld, "Authoritarian Liberalism," 2.
117 Clarke, "Global Accumulation," 146.
118 Such Keynesian critiques of neoliberal inequality can be seen, perhaps most prominently, in Thomas Piketty's *Capital in the Twenty-First Century* (Cambridge: Harvard University Press, 2014).
119 Adorno, "Late Capitalism," 122.
120 See Bonefeld: "The notion that the state has been 'brought back in' suggests a resurgent state, one that has regained some measure of control over the market. This view implies a conception of market and state as two distinct modes of social organization, and the perennial question about such a conception is whether the market has autonomy vis-à-vis the state, or the state vis-à-vis the market. The social constitution of state and market as distinct forms of social relations is not raised." Bonefeld, "Free Economy and the Strong State: Some Notes on the State," *Capital and Class*, 34, no. 1 (2010): 16.
121 Adorno, "Late Capital," 123–24.
122 Clarke, "Global Accumulation," 146.
123 See Aaron Benanav and John Clegg, "Crisis and Immiseration Theory: Critical Theory Today," in *The SAGE Handbook*, 1635. One further source of fragmentation within the working class—beyond the scope of this chapter—consists in reactions to the Vietnam, anti-war movement. For an account of the split between the student movement and the American working class, see Robert O. Self's *All in the Family*: "The class politics of the war, in which American policy burdened its most economically vulnerable citizens with the bulk of wartime sacrifice, fed a politics of reactionary resentment against an

educated, urban elite." Self, *All in the Family: The Realignment of American Democracy since the 1960s* (New York: Hill and Wang, 2012), 74.

124 For details regarding the internal differentiation within the 1960s dissident movements, see Benanav and Clegg, "Crisis and Immiseration," 1634–35. A related development, detailed in Luc Boltanski and Eve Chiapello's sociological history of management, delineates the assimilation of the May '68 "artistic critique" of the managerial labor. See Luc Boltanski and Eve Chiapello, *The New Spirit of Capitalism*, trans. Gregory Elliot (London: Verso, 2007).

125 Clarke, "Global Accumulation," 146.

126 See Benanav and Clegg, "Crisis and Immiseration," 1639.

127 Marx Horkheimer and Theodor W. Adorno, *Dialectic of Enlightenment: Philosophical Fragments,* trans. Edmund Jephcott (Stanford: Stanford University Press, 2002), 29.

128 According to Michel Foucault's analysis of neoliberal governmentality, neoliberalism is not "orientated towards the commodity and the uniformity of the commodity, but towards the multiplicity and differentiation of enterprises." Foucault, *The Birth of Biopolitics*, 149. Wendy Brown's genealogical critique similarly argues: "Competition replaces exchange; inequality replaces equality. In neoliberalism, competition replaces the liberal economic emphasis on exchange as the fundamental principle and dynamic of the market." Brown, *Undoing the Demos*, 64.

129 In spite of the neoliberal critique of monopoly in Milton Friedman's popular texts, the Chicago school played a key role in undermining antitrust legislation. For details, see Will Davies, *The Limits of Neoliberalism*: "The most obvious historical consequence of the Chicago revolution in anti-trust (and in regulation more broadly) was far greater freedom for dominant competitors within the overall contest of capitalism. The new assumption, that efficiency is the goal of anti-trust and that monopolistic and exploitative practices are often efficient, led to a mode of regulation that was far more sympathetic to the interests of large business than during the 1950s and 1960s. This created the regulatory climate that would permit the rise of 'shareholder value' as the legitimate goal of corporate governance during the 1980s and 1990s." Davies, *The Limits of Neoliberalism: Authority, Sovereignty, and the Logic of Competition* (London: Sage, 2014), 104–05.

130 William Lazonick, "The Financialization of the U.S. Corporation: What Has Been Lost, and How It Can Be Regained," *Seattle University Law Review*, 36 (2013): 859.

131 According to Mattick, "The slowdown in productive investment meant that money was increasingly available for other purposes. Corporations began to spend vast sums they might earlier have used to expand production to buy up and reconfigure existing companies, selling off parts of them for quick profits and manipulating share prices to make money on the stock market." Mattick, *Business as Usual*, 60.

132 See Lazonick, "Financial Commitment and Economic Performance: Ownership and Control in the American Industrial Corporation," *Business and Economic*

History, 17 (1988): 123. As Cook argues, criticizing Foucault's analysis of neoliberal governmentality, "Yet one problem with Foucault's own analysis is its failure to assess the extent to which neoliberalism successfully steered the West away from a market society based on exchange towards an enterprise society based on competition. Indeed, Adorno was not criticizing economic theories. Rather, he was criticizing what he saw as really existing tendencies within society: the material forces that shape society and orient its trajectory (forces that are analogous to disciplinary power and biopower themselves)." Cook, *Adorno, Foucault and the Critique of the West*, 94.

133 According to Lazonick and Mary O'Sullivan, "Increasingly during the 1980s, and even more so in the 1990s, support for corporate governance on the principle of creating shareholder value came from an even more powerful and enduring source than the takeover market. In the name of 'creating shareholder value,' the past two decades have witnessed a marked shift in the strategic orientation of top corporate managers in the allocation of corporate resources and returns away from 'retain and reinvest' and towards 'downsize and distribute.' Under the new regime, top managers downsize the corporations they control, with a particular emphasis on cutting the size of the labour forces they employ, in an attempt to increase the return on equity." Lazonick and O'Sullivan, "Maximizing Shareholder Value: A New Ideology for Corporate Governance," *Economy and Society*, 29, no. 1 (2000): 18.

134 For an account of inequality in the United States, see Lawrence Mishel, Josh Bivens, Elise Gould, and Heidi Shierholz, *The State of Working America* (Ithaca: Cornell University Press, 2012).

135 Adorno, "Marx and the Basic Concepts," 8.

136 Bonefeld, *Critical Theory*, 156.

137 For example, the recessions of 1987 and 1990, the Mexican crisis of 1994, and the East Asian crisis of 1997. See Holloway, "Global Capital and the National State," 116–40.

138 McNally, *Global Slump*, 197.

139 Cited in Bonefeld, "Strong Economy," 15–16.

140 Bonefeld, *Critical Theory*, 156.

141 Abromeit, "Frankfurt School Critical Theory," 3–27.

142 Ibid., 10. For an analysis that connects right-wing critiques of capitalism with the ideology of anti-Semitism, see Moishe Postone's "Anti-Semitism and National Socialism: Notes on the German Reaction to the Holocaust," *New German Critique*, no. 19 (1980): 97–115.

143 "The false critique of capitalist society recognizes the misery of the many and offers nationalist solutions, sometimes in the name of socialism and sometimes in the name of patriotism," Bonefeld, "Authoritarian Liberalism," 7.

144 Horkheimer and Adorno, *Dialectic of Enlightenment*, 142.

145 Ibid., 165.

3

Natural-History and the Critique of Neoliberal Theory

Economics is the science of the laws that govern society. However, economics does not recognize the social genesis of its concepts. Indeed, economists represent the phenomena of markets and prices through strictly defined models, but they fail to identify the fetishistic properties of their objects. Adorno in fact hated the separation of economics and sociology; in their division, neither discipline can apprehend the contradictory form of capitalist wealth.[1] His dialectics enjoins us to consider the actual human relations of exploitation that subsist within the concepts the economists presuppose. According to Backhaus, Adorno's major contribution to critical theory was to "thematise what Marx terms 'the objective illusion' of economic categories."[2] As previously shown, Adorno's critical theory exposes the antagonistic movement of society and the mediation of individuals by exchange. His critique of fetishism specifies the substitution of individual relations into relations between commodities. Indeed, capitalism is governed by abstract laws that manifest the relations of society as relations of objective things. Adorno's critical theory of capitalist society interprets the totalizing "relations of production," in their appearance as "second nature."[3] But if commodity fetishism pervades every moment of reality as completely as Adorno suggests, how could the totality appear as anything but a natural, and therefore unchangeable, object? To put it another way, how could economic relations appear to us as the products of human practice?

Just as the liberal tradition of classical political economy depicted the relations of society as the work of the "invisible hand" of the market, today's neoliberal theory similarly transfigures its concepts into a "mystified law[s] of nature."[4] Neoliberal economics, as I intend to show, can be criticized as the ideological expression of the capitalist object. "Since every social theory is interwoven with real society," as Adorno suggests, "every social theory can certainly be misused ideologically or operationalized in a distorted manner."[5] Neoliberal economic theory plays a significant institutional role today, extending far beyond the confines of the academy.⁶ According to the most influential strands of neoliberal economic thinking, the free market is not only the most natural form of human organization but also the only available site of "truth" for society. But the neoliberal concept of truth is the inverted reflection of an untrue capitalist world. In what follows, I argue that Adorno's materialist concept of "natural-history" (*Naturgeschichte*) can provide a critical framework for deciphering the dominant concepts of neoliberal economic theory. An immanent critique of neoliberalism, I suggest, should reveal the constitutive social, and historically produced, relations that appear natural in the economic sciences. According to Adorno, "Economic and social relations and ideologies are inextricably interwoven."⁷ His idea of natural-history can help us grasp how capitalism generates the concepts of economics, and how these concepts become moments of the social whole they reinforce. Additionally, I return to Adorno's critique of positivism in sociology to show how the economic sciences similarly reify capitalist social relations. I develop the idea of natural-history with reference to the following concepts and categories: (1) natural-history, (2) neoclassical economics and positivist sociology, (3) neoliberal economics and Hayek's theory of information, and (4) neoliberal "second nature." Through a reconstruction of neoliberal concepts and categories I argue that the concept of the "information economy" can be grasped with reference to Adorno's critique of "second nature," which is to say, an objective context that naturalizes the historical relations of capitalist society.

The Idea of Natural-History

In order to organize Adorno's framework for criticizing economic theory, I must first clarify the details of his approach to natural-history. Unfortunately, the idea of natural-history defies straightforward definition. Adorno first presented "The Idea of Natural-History" in 1932 to the Frankfurt chapter of the *Kant-Gesellschaft*, which was disputing the problem of historiographical methodology at the time.⁸ Adorno developed his materialist critique of the idealisms of neo-Kantianism and Heidegger's "neo-ontology" respectively, by establishing a dialectical framework for the interpretation of historical phenomena.⁹ Influenced by Georg Lukács's Hegelian concept of "second nature," "The Idea of Natural-History" indexes Adorno's first attempt to liberate dialectics from the system of traditional Marxism. By "natural-history," Adorno does not mean the "history of nature," in the sense of progress, linearity, or natural evolution. Moreover, his concept of nature does not refer to the objects of "natural science."[10] The concepts of nature and history form an internal, dialectical tension, in which both concepts are "mediated in their apparent difference."[11] The concepts are set in motion to disarticulate the sedimentation of capitalist relations in their objective, naturalized appearance. Adorno's natural-history rejects both the neo-Kantian and neo-ontological frameworks of historiography:

> If the question of the relation of history is to be seriously posed, then it only offers any chance of solution if it is possible to *comprehend historical being in its most extreme historical determinacy, where it is most historical, as natural being, or if it were possible to comprehend nature as historical being where it seems to rest most deeply in itself as nature.*[12]

Adorno's dialectics disrupts ontology's fatalism. This framework, he suggests, allows us to comprehend an object as natural where it appears most historical, and as historical where it appears most natural, thus shattering the semblance of history as natural, predetermined fate.[13]

Adorno indicates that the enlightenment's classical representations of nature have inherited mythological cosmologies. By "myth," Adorno suggests that nature is depicted as an order of cyclical repetition, eternal necessity, and preordained fate. Mythic nature, he continues, signifies "what has always been, what as fatefully arranged predetermined being underlies history and appears in history, it is substance in history."[14] Mythic nature is defined by empty, homogeneous space and time. But the concept of mythic nature contains its own dialectic; mythic repetition is mediated by history—by the appearance of new forms. Hullot-Kentor writes: "The historical is mythical and the mythical historical. Not only are they intertwined, but the historical new appears in the mythical."[15] Just as socially produced forms can ossify into naturalized appearances, the very same appearances can fracture under the pressure of historical transformation.

To develop the dialectic of natural-history further, Adorno draws from Lukács's distinction between "first" and "second" nature to delineate the naturalization of social relations in capitalist modernity.[16] By "first nature," Adorno means the representation of nature by the mathematical sciences. The concept of history, by contrast, refers to human practice, to the constitution of novel forms of life. History is "that mode of conduct established by tradition that is characterized primarily by the occurrence of the qualitatively new; it is a movement that gains its true character through what appears in it as new."[17] History therefore contains potentials for breaking the seeming invariance of naturalized social forms. Adorno's dialectic suggests that our experience of "first nature" is mediated by "second nature"—that is, by the commodity-form and the fetishistic properties possessed by the commodity.

In *Negative Dialectics*, Adorno returns to the idea of natural-history to develop its Marxist implications for ideology critique. In this "model" in his late opus, Adorno pursues the critique of commodity fetishism through the prism of natural history to analyze the seeming "inescapability" of the capitalist relations of production.[18] The capitalist totality possesses the semblance of natural necessity: "The natural growth of capitalist society," Adorno writes, "is real and at the same time semblance."[19] The law of capitalist accumulation expresses the necessity of exploitation; the constant need to expand and reproduce the relations of society is the mystification of capital. The "natural-rootedness" of capitalist society, Adorno continues, "is grounded in the abstraction, which counts as essential for the process of exchange."[20] The exchange abstraction depends on society's "disregard" for living human beings.[21] The semblance of inescapability in the life process of capitalism, then, is "value as a thing-in-itself, as 'nature.'"[22] The naturalness of value, however, is real as the unconscious "law of motion" of capital. To the degree that it is "hypostasized" as an immutable fact of nature, the putative "natural lawfulness" of society is ideology.[23] But for Adorno, ideology is not at all a simple delusion of the masses; ideology, he insists, is not a "detachable layer" of the social process. Ideology "precedes the false consciousness of all" and reflects the practices of human beings in an untrue world.[24]

But if the social process is as beset with illusions as Adorno's critique of ideology suggests, what are the implications for the theory of society? Adorno follows Marx's immanent critique of the classical theory of liberalism by confronting the concept of society with its object. The naturalization of economic concepts (e.g., utility, price, and profit), form moments of the totality that manifests behind the backs of the individuals in their work. The socially constituted context of "second nature" mediates the disciplines of economics and sociology, reifying social relations into purportedly scientific "laws." For Adorno economics is identity thinking.[25] It identifies the movements of prices with the rational preferences of individuals, but it does not conceptualize the irrational organization of a totality that reduces needs to exchange-value. The modern discipline of "subjective economics," as Adorno calls it, "is essentially an analysis of the market processes in which established market relations are already presupposed."[26] Subjective economics "elegantly formalizes" historically produced processes but fails to question the constitution of its objects.[27] Insofar as the positivist methods of economics and sociology presuppose capitalist relations, they arrest the movement of society into putatively scientific doctrines. In the hands of economists, society appears to govern individuals in the providential form of the "invisible hand" of the market, which "takes care of both beggar and king."[28]

Liberalism: Economy as First Nature

The political economy of Adam Smith and David Ricardo divided the economy into three spheres of activity: production, exchange, and consumption. To Smith, the historical development of "commercial society" manifested through the natural human propensity to "truck, barter, and exchange."[29] The classical "labor theory of value" can be understood as a "metaphysics" of value. For Smith and Ricardo, value expresses an invariant substance underlying the transformations of society. Dividing labor into the so-called "productive" sphere of manufacture and the "unproductive" labor of service and reproduction, Smith's political economy affirmed a physicalist concept of value as the foundation of wealth.[30] Insofar as they reified value by reducing it to an invariant substance, classical political economy imagined it could formalize its phenomena as laws of first nature. As Thorstein Veblen later remarked in his critique of economics, Smith and Ricardo's "resulting economic theory is formulated as an analysis of the 'natural' course of the life of the community, the ultimate theoretical postulate of which . . . might be stated as some sort of law of the conservation of economic energy."[31] Metaphors of balance, motion, and energy suffused the classical tradition, thereby establishing the natural basis for conceptualizing the capitalist object.

According to Adorno, Marx did not have to develop an alternative theory to political economy. He "needed only to inquire whether capitalism fit into this system in order to produce a quasi-systematic theory of his own, in determinate negation of the system he found before him."[32] Marx's critique of political economy turns on his repudiation of Smith and Ricardo's labor theory of value. For Marx, Smith and Ricardo developed a naturalistic theory of value based on the expenditure of labor time. Such an approach, however, was carried out independently of any theory of the social form of production.[33] Against the substance theory of value, Marx's theory of value as a "social form" recognizes the historically specific relations of the capitalist mode of production, as well as the fetish character of value that appears disconnected from the activity of laborers, only to confront them as the natural properties of things. By holding fast to the validity of equal exchange in a system of private commodity producers, Marx exposed the constitutive violence underlying the appearance of equal exchange, as well as the appropriation of abstract wealth in a system of legally free and equal subjects.[34]

The succeeding discipline of "subjective economics" indexes an attempt by liberalism to respond to Marx's critique of classical political economy. The liberal response to the critique of political economy aimed to establish the moral and political legitimacy of capitalism on an individualist basis. This individualism was undertaken by breaking from Smith and Ricardo's classical "cost of production theory of value" and replacing it with a subjective theory of value. The so-called Marginalist Revolution of the 1870s in economics therefore defined value as "utility," deriving the rationality of capitalism from the rational actions of individuals. Moreover, for marginalists like William Stanley Jevons, Leon Walras, Vilfredo Pareto, and Francis Edgeworth, economics was reconceptualized as positive science that mathematically formalized the laws of market equilibrium.[35]

In a well-known formulation, Lionel Robbins defined economics as "the science which studies human behavior as a relationship between ends and scarce means which have alternative uses."[36] By "utility," neoclassicals mean the amount or degree of satisfaction derived from the consumption of a commodity. In order to formalize the allocation of resources in markets, neoclassicals appropriated the energy concept from "proto-energetics physics."[37] As economic historian Philip Mirowski has argued in detail, the neoclassical tradition explicitly modeled the utility concept as an analogy with potential energy.[38] In determining value as utility, neoclassicals displaced the commensurability of economic value from production to circulation. This displacement—in effect—shifted the substance of economic value from labor to the rational optimization of individuals.

But insofar as the Marginalist Revolution modeled the laws of market equilibrium through the concept of utility, the theory held fast to the following assumptions: (1) the economic agent is "rational" vis-à-vis market prices, (2) the agent "maximizes" its utility preferences in every exchange, and (3) the agent possesses *all relevant information* regarding market prices. The neoclassicals "ascribe subjective power to economic things" and naturalize the relations of society into mathematical expressions of historical phenomena.[39] Within the neoclassical paradigm, the categories of wages, rent, and profit are dissociated from their genesis; the social constitution of the economic agent—*homo oeconomicus*—never appears in the laws of supply and demand. Moreover, the neoclassical concept of rationality abstracts the preferences of agents from the mediations of experience. This concept of rationality—in repressing the priority of the social object—is a case of identity thinking. In its indifference to the psychological, anthropological, and historical constituents of experience, the figure of *homo economicus* indexes the indifference of the real abstractions of capital, the reduction of subjects to bearers of exchange-value.

The neoclassical vision regarding economic rationality, general equilibrium, and optimality expresses the semblance of mythic nature. Marginalists largely abandoned questions regarding class and the social constitution of production relations to conceptualize utility, efficiency, and price on a narrow, individualist basis. As Clarke maintains, marginalism can "only make economics a 'natural science' because it 'naturalises' the fundamental relationships of capitalist society."[40] By ignoring the constitution of capitalist categories, the market appears in abstraction from the actual relations of society, thus reifying its findings as the constituents of first nature. Neoclassicals unmoor market prices from the contradictory relations of production; in the putative identity of price and value, their vision of utility maximization expresses the universal principle of socialization, but rather than grasping the mediations of market price with reference to the contradictory moments of the commodity-form, neoclassicals reduce value to price.[41] The exchange relation is not an immediate function between rational agents, but rather an objective form of interdependence that belongs to a system of private commodity producers. Exchange-value appears through the money form as the universal equivalent. Marginal utility theory assumes that market prices can exist without a determinate social form.

The discipline of subjective economics, Adorno suggests, is the "apology" for bourgeois society.[42] By cutting off its analyses of price from the constituents of the capitalist totality, subjective economics quantifies its objects in abstraction from their historical development. This theoretical abstraction, however, is the work of the objective exchange abstraction—that is, the practical abstraction that individuals realize independently of their private reflection. Without the real moment of "conceptuality in reality" itself, the objects of economic science could not "come into existence."[43] The total absence of empirical contents from its representations bears the mark of real abstraction—that is, the constitution of ideal "thought forms" by social forms. As discussed in Chapter 1, the exchange abstraction produces really existing idealities. Neoclassical economic theory is possible on the basis of the objective conceptuality of capitalist society. The concepts of neoclassical theory express more than they intend.

Adorno regarded subjective economics and empirical sociology as manifestations of the same positivist imperative: the desire to classify the phenomena of society scientifically. Indeed, the development of marginalism in economics provided the basis for the modern sociology of voluntary individual action.[44] Subjective economics is informed by the neo-Kantian tradition from which it arose. Insofar as marginalists grant validity to their formal method independently of any consideration of the constitution of their objects, they depend on what Adorno criticizes as "methodologism" in social science.[45] As Adorno remarked in his debate with Karl Popper during the *Positivist Dispute*, "The predominant positivistic sociology can rightly be termed subjective in the same sense as subjective economics."[46] Positivism begins with the data of individual opinions, attitudes regarding status, and modes of behavior. In this conception, Adorno argues, "society is largely what must be investigated statistically: the average consciousness or unconsciousness of societalized and socially acting subjects, and not the medium in which they move."[47] The positivistic sociology of Vilfredo Pareto, for example, reduces society to "nothing but the average value of individual modes of reaction," just as subjective economics reduces the form of society to individual preferences.[48] Both disciplines identify human action with the surface facts of society.

By treating society as the "objective" average of individual facts, positivism "objectivates" what "really causes objectivation" in reality, namely, the estrangement of individuals from each other and from the totality.[49] Recall that for Adorno, society is at once "subject and object."[50] Sociology, therefore, has a "dual character."[51] The methods of positivism reify society by eliminating its subjective moment—that is, the "human beings who form it."[52] In neglecting to grasp society as subject and object, positivism falls short of its supposed objectivity. The reification of method is just as discernible in economics. The economists who study the struggle over the distribution of wealth, for example, rightly identify the primacy of social conflict in capitalism. However, economics fails to see that "this conflict of interests, as manifested in competition, is itself a dilute derivative of much deeper conflicts, those between classes."[53] The conflicts of interests over the distribution of wealth, as Adorno maintains, "are really the ones which take place after the central conflict over the means of production has already been decided, so that the competition is carried on within the sphere of an already appropriated surplus value."[54] Positivist approaches lack the standpoint that would allow theory to conceptualize the social "essence which shapes appearances."[55] The rationality imputed to actors by positivism is possible on the basis of the rationality of society's real conceptuality—that is, of the exchange principle that abstracts from objects. The methods of positivism, according to Adorno, are "so blinded by society that it regards second nature as first nature and identifies the data of society with the data of natural science."⁵⁶ The neoclassical school perpetuates the real abstraction of society conceptually, forming a moment within the total context of exchange relations in their naturalized appearance. By treating the relations of society as the objective expressions of individual preferences, economics accepts reification and "repeats it," in theory, thus losing "the perspective in which society and its law would first reveal themselves."⁵⁷

Neoliberal Theory and the Economics of Information

Neoliberal economics is often mistakenly conflated with its neoclassical predecessor.⁵⁸ While there are significant points of contact between neoclassical and neoliberal theory, the latter tradition also differs from many of the assumptions of the Marginalist Revolution. Moreover, the origins of neoliberal economics, in fact, predate the body of theory associated with the Chicago school of economics, and can be traced to the Austrian school in the 1920s.⁵⁹ Neoliberal theory, in fact, began as a critique of laissez-faire liberalism and market socialism. In addition to the influential contributions of Carl Menger and Ludwig von Mises, the Austrian school produced Friedrich von Hayek, perhaps the most decisive social thinker within this tradition. Trained originally in biology, brain science, psychology, and neo-Kantisan epistemology, Hayek's contribution to the "Socialist Calculation Debate" in the 1920s provided the foundation for the articulation of a new concept of the free market.⁶⁰

The problem of economic calculation began as a confrontation between Ludwig von Mises and Oscar Lange regarding the possibility of market simulation within a socialist planning board. Against Lange, who had argued affirmatively in favor of planning, von Mises insisted that an economy could never "calculate" the optimal allocation of goods without market prices.⁶¹ Although for many economic liberals, von Mises's critique of central planning was sufficient for abandoning market socialism, Hayek's participation in the debate would be regarded as the most influential body of theory in neoliberal economics.⁶² Hayek shifted the terms of the Socialist Calculation Debate by reframing the problem of resource allocation into a problem of knowledge and information. The inescapable mistake of socialist planning, he argued, consisted in trying to do what only the market could—namely communicate information. By pointing to the limits of central planning, and by naming the free market as the true site of information for economic coordination, Hayek initiated a wider turn within the economics profession that would converge in a new epistemology of markets. This shift can be seen perhaps most famously, in his 1945 essay, "The Use of Knowledge in Society," in which he asks,

> What is the problem we try to solve when we try to construct a rational economic order? On certain familiar assumptions the answer is simple enough. If we possess all the relevant information, if we can start out from a given system of preferences, and if we command complete knowledge of the available means, the problem which remains is purely one of logic. . . . This, however, is emphatically not the economic problem which society faces. . . . The peculiar problem of a rational economic order is determined precisely by the fact that the knowledge of the circumstances of which we must make use never exists in concentrated or integrated form but solely as dispersed bits of incomplete and frequently contradictory knowledge which all the separate individuals possess. The economic problem of society is thus not merely a problem of how to allocate "given" resources; . . . it is a problem of the utilization of knowledge not given to anyone in its totality.[63]

Hayek's theory breaks from classical laissez-faire notions regarding general equilibrium, and refocuses the problem of economic allocation by privileging the role of information. The free market—now redefined as an information processor—does not primarily allocate goods, but rather discovers and broadcasts information to individuals. The attempt to replace the market system with public planning then, according to Hayek, cannot solve the problem of economic calculation, because no planning board can convey the fragmented bits of knowledge individual entrepreneurs need. According to Clarke, for "the neo-Austrian model it is no longer necessary to assume that every individual has perfect knowledge and perfect foresight, because knowledge is no longer an attribute of the individual, but is conveyed by market prices."[64] The problem of economic calculation is therefore epistemic: How can the relevant knowledge be distributed, as Hayek suggests, if the relevant knowledge is never given to anyone in its totality?

Hayek replaced the concept of "knowledge" with "information" to decenter the neoclassical, rational individual. Information, he argues, refers to an entity that only the price mechanism can discover—information does *not* refer to the agent's cognition. The concept of information therefore refers to a "mind-independent" entity, existing only as an object of the market's epistemic faculties. The relevant information in an "economy of knowledge," he maintains, depends on the partial knowledge of individuals.[65] Because information is dispersed, fragmented, and largely practical, Hayek favored the activity of individual entrepreneurs who respond and adapt to local and unpredictable circumstances. The limited knowledge of central planning thus provided the fulcrum of his famous critique of socialism in *The Road to Serfdom* (1944). "This is precisely what the price system does under competition," he writes. "It enables entrepreneurs, by watching the movement of comparatively few prices, as an engineer watches the hands of a few dials, to adjust their activities to those of their fellows."[66] The limited knowledge and rationality of the agent indexes a radical break from the neoclassical tradition: rather than attributing the rationality of markets to the preferences of individuals, Hayek's theory specifies the immanent capacity of markets to process information as the key to a rational economic order. The information produced through prices is usable by all competing entrepreneurs, but would be possessed by none in the absence of the market system. The self-regulating market thus emerges, as his theory suggests, as the only available means of differentiating signal from noise.[67]

But Hayek starkly differentiates his information theory from the liberal notions regarding any purported "equality of knowledge," as his interlocutor, Karl Popper, would champion in the latter's concept of an "open society."[68] Hayek's economy of information stressed the inequality of agents in markets, pointing to the need for fiercely competitive relations between individuals. "Epistemology," he argues, "is governed by competition as a procedure for the discovery of such facts as, without resort to it, would not be known to anyone."[69] The relevant knowledge in question, Hayek maintains, is only communicable to agents who avail themselves of the market's signals. According to the theory, forms of knowledge exist that are only "known" by markets.[70] Insofar as Hayek positions information as the exclusive property of markets, he effectively subordinates individuals to the ostensibly superior cognitive faculties of markets.

Hayek's theory also turned to psychology to establish its concepts of cognition and intentionality. In his early text, *The Sensory Order*, published later in 1952, he developed an account of cognition that drew from associationist psychology, portraying the mind as a hierarchical set of classifying algorithms. Hayek's epistemology appropriated Gilbert Ryle and Michael Polanyi's theory of "tacit knowledge."[71] The concept of tacit knowledge suggests the primacy of implicit, non-articulable knowledge as being fundamental to cognition. Grounded in an order of non-articulable classifying systems, Hayek's theory of mind radically decentered the individual's rationality. As Mirowski and Nik-Khah indicate, for Hayek "it was *rationality that was largely unconscious*, with conscious perception and drives constituting the veneer of intentionality and desires floating on top of a sea of obscure and inaccessible rule structures."[72] But if the individual agent acts by responding to information and signals, as Hayek claims, what social structure can occasion the use of the mind's unconscious rules?

The ordered structure Hayek proposes, unsurprisingly, is a market system, because such a system is structured by the rules of private property, voluntary exchange, and competition. Guided by the ordering constituents of a market system, the individual no longer needs to design, plan, or regulate society. Information, in his theory, is increasingly abstracted from the individual knower; the relevant information is largely the result of imitation, rule-following, and local adaptations to the market's signals. As Hayek argues in the "The Primacy of the Abstract," "the formation of a new abstraction seems *never* to be the outcome of a conscious process, not something at which the mind can deliberately aim, but always a discovery of something which already guides its operation."[73] Information then, to Hayek's mind, is largely the work of the network of exchange relations in commercial society. By attributing ignorance to the agent primarily, and by subordinating the agent to the "spontaneous order" that knows more than any agent, the market system emerges as the only possible form of rational social organization.

Neoliberal theory, therefore, not only naturalizes markets but also treats the human mind as "market-like" in its structure.[74] In *The Sensory Order*, Hayek draws a clear analogy between the human brain and the market system:

> In both cases we have complex phenomena in which there is a need for a method of utilizing widely dispersed knowledge. The essential point is that each member (neuron, or buyer, or seller) is induced to do what in the total circumstances benefits the system. Each member can be used to serve needs of which he doesn't know anything at all. Now that means that in the larger (say, economic), order knowledge is utilized that is not planned or centralized or even conscious. . . . In our whole system of actions, we are individually steered by local information—information about more facts than any other person or authority can possibly possess. And the price and market system is in that sense a system of communication, which passes on (in the form of prices, determined only in the competitive market) the available information that each individual needs to act, and to act rationally.[75]

For Hayek the human mind and the market system are each, self-ordering systems. Just as consciousness is the by-product of unknown neuronal firing, the market is the unplanned result of exchanges between buyers and sellers. The faculties of the brain and economy, according to Hayek, are formed as wholes that are designed by parts unknown to any individual. The communication of information is the condition of possibility of social order. Hayek's philosophy of mind conceptualizes the essentially practical structure of knowledge. To the degree that the subject's cognition is only relevant insofar as cognition is already concordant with properties of the market, the subject's intentions and experiences are largely irrelevant for the development of the system. As Quinn puts it, "The vanishing of the subject is consistent with system theory in general, where the system itself becomes the protagonist."[76]

Although Hayek regularly criticized economists who modeled markets with scientific concepts, his later work is clearly informed by the postwar efflorescence of information theory, computer science, and cybernetics. If the neoclassical tradition naturalized its concepts and categories by imitating the laws of physics, neoliberal theory developed through a complex, reciprocally determining encounter with the emerging cybernetic sciences. Derived from the Greek "*kybernesis*" (or "steersman"), cybernetics is, as Norbert Wiener defined it, "the scientific study of control and communication in the animal and machine."[77] The science of cybernetics originated in the famed "Macy Conferences" in 1941 in the United States, and became a key resource for the interdisciplinary study of self-ordering systems.[78] Articulated throughout the course of several waves of research, cybernetics provided the basis for theorizing social forms with reference to its notions of information, communication, and control. As Mirowski shows in detail in *Machine Dreams* (2002), "Cybernetics became the vehicle for a unified science of people and things."[79] For neoliberals like Hayek, insofar as the market system can elaborate itself in the absence of interference, it can act as a "steersman" of human agents. Insofar as it aimed to blur the boundaries between the organic and the mechanical, as well mind and machine, cybernetics established a framework in which economists could conceptualize information as a "fungible commodity."[80]

Hayek's later work turned to the cybernetic sciences to conceptualize the free market as a system of "order." Spanning a body of work that did more than any other economist to reconceptualize markets, Hayek's epistemology connects the concept of information with a *political* vision of a market society. In his later work, Hayek increasingly describes markets as a "spontaneous order"—that is, a form of human practice that generates more complex structures of organization than could ever be constructed by individuals or states. The free market, according to Hayek, is an ideal example of the spontaneous order, because it is a form of social organization that determines itself through the unconscious actions of those who constitute it. Rather than prioritizing the rationality of individual agents (as the neoclassical schools had done), Hayek's epistemology prioritized the ordered properties of markets. As Quinn Slobodian suggests, "It may be more accurate to see Hayek as more a proponent of the idea of *Homo regularis* than of the idea of *Homo economicus*."[81] In his vision, prices are not merely instruments of utility maximization: they function as rules that facilitate the development of a free, liberal society.

In an effort to find theoretical resources for his "economy of knowledge," Hayek turned to developments cybernetics, systems theory, and biology. For example, in 1968, he attended the Alpbach cybernetics conference, announcing, "Order is not an object," but an "order of events."[82] Hayek therefore defines "order" as the product of humanity's innate capacity to respond to signals and rules. This capacity, however, is not primarily the achievement of knowledge, but exists immanently in organic life: "Man does not know most of the rules on which he acts; and even what we call his intelligence is largely a system of rules which operate on him but which he does not know."[83] By displacing cognition from the neoclassical figure of *homo economicus* to the supra-individual properties of market orders, Hayek's epistemology defines cognition as the emergent outcome of ignorant agents under conditions of free market competition.[84]

For Hayek, the priority of the system over the subject is articulated in cybernetics—a discipline that focused on the self-correcting properties of systems. The cybernetic concept of "negative feedback," in particular, became a key reference point in Hayek's epistemology. Negative feedback refers to the inherent tendency of an organism, machine, or system to correct itself through the output of information. Hayek would explicitly describe the price movements of market systems as a type of negative feedback:

> The correspondence of expectations that makes it possible for all parties to achieve what they are striving for is in fact brought about by a process of learning by trial and error which must involve a constant disappointment of some expectations. The process of adaptation operates, as do the adjustments of any self-organizing system, by what cybernetics has taught to call negative feedback: responses to the differences between the expected and the actual results of actions so that these differences will be reduced . . . so long as the price mechanism operates as a medium of communicating knowledge which brings it about that the facts which become known to some, through their effects of their actions on prices, are made to influence the decisions of others.[85]

Opting for the self-reflexive notion of negative feedback, Hayek's information theory stresses the interaction of expectations between individuals in markets as the key to self-regulation. Rational calculation—in this model—is ultimately the work of economic competition, in that competing individuals reduce uncertainty by following market signals. While he rejects all laissez-faire doctrines regarding the "night watchman state," Hayek persisted in the claim that market systems could (in principle) order themselves immanently without any external mediation.

Hayek also turned to later developments in cybernetic theory to model economics through the biological notions of organism, adaptation, and cultural evolution. Naturalistic metaphors of competition proliferate throughout his final work. For example, in 1979, Hayek argued that in order to "explain the economic aspects of large social systems, we have to account for the course of a flowing stream, constantly adapting itself as a whole to changes in circumstances."[86] The adaptational properties of social structures assumed greater prominence as he naturalized the origins of the spontaneous order within a more general theory of "civilization." Garrett Hardin's social Darwinism was particularly influential for Hayek, lending him further resources for defining economic competition as a process of natural evolution.[87] Hardin portrayed natural selection as a cybernetic process, arguing that the speciation is analogous to the self-correcting properties of negative feedback.[88] Moreover, Hardin did not hesitate to identify the work of negative feedback in commercial markets, arguing that the Darwinian "concept of the fittest" has the same normalizing role as that played by the "natural" process of commodities in labor markets.[89]

Hayek freely appropriated social-Darwinian concepts for his articulation of the spontaneous order. His late work attributes the self-regulating properties of biological adaptation to the economy in general. The spontaneous order, in his understanding, emerges through the competitive relations of buying and selling, trade, and rule-selection; the emerging patterns and structures constitute the order needed for the reproduction of society. Through adaptations to their environment, Hayek supposes, the individuals who constitute the system enable it to order itself. As Hayek indicates,

> The information that individuals or organisations can use to adapt to the unknown is necessarily partial, and is conveyed by signals (e.g., prices) through long chains of individuals, each person passing on in modified form a combination of streams of abstract market signals. Nonetheless, the *whole structure of activities tends to adapt, through these partial and fragmentary signals, to conditions foreseen by and known to no individual*, even if this adaptation is never perfect.[90]

The mediations of the price system signal to individuals the relevant information needed for the future. Organized within the adequate legal framework of private property and exchange, Hayek suggests, human civilization as a whole "evolves" through the competitive selection of "fit" behaviors, and the inheritance of socially structuring rules.[91]

Hayek's final articulation of the spontaneous order appears in a collection of lectures, *The Fatal Conceit: The Errors of Socialism* (1988). Here, he focuses upon the origins of markets, tracing the selection of fit rules for self-preservation. He pronounces: "The extended order is perfectly natural: in the sense that it has itself, like similar biological phenomena, evolved naturally in the course of natural selection."[92] Natural history amounts, in his account, to the objective unfolding of competitive relations, facilitating the emergence of markets through the institutions of trade and private property. "Such an order forms itself," Hayek remarks. "That rules became increasingly better adjusted to generate order happened not because men better understood their function, but because those groups prospered who happened to change them in a way that rendered them increasingly adaptive."[93] The similarities between evolution and commerce accumulate throughout his remarks, stressing the need for an ordered system for the market's development.

Increasingly, Hayek focuses on the formation of private property as the fundamental institution of a market system. However, unlike the liberal tradition of John Locke, which grounds property rights in labor, Hayek's account of property rights defends the right of private property as the natural property of competitive relations. In *The Fatal Conceit*, Hayek maintains that the generalization of property relations by competitive individuals is the legitimate foundation of the spontaneous order: "Protection of several property, not the direction of its use by the government, laid the foundations for the growth of the dense network of exchange and services that shaped the extended order."[94] The spontaneous order therefore emerges on the natural basis of private property, coordinating human practice in harmony with the naturally inherited, competitive traits of individuals. Although the selection of competitive rules and an institutionalized system of private property is never guaranteed by history (as the market can always be subverted by governments), Hayek's vision for a market system points to the natural bias in human nature for selecting capitalist forms of association. Moreover, insofar as he defines rationality as a constituent property of the market, Hayek's epistemology preempts the capacity to articulate a concept of reason that would not refer to society's subordination to the market order.

On one level, it might seem that Hayek's concept of the spontaneous order has subverted the intention of Adorno's critique of "mythic nature." Cast as a dynamic, heterogenous, and largely unknowable order of complexity and contingency, Hayek's epistemology of markets is decidedly at odds with many of the core assumptions of "subjective economics." However, Hayek's concept of the market is firmly mediated by the naturalized context of capital as "second nature." To his way of thinking, the market order is the best of all possible social orders, because markets already possess what is most rational about first nature. But by deriving the origins of markets from the putatively natural properties of the spontaneous order, Hayek's theory cuts off the determinacy of capitalist relations from their historical specificity. The "facts of nature," he suggests, are economic in their structure: natural selection is an objective case of economizing.[95] Just as the human brain recapitulates the information processing faculties of markets, organic life in general processes information through competition. But Hayek's concept of the spontaneous order does not recognize its own constitution by the alienated form of capitalist relations. Considered as natural-history, the neoliberal affirmation of rule-bound order does not acknowledge how, as Adorno suggests, nature and history are "mediated in their apparent difference."[96] Neoliberal economics goes further in recognizing the impersonal autonomism of the capitalist object than its neoclassical predecessors, but rather than grasping this autonomism in terms of the fundamental inversion of subject and object in capitalist society, the theory remains blinded by fetish character of the exchange abstraction. Hayek's theory reifies market relations in total abstraction from their social form; he names the invisible forces that manifest as first nature without recognizing the constitution of capitalist relations as the product of history.[97]

Neoliberalism as Second Nature

Neoliberal theory, I have suggested, in articulating an epistemic vision of a market society, can be criticized as the product of second nature. The neoliberal concept of the free market, however, is not a mere apology by an economist class of intellectuals and think tank experts. For critics like Mirowski and Peck, neoliberalism is described as a political project crafted by the economics profession.[98] This approach, however, is limited by its failure to return neoliberal concepts back to their genesis in the actual relations of society. The concepts of self-regulation, information, and spontaneity all reflect the mediations of the negative, capitalist totality. The neoliberal revolution in economics has legitimated its ideals regarding "liberty," "freedom," and "private initiative" as a moment in the wider, institutional dismantlement of the welfare state. But neoliberal ideas are expressions of the real abstractions of the capitalist social form. The concepts and ideas of neoliberal thought are refractions of the "objective web of blindness" that inverts the phenomena of society into self-moving economic forces.[99] "The idea of natural laws governing history," Adorno reminds us, "the idea that social entanglements are the natural outgrowth of history, goes together with the unfreedom of the individual."[100] The more the process of socialization by exchange captures every aspect of life, the "more impossible it becomes to recollect the historical origins of that process."[101] Socialization by the exchange principle externalizes the "free market" as the semblance of natural necessity. The price system, which appears in abstract isolation from human practice, assumes the form of appearance of myth—that is, of prearranged fate.

Hayek's theory goes furthest among neoliberals in recognizing the supra-individual form of a society coordinated by the exchange principle.[102] To this extent, his theory is *ideological* in conveying the truth about a false world. But ideology, as Adorno suggests, is not separate from the structure of society: "The element of ideology is implicit in the exchange relation itself: abstracting from the specific circumstances between people and the commodities—an abstraction that is necessary in the process of exchange—gives rise to false consciousness."[103] The mediating conceptuality of exchange, Adorno continues, is "independent both of the consciousness of the human beings subjected to it and the consciousness of the scientists."[104] The exchange principle, however, is not a "general formulation of average expectations," but is the law that "provides the objectively valid model for all events."[105] Hayek recognizes the independence of society's objective conceptuality—that is, of the priority of the totality that "preserves itself" through conflicts of interest.[106] But rather than criticizing the reduction of individual interests to the economic process as illusion, as second nature, he naturalizes the coercive disunity of individuals and the totality. His theory, moreover, does not fundamentally question the validity of capitalist relations in their historical specificity. The object of his critique of socialist planning is primarily a critique of regulation from the standpoint of the transhistorical validity of markets. Such a standpoint, however, does not recognize the historical processes of dispossession that constitute the capital-labor relation. It is useful to observe Adorno's recollection of Marx's critique of economic self-interest in the *Grundrisse*,

> The economists put it this way: Everyone pursues his private interest and thus unwillingly and unwittingly serves the private interests of all, the general interests. The joke is not that everyone's pursuit of his private interest will in effect serve the entirety of private interests, that is, the general interest; from

this abstract phrase it might as well be inferred that everyone mutually inhibits the pursuit of the other's interest, and that, instead of general affirmation, the result of this *bellum omnium contra omnes* will be general negation. The point is, rather, that the private interest itself is already a socially determined interest, one that can be pursued only on the terms laid down by society—hence an interest tied to the reproduction of those terms and means. It is the interest of private persons; but its content as well as the form and means of realization are given by social conditions independent of them all.[107]

Adorno captures this apparent independence in the law of autonomization, the real movement of economic abstractions that appear in mystified form as values. This law of autonomization, however, is founded upon the production of the "doubly free laborer," that is, of the historical separation of the laborer from her means of subsistence.[108] The violence needed for the "separation of free labor from the objective conditions of its realization—from the means of production and the material labor"—appears in the form of contractual relations between free subjects.[109] The neoliberal critique of socialist calculation does not recognize the historically specific determination of exchange-value—that is, of the necessary form of appearance of value. If neoclassicals legitimated its science of economics through the translation of mechanical physics into utility, neoliberals have abandoned the category of market equilibrium altogether, preferring the notion that the market system knows more than any individual or state.

Hayek's vision of the free market is both true and false. Insofar as subjects are compelled by the autonomous movement of the totality, they really do respond to an impersonal system of external market signals. However, the autonomism of the totality is not merely the outcome of subjective preferences in competition; capitalist society is a subject-objective totality. Recall that for Adorno, society is a process of socialization determined by exchange: "When we speak of society in a strong sense . . . we are referring essentially to the element of 'socialisation,' . . . a functional connection which leaves no-one out, a connectedness in which all members of the society are entwined and which takes on a certain kind of autonomy in relation to them."[110] The genesis of value remains obscure to individuals mediated by exchange as the commodity acts "behind the backs" of individuals as a regulatory power. The concept of the information economy fixates upon the prices of commodities as the supposed representation of individual preferences. Socialized by the exchange principle, as Adorno maintains, the totality "is pre-established for all individual subjects," thus compelling them to "obey its 'contrainte' even in themselves and even in their monadological constitution."[111] Neoliberal theory names this structural interdependence of individuals, but rather than grasping the historically specific form of capitalist mediation, the theory grounds its epistemology in the putatively natural properties of exchange. Hayek ascribes "liberty" to subjects already determined as "character masks" of capital, thus repressing the fundamental subject-object inversion of a total system organized for profit.

Neoliberal economics fetishizes the real metaphysics of late capitalist society. By projecting the faculties of mind (through its concepts of information, complexity, and order) onto the economy, neoliberals position markets as the most rational tool for reducing the ignorance of a totality dominated by the commodification of the future. In its semblance of first nature, the free market, it is claimed, develops immanently through its capacity to process and convey information. But the concept of the free market is only possible on the basis of the fetishistic properties of the commodity-form. The global expansion of financial capitalism reduces human practice to identity. The semblance of nature possessed by the chains of credit cuts off value from the contradictory relations of the negative totality. The abstract and quasi-providential authority of the free market belongs to the irrational form of society organized for profit. The exchange abstraction, which consumes the particular in the universal, is extended in neoliberalism's progressive harnessing of the future to the accumulation of capital.

Neoliberal theory is the conceptual fetish of late capitalist society in its need to mortgage the exploitation of labor to the future. In Hayek's theory, as we have seen, information provides the basis for the self-ordering properties of markets. But these ordering properties are only the result of the peculiar character of a system of private producers that validates social labor in exchange. Hayek's anthropological account of the generalization of exchange fails to conceptualize the mediated form of capitalist wealth in its historical specificity. As we have seen, the capitalist mode of production is characterized by a principle of reduction—namely, the reduction to unity that allows the exchange of commodities. "What makes commodities exchangeable," Adorno maintains, "is the unity of socially necessary abstract labour time."[112] This unity is not determined by individuals and their private evaluations in exchange. "Abstract labour time," Adorno indicates, "abstracts from living opponents" who are entwined in a system that has become autonomous.[113] In failing to conceptualize exchange as the objective principle of abstraction that validates private labor as social labor, neoliberal theory attributes subjective properties to commodities as the intrinsic bearers of value. The emergence of the free market—now defined as the true cognizing subject of society—expresses the contradictory relations of society. Through the abstraction of exchange, which validates the expenditure of socially necessary labor time, commodities are imbued with social powers. But the fetish of information in today's economic theory is not simply an illusion. Fetishized perceptions, Adorno remarks, "are not an illusion either," because human beings "become dependent on those objectivities which are obscure to them."[114] Individuals are actually dependent on the fetish form of value as it is reflected back to buyers and sellers as the seemingly natural properties of things. The categories of socially necessary illusion are "in truth also categories of reality"— their epistemic authority belongs to the rationality of an irrational totality.

The condition that subjective rational interests subsist through an irrational whole makes society appear as an objectively unfolding necessity. Notwithstanding his critique of economic scientism and empiricism, Hayek's theory is captured by the positivist preoccupation with the surface facts of society.[115] Such positivism can be seen, for example, in Hayek's prohibition on the metaphysical distinction between appearance and reality in science.[116] But as Horkheimer and Adorno suggest, the positivistic dissolution of traditional metaphysical concepts promotes the fatalistic acceptance of society in its "givenness."[117] But the positivity of market facts conceals the law of value and the antagonistic essence that subsists beneath society's manifestations. Positivism "equates probability with essence."[118] A dialectical theory of society, however, does not remain fixated on the appearances of society, but seeks to understand "the societal essence which shapes appearances, appears in them and conceals itself in them."[119] According to Adorno, positivism "confuses facts and figures, the plaster model of the world, with its foundation."[120] Neoliberal theory fixates on the supposed liberty of information, communication, and self-regulation, without reflecting on the socially dominating effects of their commodification. "Without exception," Adorno insists, "what is called communication nowadays is but the noise that drowns out the silence of the spellbound."[121] By affixing economic properties to first nature in advance of any reflection on the mediations of second nature, Hayek's notions of information and spontaneity reinstate the fated order of myth. The mode of thinking that characterizes economics sustains the identity of thought and its object that is "inextricably entwined with the structure of reality itself."[122]

Hayek is right to name the abstractions of the price system as an immanent moment of the capitalist object. In supposing that markets aggregate decentralized information on the basis of competitive relations, Hayek fails to consider the manipulation of information by private monopoly capital. Policies of financial deregulation, as we have seen in Chapter 2, have largely reinforced the concentration of private wealth in neoliberalism, and just as monopoly capitalism preempts market competition it similarly distorts the free circulation of information. As I discuss at greater length in Chapter 5, monopolists have instrumentalized key technologies and computational systems for regulating behavior, such as data mining, data analytics, and target marketing.[123] In addition to managing consumer and employee behavior, such models are typically proprietary and inaccessible to public scrutiny.[124] Hayek takes for granted that only states and planning boards interfere with the price system's transmission of information; he never supposes that monopoly capital can subvert the price system through asset-price inflationism. It is difficult to see how the administrative manipulation of information and stock prices by protected corporations could be described as contributing the price system's calculations in Hayek's sense. Insofar as he identifies states and planning boards as the sole source of regulation that interferes with competition, he neglects the power of monopolists to distort the price system through the administration and control of information.

More significantly, Hayek's theory, as well as the wider tradition of neoliberal economics that he played a role in shaping, expresses the really existing abstractions of capitalist society. "Abstraction," Adorno reminds us, "is dictated by the object, by the constancy of a society which actually does not tolerate anything qualitatively different—a society which drearily repeats itself in the details."[125] In failing to conceptualize the social constitution of the exchange abstraction, the concept of the information economy transfigures historically definite relations into the natural properties of things. The social basis of the exchange principle is the reduction of labor to value-producing labor. The "universal reduction of all specific energy to the one, identical, abstract form of labor," Adorno remarks, extends from production to circulation and consumption.[126] In disregarding the historical dissolution of laboring activities into exchange-value, as well as the coercive separation of the class of laborers from the means of production, neoliberal theory naturalizes the antagonistic relations of society. "Included in the objective law-like nature of society," as Adorno puts it, "is its contradictory character, and ultimately its irrationality."[127] By naming market prices as the only valid data of economic coordination, neoliberal theory affirms the primacy of the production apparatus over needs, as well as the independence of society's irrationality from living purposes.

Exchange-value continues to dominate and replace needs, "illusion replaces reality."[128] To this extent, "society is myth and its elucidation is still as necessary as ever."[129] Adorno's dialectical framework of natural-history, I have argued, can provide the basis for a materialist critique of economics as the ideological expression of capitalist society. Critical theory, moreover, would do well to return to Adorno's understanding of *ideology critique*, because this approach grasps the mediation of economic concepts by the actual relations of the social object. Such an approach, moreover, resists the tendency by many critics of neoliberalism to reify the distinction between theory and practice (depicting neoliberalism as the by-product of the economics profession, for example), rather than conceptualizing the emergence of neoliberal ideas as expressions of human practice. Instead, a critical theory of neoliberalism should oppose the objectivity of the economy by "turning the truth" of its concepts against the "untruth that produced them."[130] The dialectic of natural-history captures the mystifications of economics as the expression of a historically specific, social form. By returning the apparently self-moving laws of economic necessity to their "social genesis," our critique is better positioned to grasp the power and influence of neoliberal ideas as the conceptual fetishes of a "false" world. As Bonefeld puts it, Adorno's negative dialectics "holds that the incomprehensible economic forces find their rational explanation in human practice and in the comprehension of this practice."[131] Manifesting in the form of abstract prices, the antagonistic relations of society today are experienced by individuals as fate. Yet this fate is only the result of historically conditioned practices. The "law which determines how the fatality of mankind unfolds itself is the law of exchange."[132] But this law is also an illusion, since the exchange of equivalents proceeds both "justly and unjustly."[133] However, the law of exchange is not an immutable, timeless necessity. The illusion of natural history, Adorno suggests, "signifies that within this society laws can only be implemented as natural processes over people's heads, while their validity arises from the form of the relations of production within which production takes place."[134]

Neoliberal society, I have argued, can be grasped as a socially constituted context of "second nature," defined by the abstract authority of markets. This authority, however, is not comprehensible on the basis of economic relations and institutions alone. As delineated in Chapter 1, Adorno's theory of society not only criticizes the objective mediation of subjects by exchange but also grasps the constitution of cognition by this process of socialization. "Identity thinking," as he describes it, best captures the mode of thinking characteristic of a society dominated by the exchange principle. Such thinking reduces particular objects to a universal concept, thus mirroring the coercive social object in which it is entwined. In Chapter 4, I develop Adorno's theory of identity thinking to criticize patterns of rational cognition that function as indexes of validation in contemporary neoliberal culture. By returning to Horkheimer and Adorno's *Dialectic of Enlightenment* and their critique of "instrumental reason," I aim to further delineate how neoliberal ideas are implicated within larger processes of social control, specifically with regard to what Horkheimer and Adorno call the "domination of nature."

Notes

1 Adorno: "The fact [is] that the strict division between economics and sociology sets aside the really central interests of both disciplines. As a result, both fail to assert the central interests and thereby fulfil their function within the existing order, by not probing the wounds which this order has and which, above all, it inflicts on each of us, even if we have not yet become the objects of wars or similar natural catastrophes of society," *Introduction to Sociology*, 144.
2 Hans-Georg Backhaus, "Between Philosophy and Science," *Open Marxism*, 1 (1992), 87.
3 Adorno, "Late Capitalism," 121.
4 Adorno, *Negative Dialectics*, 354.
5 Adorno, "Introduction," 30.
6 For an account of the proliferation of neoliberal economic theory throughout a wider set of political and institutional contexts (e.g., in business, think tanks, and the US Federal Reserve), see Mirowski, *Never Let a Serious Crisis Go to Waste*.
7 Adorno, *Negative Dialectics*, 267.
8 For discussion of the context and background of Adorno's contribution to the Frankfurt chapter of the Kant Society, see Robert Hullot-Kentor's "Introduction to Adorno's 'The Idea of Natural-History,'" in *Things Beyond Resemblance* (New York: Columbia University Press, 2006), 234–51.
9 Adorno, "The Idea of Natural-History," in *Things Beyond Resemblance*, 257.
10 Ibid., 252.
11 As Susan Buck-Morss argues, the idea of natural-history forms a framework of "*cognitive* concepts, not unlike Kant's 'regulative ideas' for critical reflection." See Buck-Morss, *The Origin of Negative Dialectics: Theodor W. Adorno, Walter Benjamin, and the Frankfurt Institute* (New York: The Free Press, 1977), 49.
12 Adorno, "The Idea of Natural-History," 260.
13 As Adorno's student, Alfred Schmidt, would later write, "Natural and human history together constitute for Marx a differentiated unity. Thus human history is not merged in pure natural history; natural history is not merged in human history." Schmidt, *The Concept of Nature in Marx*, trans. Ben Fowkes (London: NLB, 1971), 45.

14 Ibid., 253.
15 Ibid., 248.
16 For Lukács, the alienated form of social relations in capitalist modernity undermined the possibility of historical interpretation. In his *The Theory of the Novel* (1920), for example, Lukács bemoaned the sedimentation of cultural forms into a meaningless sphere of "convention," and described petrified relations as a context of "second nature." Because of the inscrutable constitution of estranged relations in capitalism, the historically constituted second nature is misrecognized as first nature. To Adorno's mind, the semblance of second nature consisted in its semblance of natural being. Adorno agreed with Lukács that the problem of historical interpretation lied in conceptualizing alienated forms *in their meaninglessness*. However, Adorno rejected Lukács's claim that second nature was immune to interpretation, arguing that the psychoanalytic model is the key to deciphering alienated forms. For discussion on this difference, see Hullot-Kentor, "Introduction," 234–51.
17 Adorno, "The Idea of Natural-History," 253.
18 Adorno, *Negative Dialectics*, 355.
19 Ibid.
20 Ibid., 347.
21 Ibid.
22 Ibid.
23 Ibid.
24 Ibid.
25 As Bonefeld puts it, "The mistake," says Adorno, . . . "in traditional thinking is that identity is taken for the goal." What is identified and what does the identity of an economic quantity or market position identify? It identifies quantitative differences, which is the measure of success, poverty, or ruin." Werner Bonefeld, "Negative Dialectics and the Critique of Economic Objectivity," *History of the Human Sciences*, 29, no. 2 (2016): 72.
26 Adorno, "Marx and the Basic Concepts," 10.
27 Ibid.
28 Adorno, *Negative Dialectics*, 251.
29 Adam Smith, *The Wealth of Nations* (New York: Bantam Dell, 2003), 22.
30 For background and discussion of Smith's substance theory of value, see Philip Mirowski, *More Heat than Light: Economics as Social Physics, Physics as Nature's Economics* (Cambridge: Cambridge University Press, 1989), 163–79.
31 Thorstein Veblen, *The Place of Science in Modern Civilization and other Essays* (New York: B.W. Huebsch, 1919), 280.
32 Adorno, "Late Capitalism," 115.
33 For a detailed analysis of Marx's critique of Smith and Ricardo's labor theory of value, see Clarke, *Marx, Marginalism, and Modern Sociology*, 42–143.

34 As Clarke argues, Marx's critique of political economy exposes the institution of private property as the presupposition of the capitalist system structured by the exchange of the alienated products of labor: "The relation of private property, as a relation between an individual and a thing, is therefore only the juridical expression of a social relation, in which the products of *social* labour are *privately* appropriated." Clarke, *Marx, Marginalism*, 7.
35 See Mirowski, *More Heat than Light*, 193–275.
36 Lionel Robbins, *An Essay on the Nature and Significance of Economic Science* (London: Macmillan and Company, 1935), 16.
37 See Mirowski, *More Heat than Light*, 193–241.
38 "The Marginalist Revolution preempted all talk of gravitational metaphors by appropriating the actual mathematical model from physics. Natural price was redefined to be the equilibrium concept in the energetics model, and market price was redefined to be the price that would clear a market at a single point in time. By choosing the static physics model of equilibrium, and avoiding the physical dynamics, the two were conflated and made identical," ibid., 240.
39 Bonefeld, "Negative Dialectics," 62.
40 Clarke, *Marx, Marginalism, and Modern Sociology*, 110.
41 Mirowski, *More Heat than Light*, 240–41.
42 Adorno, "Marx and the Basic Concepts," 11.
43 Ibid., 3.
44 See Clarke: "While social economics continued to be a branch of economics, in presupposing the rational pursuit of material self-interest to be the only basis of social action, marginalist economics also left a space for sociology. Within the framework of the theory of action, economics is defined as only the branch of the social sciences, the science that studies the consequences of rational economic action. Sociology is then the discipline that studies the consequences of non-rational action and of action oriented to other than economic goals, the discipline that takes account of the normative orientation of action and so that locates economics within the framework of the voluntaristic theory of action." Clarke, *Marx, Marginalism*, 10.
45 For an account of Adorno's critique of neo-Kantian methodologism, see Gillian Rose, *Hegel Contra Sociology* (London: Verso) 35–36. Interestingly, Rose would accuse Adorno of the very methodologism he condemned in positivist sociology.
46 Adorno, "Introduction," 7.
47 Ibid., 8.
48 Adorno, *Negative Dialectics*, 198.
49 Adorno, "Introduction," 33.
50 Ibid., 33.
51 Ibid.

52 Ibid., 43.
53 Adorno, *Introduction to Sociology*, 67.
54 Ibid.
55 Ibid., 37.
56 Adorno, "Marx and the Basic Concepts," 3.
57 Adorno, "Introduction," 34.
58 See, for example, Harvey, *A Brief History of Neoliberalism*, 20.
59 For details see Peck, *Constructions of Neoliberal Reason*.
60 For background and discussion of the Socialist Calculation Debate, see Don Lavoie, "A Critique of the Standard Account of the Socialist Calculation Debate," *The Journal of Libertarian Studies*, 5, no. 1 (1981): 41–87.
61 Ibid., 41.
62 As Mirowski and Nik-Khah remark, "Perhaps the dominant version within the MPS [Mont Pelerin Society] ... emanated from Friedrich Hayek himself, wherein *'the market' is posited to be an information processor more powerful than any human brain, but essentially patterned upon brain/computation metaphors.*" Mirowski and Edward Nik-Khah, *The Knowledge We Have Lost in Information* (Oxford: Oxford University Press, 2017), 54–5.
63 F. A. Hayek, "The Use of Knowledge in Society," *American Economic Review*, XXXV, 4 (1945): 519. Cited in Mirowski and Nik-Khah, "The Knowledge We Have Lost," 62–3.
64 Clarke, *Marx, Marginalism*, 214.
65 Hayek, "The Use of Knowledge," 526.
66 F. A. Hayek, *The Road to Serfdom*, ed. Bruce Caldwell (Chicago: The University of Chicago Press, 2007), 95.
67 The practice of competition, according to Hayek, obtains epistemic properties. As he argues, "Which goods are scarce, however, or which things are goods, or how scarce or valuable they are, is precisely one of the conditions that competition should discover: in each case it is the preliminary outcomes of market process that inform individuals where it is worthwhile to search. Utilizing widely diffused knowledge in a society with an advanced division of labor cannot be based on the condition that individuals know all the concrete uses that can be made of objects in their environment. . . . The knowledge of which I am speaking consists to a great extent of the ability to detect certain conditions—an ability that individuals can use effectively only when the market tells them what kinds of goods and services are demanded, and how urgently." F. A. Hayek, "Competition as a Discovery Procedure," trans. Marcellus S. Snow, *The Quarterly Journal of Austrian Economics*, 5, no. 3 (2002): 13.
68 For details regarding Karl Popper's influence on Hayek, as well as his participation in the Mont Pelerin Society, consult Daniel Steadman Jones, *Masters of the Universe: Hayek, Friedman, and the Birth of Neoliberal Politics* (Princeton: Princeton University Press, 2012).

69 Friedrich Hayek, *New Studies in Philosophy, Politics, and the History of Ideas* (Chicago: The University of Chicago Press, 1978), 179.
70 Ibid.
71 Friedrich Hayek, *The Sensory Order: An Inquiry into the Foundations of Theoretical Psychology* (Chicago: The University of Chicago Press, 2014), 48–54.
72 Mirowski and Nik-Khah, *The Knowledge We Have Lost*, 68.
73 Friedrich Hayek, "Primacy of the Abstract," in *Beyond Reductionism: New Perspectives in the Life Sciences*, ed. Arthur Koestler and J. R. Smythies (London: Macmillan and Co., 1969), 46.
74 See Mirowski and Nik-Khah, *The Knowledge We Have Lost*, 55.
75 Friedrich Hayek, "Wiemer-Hayek Discussion," in *Cognition and the Symbolic Processes, Vol. 2*, ed. Walter B. Wiemer and David S. Palermo (Hillsdale: Lawrence Erlbaum Associates, Publishers, 1974), 325–26.
76 Quinn Slobodian, *Globalists: The End of Empire and the Birth of Neoliberalism* (Cambridge: Harvard University Press, 2018), 232.
77 Norbert Wiener, *Cybernetics: Or Control and Communication in the Animal and the Machine* (Cambridge: The MIT Press, 1985).
78 For an excellent account, see Steve Joshua Heims, *The Cybernetics Group* (Cambridge: The MIT Press, 1991).
79 Philip Mirowski, *Machine Dreams: Economics Becomes a Cyborg Science* (Cambridge: Cambridge University Press, 2002), 54.
80 To name just one example within the cybernetic sciences, Claude Shannon's "information theory" is regarded as a significant development that would later persuade economists to conceptualize information as a commodity. Developed with Warren Weaver in 1948, Shannon's mathematical theory defined the concept of information as a physical system. Beginning as an engineering notion in cryptography, Shannon measured the transmission of symbols through noise-distorted communication channels by treating strings of symbols as a stochastic process—with each symbol possessing its own probability. By quantifying the amount of uncertainty expressed by a string of symbols as physical entropy, Shannon could define information in total abstraction from all semantic content. His notion was quickly appropriated by communications engineers working at Bell Labs, and emerged as a key concept for the burgeoning computer sciences. Although Shannon opposed the use of information theory in the social sciences, economists soon borrowed the concept for their own purposes. As Mirowski and Nik-Khah suggest, the proliferation of Shannon's information theory "had the unintended consequence of bolstering the general impression that scientists could and should treat information as a quantifiable thing, or even a *commodity*." Mirowski and Nik-Khah, *The Knowledge We Have Lost*, 105.
81 Slobodian, *Globalists*, 231.
82 Ibid., 230.

83 Ibid., 229.
84 Despite the pervasiveness of the figure of "*homo economicus*" in critiques of neoliberalism, most neoliberals largely abandoned the neoclassical models of utility maximization and Walrasian general equilibrium. For details regarding the often-contentious relationship between the neoclassical, "econometric" tradition of the Cowles Commission and the Chicago school, see Mirowski, *Machine Dreams*, 207–22.
85 Friedrich, *Law, Legislation and Liberty* (London: Routledge, 1998), 124–25.
86 Cited in Slobodian, *Globalists*, 228.
87 See Gabriel Oliva, "The Road to Servomechanisms: The Influence of Cybernetics on Hayek from *The Sensory Order* to the Social Order," *Research in the History of Economic Thought and Methodology*, 34A (2016): 161–98.
88 Ibid.
89 Garrett Hardin, *Nature and Man's Fate* (New York: Rinehart & Company, Inc., 1958), 55. Given Hardin's explicitly racist and ethnonationalist defense of the commons, it would be useful to consider the racialized implications regarding the revival of organicist theories of cultural evolution in neoliberal thought. Moishe Postone, for example, argues that the proliferation of "racial theories and the rise of Social Darwinism" in the late nineteenth century can be understood as expressions of the commodity-form. See Postone, "Anti-Semitism and National Socialism: Notes on the German Reaction to 'Holocaust,'" in *Germans and Jews Since the Holocaust*, ed. Anson Rabinbach and Jack Zipes (New York: Holmes and Meier, 1986), 302–14.
90 Friedrich Hayek, *The Fatal Conceit: The Errors of Socialism*, ed. W. W. Bartley III (Chicago: The University of Chicago Press, 1988), 76.
91 Hayek, *New Studies*, 96.
92 Hayek, *The Fatal Conceit*, 19.
93 Ibid., 20.
94 Ibid., 33.
95 Ibid., 41.
96 Adorno, "The Idea of Natural-History," 253.
97 Note that Hayek recognizes the difficulty in his own approach to natural history. For example, in his "The Results of Human Action but not of Human Design," he argues in favor of overcoming the classical Greek distinction between the natural (*phusei*) and the artificial (*thesei*), by differentiating between practices that are intentional, and unintentional practices that exhibit design. Positioned between artificially designed institutions (*taxis*), on the one hand, and a natural order (*kosmos*), on the other, Hayek's notion of "catallaxy" refers to an order of human practice, which is the emergent outcome of unconscious adaptations. See Friedrich Hayek, "The Results of Human Action But Not of Design," in *New Studies in Philosophy, Politics, and the History of Ideas*.

98 This approach can be seen, for example, in Mirowski's notion of a "Neoliberal Thought Collective." By thought collective, Mirowski means an interlocking network of private think tanks (e.g., the Mont Pelerin Society, the American Enterprise Institute, Heartland, etc.) that has worked in concert to build its vision of a market society. While this institutional network is undoubtedly an important aspect of the history of neoliberalization, such an approach fails to explain how the thought collective could mobilize its politics on the basis of the objective conditions of society. As Mirowski argues, "Economic doctrines rise to dominance because they have been built up from compelling intellectual trends located elsewhere in the culture, and often, in other sciences; and, in turn, depend upon promoters and funders to impress their importance upon other economists, and thenceforward the larger world." See Mirowksi, *Never Let a Serious Crisis*, 13.

99 Adorno, *Negative Dialectics*, 406. Translation modified.

100 Adorno, *History and Freedom*, 117.

101 Ibid., 121.

102 For example, Hayek's work connects the practice of exchange to forms of thought: "The moment that barter is replaced by indirect exchange mediated by money, ready intelligibility ceases and abstract interpersonal processes begin that far transcend even the most enlightened individual perception." Hayek, *The Fatal Conceit*, 101.

103 Adorno, *History and Freedom*, 119.

104 Adorno, "Sociology and Empirical Research," 80.

105 Ibid.

106 Adorno, *Negative Dialectics*, 306.

107 Ibid., 335.

108 As Bonefeld argues, connecting Adorno's law of autonomization to primitive accumulation, "This law of autonomisation is however a double-edge sword in that it carries its historical foundation in the separation of the labourer from her means of existence within the law of its movement." Bonefeld, *Critical Theory*, 84.

109 Marx, *Grundrisse*, 471.

110 Adorno, *Introduction to Sociology*, 29–30.

111 Adorno, "Introduction," 32.

112 Adorno, "Marx and the Basic Concepts," 6.

113 Ibid.

114 Ibid., 7.

115 For a detailed critique of what Hayek calls "scientism," see *The Counter-Revolution of Science: Studies on the Abuse of Reason* (Glencoe: The Free Press, 1952).

116 See Hayek, *The Sensory Order*, 5, 93.

117 See, for example, Horkheimer and Adorno: "The blocking of theoretical imagination has paved the way for political delusion." *Dialectic of Enlightenment*, xvi.

118 Ibid., 17.
119 Adorno, "Introduction," 37.
120 Adorno, *Hegel: Three Studies*, 74.
121 Adorno, *Negative Dialectics*, 348.
122 Adorno, *Lectures on Negative Dialectics*, 20.
123 For a critical discussion of the instrumental use of such models by private monopolies, see David Golumbia's *The Cultural Logic of Computation* (Cambridge: Harvard University Press, 2009), 129–77.
124 Ibid.
125 Adorno, "Introduction," *The Positivist Dispute*, 39.
126 Horkheimer and Adorno, *Dialectic of Enlightenment*, 172.
127 Adorno, "Introduction," 42–43.
128 Adorno, "Sociology and Empirical Research," 80.
129 Ibid.
130 Adorno, "Reflections on Class Theory," 102.
131 Bonefeld, "Negative Dialectics," 66.
132 Adorno, "Sociology and Empirical Research," 80.
133 Ibid.
134 Adorno, *History and Freedom*, 118.

4

Neoliberal Reason

The Domination of Nature

As we have seen, in neoliberalism, the abstract and impersonal network of exchange that mediates individuals is just as decisive for the prevailing forms of thought in society. The framework of Chapter 3 developed Adorno's idea of natural-history to criticize the ideological function of neoliberal economic theory. Adorno's critical theory suggests that in late capitalism, the fetish character of commodities casts an inscrutable "spell" over individuals, compelling them to accept exchange relations as immutable and natural. Adorno characterizes the history of society as the "control of nature, progressing domination over human beings and ultimately over humans' inner nature."[1] His critical theory suggests, following Marx, capitalism is an inverted world where nature is mediated by historical processes and social relations are naturalized, appearing to individuals as "second nature." Neoliberal economics contributes to this context of second nature in theory. This participation in the context of second nature, however, can be further explored through Adorno's critique of "instrumental reason," which he develops with Max Horkheimer in the *Dialectic of Enlightenment*. This chapter returns to this dialectic to engage the relation between reason and domination that is operative in the neoliberal period, particularly as it is emerging today as the domination of nature.

As discussed previously, neoliberal theory has largely defined "truth" as a property of markets. But if individuals today live under increasing conditions of economic austerity and inequality, why do they internalize neoliberal ideas regarding the alleged superiority of the free market's knowledge? In what follows I argue that Horkheimer and Adorno's *Dialectic of Enlightenment* can illuminate how forms of historically produced coercion can appear rational, and necessary. I argue that the concept of "neoliberal reason" expands social domination by reducing reason to an instrument of the economy. At the center of this dialectic, I want to suggest, lies a logic of sacrifice that unfolds as the universal need to harness the future capital accumulation. Moreover, insofar as reason now appears as the exclusive property of economic calculation, I argue that neoliberalism has significantly undermined the capacity to resist the ongoing crises of ecology. This chapter connects Horkheimer and Adorno's critique of instrumental reason to the current crises of ecology by arguing that neoliberalism has reduced reason to its "economic" position in the reproduction of capital. To develop this claim, I engage the following concepts and categories: (1) Horkheimer and Adorno's anthropology of reason, (2) sacrifice, (3) the "organic composition" of humanity, (4) the computational theory of mind, and (5) the domination of external nature. The chapter asks us to consider how we can resist the dynamic of rationalization that subsumes nature under exchange-value, while threatening to undermine the sustainability of life on a planetary scale.

Dialectic of Enlightenment

In the *Dialectic of Enlightenment*, Horkheimer and Adorno adopt an anthropological perspective to expand their critique of social domination. The intention of the book, they indicate, "is to explain why humanity, instead of entering a truly human state, is sinking into a new kind of barbarism."[2] The origins of this barbarism can be explained in terms of the process of civilization that is conditioned by self-preservation. The progress of civilization, they argue, depends on the progress of enlightenment reason. However, the progress of enlightenment, Horkheimer and Adorno argue, is ineluctably tied to the need to survive, to humanity's instinct for surviving the threats of nature. Through the use of reason, human beings can order, manipulate, and control nature: "What human beings seek to learn from nature is how to use it to dominate wholly both it and human beings."[3] For Horkheimer and Adorno, the progress of civilization therefore depends on the instrumental use of reason to know and master "inner" and "outer" nature. Enlightenment explains nature by instrumentally reducing it to an object; nature becomes a unified context amenable to human control. The progress of enlightenment, then, is revealed throughout the course of the *Dialectic of Enlightenment* to depend on the reduction of reason to a mere instrument of self-preservation, a reduction that inscribes the progress of enlightenment within a coercive, self-undermining logic.

By broadening the scope of their analysis to the anthropological, premodern account of civilization, Horkheimer and Adorno's theory connects the genesis of the modern, bourgeois subject to broader patterns of domination. Their anthropological perspective not only refuses all affirmations regarding a mythological, precapitalist past but also exposes the survival of primitive forms of compulsion within capitalist modernity. As Marcel Stoetzler suggests, "The emphasis on the concept of self-preservation points to the economic core of enlightenment and civilization."[4] Horkheimer and Adorno's anthropology illuminates the mediation of human nature by the demands of civilization; by repressing the instincts, they argue, human beings achieve greater resources for surviving, but this facility is purchased at the price of forgetting humanity's affinity *with* nature. If reason developed as an adaptive tool for survival, as Horkheimer and Adorno claim, it never entirely left behind its perception that nature is essentially hostile and threatening. That anything could escape the grasp of reason motivates its desire for unity: "Nothing is allowed to remain outside, since the mere idea of an 'outside' is the real source of fear."[5] Civilization's progress, then, insofar as it is grounded in the needs of self-preservation, remains a form of compulsion that relates to nature through its domination.

Horkheimer and Adorno's narrative captures the double-sided process of civilization by suggesting that the progress of reason is caught in a dialectical contradiction with "myth." Their narrative famously begins, "Myth is already enlightenment, and enlightenment reverts to mythology."[6] By myth, Horkheimer and Adorno mean irrational depictions of nature, god, or the cosmos; myths are anthropomorphic explanations of natural phenomena. Moreover, myths are forms of self-representation, developed by humans who imbue reality with a sense fated necessity. From the standpoint of modern enlightenment reason, myths are irrational relics belonging to a less advanced stage of development. However, myths already prefigure a key aspect of enlightenment reason, namely the need to explain, order, and control nature for survival. "Myth sought to report, to name, to tell of origins—but therefore also to narrate, record, explain."[7] Because myth is a practice of self-preservation it is implicated in the civilizational process, which depends on enlightenment to master nature by comprehending it. Enlightenment, by contrast, is defined by the "disenchantment of the world."[8] It seeks to master nature through the disavowal of anthropomorphic myths. Enlightenment masters nature by objectifying it. In modern science, for example, enlightenment reason controls nature by eliminating all anthropomorphic properties, reducing nature to a disenchanted, causal nexus of lawlike objectivity.

The entwinement of myth and enlightenment converges in what Horkheimer and Adorno call the "principle of immanence."[9] Myths use the principle of immanence by explaining natural objects according to repeatable, cyclical patterns. The world myth explained was repetitive, timeless, and purposive. The principle of myth as a whole, therefore, is a principle of immanence, because its grasp of nature depends on the structural iterability of natural objects. Similarly, enlightenment develops the principle of immanence by instrumentalizing what is repeatable in nature: "The principle of immanence, the explanation of every event as repetition, which enlightenment upholds against mythical imagination, is that of myth itself."[10] The principle of immanence ties enlightenment to myth, and likewise, rationality to instrumentality. Abstracting from the concrete particularity of objects, enlightenment controls nature to satisfy the imperatives of self-preservation. To the extent that the progress of civilization depends on enlightenment reason, this progress is founded upon an originary compulsion that reduces both thinking and the world to mere objects of control.

Sacrifice: The Entwinement of Myth and Enlightenment

Horkheimer and Adorno explore the implications of enlightenment's compulsory trajectory by delineating the genesis of modern subjectivity. The origins of consciousness, they argue, are bound up with the struggle for survival, a struggle that continues to mediate thought in the present. Underlying the origins of the subject, they argue, is a process of rationalization characterized by the repression of the instincts, as well as the denial of the moment of naturalness within subjectivity. The key to their argument lies in the concept of "sacrifice." For Horkheimer and Adorno, the logic of sacrifice connects the properties of domination within capitalist modernity to the prehistory of civilization. By "sacrifice," Horkheimer and Adorno mean a mimetic practice, or ritual, that accomplishes a level of mastery over nature through a strategy of "cunning," devised to control the gods.[11] Sacrifice anticipates the unity imposed on nature by enlightenment:

> The sacrificial animal is slain in place of the god. The substitution which takes place in sacrifice marks a step toward discursive logic. Even though the hind which was offered up for the daughter, the lamb for the firstborn, necessarily still had qualities of its own, it already represented the genus. It manifested the arbitrariness of the specimen.[12]

In sacrifice, human beings utilize objects as representatives of wholes. The apparently irrational substitution (e.g., of a lamb for the firstborn) prefigures the "universal fungibility" of things in modern scientific rationality.[13] Horkheimer and Adorno describe the substitutability of things in sacrifice as a "ruse of cunning," because the substitution in question is a form of deceit.[14] In the substitution of particular for whole, the ritual of sacrifice establishes "abstraction" as the crucial instrument of enlightenment—by abstracting from concrete particularity, natural objects can become interchangeable and subsumable under the purpose-directed activities of human beings.

Sacrifice, therefore, can be understood as a prehistorical ritual of civilization that is connected to what Adorno later called the "identity principle." Indeed, Horkheimer and Adorno connect sacrifice to the modern practice of commodity exchange: "If exchange represents the secularization of sacrifice, the sacrifice itself, like the magic schema of rational exchange, appears as a human contrivance intended to control the gods, who are overthrown precisely by the system created to honor them."[15] Sacrifice establishes the really existing abstraction in practice that relates heterogeneous objects to a unified standard of comparison. Just as in exchange two objects are equated to money as an external universal, sacrifice establishes the framework in which particulars can function as representatives of universals. For Horkheimer and Adorno, the unity of modern science is the result of the sacrificial abstraction that subsumes the particularity of objects under universals:

> Abstraction, the instrument of enlightenment, stands in the same relationship to its objects as fate, whose concept it eradicates: as liquidation. Under the leveling rule of abstraction, which makes everything in nature repeatable, and of industry, for which abstraction prepared the way, the liberated finally themselves become the "herd" (*Trüpp*), which Hegel identified as the outcome of enlightenment.[16]

The practice of sacrifice is bound up with the civilizational process that reduces reason to a tool of preservation. Despite humanity's affinity with nature, this affinity is largely banished from conscious reflection. The progress of civilization, which depends on the separation of humanity from nature, recapitulates sacrifice as a societal process that dominates external nature.

Horkheimer and Adorno describe the birth of the modern, bourgeois individual as a process of self-preservation that "introverts" the sacrificial logic within the subject. In a Freudian analysis of subject formation, the *Dialectic of Enlightenment* articulates the origins of modern subjectivity as a process of renunciation. "The history of civilization," they argue, "is the history of the introversion of sacrifice—in other words, the history of renunciation."[17] The achievement of the subject's unity, they argue, is best understood as a sacrificial transaction, because the subject can only preserve itself through the renunciation of its natural instincts. As Breuer remarks, "Individuality rests upon affect control and suppression of instincts, upon the denial and repression of the natural dimension for the purpose of self-preservation: the introversion of sacrifice."[18] According to Horkheimer and Adorno, the process of civilization is sacrificial because it transfigures the compulsion required for survival into an internal compulsion within the subject.[19] Through repression the subject achieves its unity by sacrificing its own particularity to itself as a universal member of civilization. The specifically dominating properties of this introversion consist in the self's relinquishment of its own particularity. The self-preserving power of the self, in other words, is a function of self-domination. Individuality depends on the denial and repression of the natural dimension of humanity, a dependence that is forgotten throughout the civilizational process.

According to Horkheimer and Adorno, the domination within the process of civilization only deepens in the historical, "enlightenment," period of modernity. In the modern period, the principal of reason "serves as a universal tool for the fabrication of all other tools," and remains as grounded as ever in the "compulsive character of self-preservation."[20] The "internalization of repression" makes possible increases in economic productivity in modernity.[21] As enlightenment enters a historic condition of capitalist social relations, the instrumentalization of reason intensifies. The *Dialectic of Enlightenment* traces the genesis of subjectivity back to Homer's *Odyssey*, where Horkheimer and Adorno interpret the figure of Odysseus as prototype of the modern, bourgeois individual. According to their analysis, the birth of the modern individual is ineluctably entwined with economic competition: "Emancipated from the tutelage of earlier economic stages, individuals fended for themselves alone: as proletarians by hiring themselves out through the labor market and by constant adaptation to new economic conditions, as entrepreneurs by tirelessly realizing the ideal type of *homo oeconomicus*."[22] The civilizational process unfolds in capitalist modernity as a double-sided process that emancipates individuals from the directly coercive bonds of feudalism, but in turn, binds them to the indirect domination of the market. The dialectic of freedom and compulsion within the social form of capitalist modernity is reinstated within the individual, who must survive by adapting to the generalization of commodity exchange.

Horkheimer and Adorno's presentation of enlightenment thus stresses the development of thought as being a process of socialization and adaptation. The *Dialectic of Enlightenment* presents the civilizational process in terms of the unity of scientific rationalism and social rationalization. As the capitalist mode of production fragments individuals through an increasingly complex division of labor, the bourgeois individual must adapt to the impersonal form of the social whole:

> In the bourgeois economy the social work of each individual is mediated by the principle of the self; for some this labor is supposed to yield increased capital, for others the strength for extra work. But the more heavily the process of self-preservation is based on the bourgeois division of labor, the more it enforces the self-alienation of individuals, who must mold themselves to the technical apparatus body and soul.[23]

The modern bourgeois individual gives its individuality over to the social process to survive. The rationalization of reason thus underlies the historical development of enlightenment, as well as the corresponding reduction of the self to its functional position in economic relations.

Horkheimer and Adorno's *Dialectic of Enlightenment* therefore suggests that society conditions thought just as much as nature. Rather than overcoming the illusions of metaphysics, enlightenment reason is itself a moment in the real metaphysics of capital. The entwinement of reason with domination culminates in capitalist modernity, where the rationalization of the labor process finds its reflexive articulation in the Kantian transcendental subject of enlightenment philosophy: "Enlightened thinking has an answer for this, too: finally, the transcendental subject of knowledge, as the last reminder of subjectivity, is itself seemingly abolished and replaced by the operations of the automatic mechanisms of order, which therefore run all the more smoothly."[24] In capitalist modernity, the instrumental use of reason is tied to economic calculation. The abstract form of exchange society privileges formalizable thinking. As Stoetzler suggests, "Excessively formal thinking follows from the preponderance of social forms over social individuals and their concrete needs."[25] The instrumentalization of reason assumes an overly formal and abstract character in capitalist society, reflecting the objective abstraction of the exchange principle as it levels diverse, heterogeneous objects to sameness and uniformity.

For Horkheimer and Adorno, the reduction of reason to a mere tool finds its ultimate expression in positivist thought. Positivism, they argue, severs cognition from subjectivity entirely; thought becomes merely the stuff of logical processes. Unmoored from critical reflection, logical positivism cuts off cognition from its social constitution. As Horkheimer and Adorno put it, positivism "eliminated the last intervening agency between individual action and the social norm."[26] By isolating cognition from subjectivity and experience, positivism renders cognition "thingly." This reification of thought, moreover, functions as a claim by society regarding the putative, "value-free" neutrality of scientific rationality.[27] This claim to value-neutrality, however, is contradicted by reason's mediation by the needs of preservation. Reduced to an intellectual branch of the advanced technological state of capitalist society, logical positivism instrumentalizes philosophy by subordinating it to science: "It is supposed, like a kind of intellectual Taylorism, to improve scientific production methods, to rationalize the accumulation of knowledge, and prevent the waste of mental energy."[28] Positivism's "ultimate product," Horkheimer and Adorno suggest, is "pure immanence," which is "nothing other than a form of universal taboo."[29] Anything that cannot be manipulated fails to count as valid knowledge.

The development of modern rationality, particularly in logical positivism, mirrors what is dominating about capitalist society. Similar to the rationalization of the labor process, positivism eliminates human experience from cognition: "Reason itself has become merely an aid to the all-encompassing economic apparatus."[30] Recall that according to Adorno, the fetish character of the commodity determines the reification of thought. With its prioritization of binary thinking and the law of noncontradiction, positivism indexes the real dualisms of the capitalist social form. In late capitalism reason becomes "rigidly-purpose directed and as calamitous as the precisely calculated operations of material production," which mold thinking to the imperatives of abstract labor.[31] The hegemonic rise of logical positivism in the twentieth century, Horkheimer and Adorno suggest, can be attributed to the reified relations of production: "The expulsion of thought from logic ratifies in the lecture hall the reification of human beings in the factory and office."[32] In the totally administered world of late capitalism, cognition is only useful to the extent that it classifies, subsumes, and manages its objects.

As soon as the totally administered society rationalizes thinking as a tool of production, reason lives merely as a historically obsolete rudiment that belonged to a previous stage of development. Horkheimer and Adorno suggest that reason has outlived its purpose in advanced industrial societies: "Now that self-preservation has been finally automated, reason is dismissed by those who, as controllers of production, have taken over its inheritance and fear it in the disinherited."[33] The historical obsolescence of reason corresponds to what Adorno called the "liquidation" of the individual.[34] "In the age of the individual's liquidation," Adorno suggests, "the question of individuality must be raised anew."[35] Due to the advanced, techno-scientific forces of production in late capitalism, the individual must not only adapt to its function within the division of labor but also mold its thought patterns to fit the mechanical structure of production. As Adorno would later remark,

> People are still what they were in Marx's analysis in the middle of the nineteenth century: appendages of the machine, not just literally workers who have to adapt themselves to the nature of the machines they use, but far beyond that, figuratively, workers who are compelled right down to their intimate impulses to subordinate themselves to the mechanisms of society and to adopt specific roles without reservation.[36]

Self-preservation in late capitalism means adapting to a labor process that is increasingly mechanical and automated. Individuals must relinquish their individuality to the impersonal demands of large-scale production. "In the midst of the standardized and administered human units," Adorno writes, "the individual wastes away."[37] The process of rationalization in production thus drags subjectivity along as a mere function, and individuals must conform to their "fungible" role as mere character masks of capitalism.

The Organic Composition of Humanity

Adorno later focuses on the rationalization of subjects in *Minima Moralia*, where he details the integration of subjects into the labor process. Adorno theorizes the social and psychoanalytic aspects of reification in an inversion of Marx's concept regarding the "organic composition of capital." In Marx, this notion refers to the "law of the tendential fall in the rate of profit," where capitalist competition leads to the constant revolutionizing of the productive forces. Investment in machines in technology increases productivity, but leads to declines in the share of living labor.[38]

Adorno shifts this tendency to a negative anthropology that describes the mechanization of cognition and behavior in terms of the rising "organic composition of man."[39] According to Adorno, the advanced technological forces of production not only replace "living" with "dead" labor in machines but also entail a process of "deadening" within subjectivity itself. The organic composition of the human being indexes the extension of the technical composition of capital into the organic composition within living individuals.[40] He writes in §147: "The organic composition of man is growing. That which determines subjects as means of production and not as living purposes, increases with the proportion of machines to variable capital."[41] Accumulation, according to Adorno, not only extracts surplus-value in production but also transforms the minds and bodies of workers.

Adorno thus refers to the birth of a "new type of human being," who gives up its individuality by "blurring the boundary and itself and its surroundings, and sacrificing most of its independence and autonomy."[42] Much as the individual loses its individuality because of its integration in labor, subjectivity and cognition similarly undergo a process of reification, where thinking is repurposed by the imperatives of accumulation. The mediation of cognition by machines is a key aspect of Adorno's understanding of reification, and can help illuminate a number of dynamics regarding the turn to an "information economy" in neoliberalism. According to Massimiliano Tomba, Adorno's shift to the anthropological perspective in his critique of the organic composition of humanity suggests an attempt to comprehend the "interpermeation of humans and machines under late capitalism."[43] For Adorno, subjects no longer simply adapt to machines in production—cognition is now administered and manufactured as exchangeable information. As Tomba suggests,

> The knowledge objectified in machines becomes organised in packages of information. This new form of information retroacts on human cognitive processes themselves so that individuals are producing knowledge and institutions are producing education in the form of objectifiable information. An enormous mass of knowledge can now be objectified not because machines are more powerful but because knowledge is already produced as objectifiable packages of information.[44]

This new type of human being lives according to prepackaged experiences and bits of information. In their organization by society and the "formally commensurable variations of the exchange relationship," individuals today find their innermost impulses readily available for manipulation.[45] The new type of human being, therefore, is easily susceptible to totalitarian control. The organic composition of humanity manifests as the "transition from firm characteristics to push-button behavior-patterns," a development within society that establishes "the person as a measuring instrument deployed and calibrated by a central authority."[46] The primary social character, therefore, is a "subjectless subject," that participates in "self-preservation without a self."[47] The process that begins with the transformation of living labor into a commodity, Adorno insists, has "permeated men through and through," deforming their interior mental life to better fit the mold of the social object.[48]

Adorno sees a dynamic in the organization of work that is also transforming intellectual labor. The reification of knowledge and labor in production recoils on subjects, reducing reason to formal calculation and rule-following.

The transformations within work pervade consciousness, reshaping human experience according to the formal properties of computation and measurement. Such changes, Adorno writes, "extend from actual industrial work with machines through the whole of society, even infiltrating the realm of 'intellectual' work, where experience-based thought is already beginning to be replaced by technical, formal-logical manipulations."[49] The new type of human being who is mediated by the advanced, technical apparatus of late capitalism, is capable of new strategies of self-management and discipline. Internalizing the division of labor, the individual acquires independent functions in a manner that resembles the "units of a factory."[50] According to Adorno, the wide array of technical devices in mass consumer society overwhelms the individual's spontaneity: "People must 'adapt' in their use to everyday devices to an incomparably higher degree than ever before."[51] This adaptation extends reification from the workplace to the home: "A single path leads from the conveyor belt via the office machine to the 'capturing' of spontaneous intellectual acts through reified, quantified processes."[52] The atomistic division of individuals in the advanced industrial societies reduces them to functions, and individuals increasingly regard themselves as interchangeable, similar to the mass-produced commodities they consume.

Neoliberal Reason: Computation, Mechanization, and Mind

The *Dialectic of Enlightenment*, as we have seen, delineates the rationalization of reason by the process of civilization. In refining the techniques of self-preservation, humanity represses its instincts and denies its own affinity with nature to survive. Capitalist modernity, Horkheimer and Adorno suggest, is founded upon the internalization of the founding compulsion that reduces nature to an object of control. This mastery and domination of nature, however, means that the key tool of enlightenment, reason, becomes an instrument of coercion rather than freedom. The progress of civilization is caught in an ineluctably regressive logic, characterized by the reduction of "internal" and "external" nature to human purposes.[53] The civilizational process depicted in the *Dialectic of Enlightenment* describes the unity of scientific and social rationalization, culminating in what Adorno later calls "identity thinking."[54] Late capitalist society "liquidates" the bourgeois individual in their total mediation by the network of exchange, the universal whole that "preserves itself" through the activity of individuals.[55] The exchange principle, we have seen, connects every member of society to an autonomous totality that asserts itself as an objective second nature, integrating individuals as the "character masks" of capitalist imperatives. In the joint administration of production, circulation, and consumption, the total character of late capitalist society perfects the compulsory logic of instrumental reason, rationalizing the accumulation of knowledge in science and technology.

Neoliberalism, I want to suggest, is expanding the scope of this rationalization. The unity of scientific and social rationalization, as expressed in Adorno's critique of enlightenment, can be observed in the prevailing neoliberal notions regarding "information," "calculation," and "complexity." Such categories reinstate the economic form of self-preservation at a higher level of abstraction. The very idea of an "information economy" abandons the subject's cognition entirely, situating knowledge and truth exclusively in financial markets. The neoliberal epistemology of markets belongs to the wider societal process of rationalization in capitalist society, a process that reshapes the relation between labor, technology, and cognition.

Today's neoliberal subject must adapt to fragmentary and unpredictable bits of market information that appear authoritative and omniscient. In shifting to a mode of self-preservation that is increasingly mediated, formal, and abstract, the neoliberal individual prioritizes flexibility and adaptability over unity. Reason is instrumental as a tool for self-manipulation; the prevailing social subject in neoliberalism engages in "self-preservation without a self," and is defined, as Adorno puts it, by a "scattered, disconnected, interchangeable and ephemeral state of 'informedness' which one can see will be erased the very next moment to be replaced by new information."[56] Neoliberalism subordinates individuals to the abstract signals of financial institutions. This subordination has laid the basis for the contemporary preoccupation with computation and data. "Cybernetic machines," as Adorno remarked, "graphically demonstrate to people the nullity of formalized thinking abstracted from its contents," but "such machines perform better than thinking subjects much of what used to be the proud achievement of the method of subjective reason."[57] Subjects today imitate the machines in theory and action, extending the scope of reason's status as a disembodied tool of adaptation.

In neoliberal capitalism, reason is reduced to calculation. This development can be observed in the domain of theory, particularly in the "computationalist theory of mind" that rose to prominence in philosophy, cognitive science, and economics.[58] Identifying computation (or symbol manipulation) as the essence of thinking, the computational paradigm unifies mind and nature under abstract identity. In his historical account of cognitive science, Jean-Pierre Dupuy describes this turn: "The aim of cognitive science always was mechanization of mind, not the humanization of machine."[59] Within this paradigm both mind and nature are computational machines; human cognition operates by processing formal symbols. As a number of commentators have observed, the introduction of the first digital computers certainly shifted the dominant theoretical concepts of cognition to notions of computation and symbol manipulation. Among other key contributors to the computationalist turn, Warren McCulloch and Walter Pitts argued that the brain was no different in principle from a digital machine, that neurons were binary switches.[60] The computational paradigm unfolded through the reciprocal imitation of mind and machine. Edwin Hutchins describes this peculiar back-and-forth: "The last 30 years of cognitive science can be seen as attempts to remake the person in the image of the computer."[61]

The model of mind as computation similarly echoed in Anglo-American philosophy, particularly in the so-called "functionalist" school.[62] The computer model of mind explicitly defined cognitions, intentions, and linguistic utterances as formal symbol manipulations.[63] As Hubert Dreyfus remarked, the computer model of mind was rooted in the "Cartesian idea that all understanding consists in forming and using appropriate symbolic representations."[64] By conceptualizing mentality as a computing faculty, the machine functionalist theory of mind reduces subjective states to the determinacy of formal rules. Mentality, now abstracted from its material inscription, is merely the representation of a mathematically defined, logical system. In cutting off thinking from experience, theory reflects the objective reification of the totally administered society. Insofar as machine functionalists isolate cognition from its mediation by matter, theory taboos reflection. "The computer," Adorno writes, "which thinking wants to make its own equal and to whose greater glory it would like nothing better than to eliminate itself—is the bankruptcy petition of consciousness in the face of a reality which at the present stage is not given intuitively but functionally, an abstract in itself."[65] Subjects see themselves reflected in machines because they have ceased to be subjects. "They approach the machine in the guise of its imperfect replica."[66] In modeling thinking subjects according to the notion of computation, theory reduces subject to object, and in doing so, theory reduces both to mere nature.

Cognitive science, I am suggesting, can be understood to have radicalized the unifying aspirations of enlightenment. Springing from the fear of society's total instrumentalization, the functionalist theory of mind reified cognition in anticipation of its real liquidation by the social process. The machine model of mind points to the actual superfluity of living subjects. The theoretical reification of thinking is determined by practice; as the individual has been rationalized out of existence in labor, such processes reflexively shape society's image of mentality. As Tomba remarks, "Modern technology creates a completely new relationship between machines and labourers, whose cognitive processes are more and more incorporated in hardware and software."[67] The mechanization of mind can rightly be understood as a development within the wider civilization process Horkheimer and Adorno detailed. In revolutionizing the means of self-preservation through science, reason treats itself as a thing by objectifying the subject. However, in failing to reflexively account for the interested, purpose-driven character that motivates the unity of mind and nature in theory, reason can only perpetuate the compulsory logic of enlightenment's progress. Horkheimer and Adorno write: "Thought is reified as an autonomous, automatic process, aping the machine it has itself produced, so that it can finally be replaced by the machine."[68] The total automation of self-preservation in advanced industrial societies "equates thought with mathematics" and reduces thinking to calculation, to mere rule-following.[69]

The ways in which today's neoliberal patterns of cognition expand social domination can be grasped as a process of internal reification, where subjects adapt to what Adorno calls the "really abstract" culture that socializes individuals through exchange.[70] The reified character of thinking reflects the condition that neoliberal society's form prioritizes the abstract imperatives of exchange-value over needs, of formal thinking over concrete experience. "Not only is domination paid for with the estrangement of human beings from the dominated objects," Horkheimer and Adorno write, "but the relationships of human beings, including the relationship of individuals to themselves, have themselves been bewitched by the objectification of mind."[71] Such human relations are submitted to the cold binary logic of computation that coordinates life through statistics and date. Instrumental reason in neoliberalism identifies subjects according to standardized dualisms. "The ways in which the capitalist dynamic ever again produces sameness," Stoetzler writes, include "racialization, sexing, and normalization—which are processes that naturalize and hypostatize differences."[72] In classifying the phenomena of experience according to easily specifiable dualisms, capitalist society bends life to its dual-sided form. Such thinking reinforces the "economic" character of life as a process of self-preservation, characterized by the ongoing domination of inner and outer nature.

Recall that for the majority of neoliberal economists, the only true form of calculation that is socially valid is the calculation that markets perform.

But the ideological neoliberal concept of the "information economy" has real effects in an age of financial speculation. The massive increases in financial exchanges throughout the 1980s coincided with key developments in computer and software engineering that became new tools for calculating risk.[73] The development of computer trading systems like "Bloomberg Terminal," for example, as well as the rise of algorithmic trading and stochastic forecasting methods accelerated the shift to the application of computation in finance.[74] In addition to submitting reality to the abstract logic of capital, finance reifies concrete, heterogenous timescales through the instruments of futures trading and derivatives. Credit-sustained accumulation, we have seen, is a speculative gamble on the exploitation of labor. The process of rationalization—that is, the "universal extension of the market system"—also reproduces the sacrificial logic of enlightenment.[75] Financial exchanges treat things identically, as homogenous and pliable. Such exchanges preserve the power of substitution implicit in the concept of enlightenment: the principle of immanence that allows the subject to manipulate objects according to their interests. Finance binds the future to accumulation, reproducing that "antagonism which could at any time bring organized society to ultimate catastrophe and destroy it."[76] The concept of computation articulated in neoliberal theory arrests cognition in the immediacy of market prices, reducing thought to functions so as to commodify the future "in the service of the present."[77] The exchangeability of diverse concrete products and timescales through the reduction to their measure, value, submits the future to abstract identity. In facing society as something alien, thinglike, and really abstract, individuals internalize the appearance of market signals as something natural, even fated.

The Domination of Nature

To summarize briefly, Horkheimer and Adorno's dialectic identifies the process of civilization as a mode of preservation that dominates external nature. This process belongs to the "economic" logic of self-preservation as a whole, which culminates in the modern bourgeois period. Humanity's relation to nature, they argue, is mediated by society, but capitalist society is not defined by human needs. Economic reason is therefore conditioned by the irrationality of the totality. Pointing to the "mythical violence" of instrumental reason's principle of immanence, Horkheimer and Adorno refer to the market as a social mediation that "only needs all."[78] The capitalist mode of production expands the domination of external nature by reducing it to the commodity-form. Both internal and external nature, therefore, have been pulled into the circuit of exchange-value. As Adorno later writes in *Negative Dialectics*, the "process of domination spews out tatters of subjugated nature undigested."[79] Human history, therefore, by failing to enter a truly human condition, is caught in a kind of permanent "prehistory," in which the "progressive natural domination" perpetuates "the unconscious one of nature, of devouring and being devoured."[80] Reduced to mere self-preservation, individuals today threaten to annihilate the natural world they depend on. Adorno captured this antagonism well: "In general the principle of the particular self-interest, which prescribes to everything individuated without exception its actions in the society, as it is, and which is the death of all."[81] As the universal extension of the market system submits the globe to capital, the exchange principle makes a claim on nature as something that can be infinitely commodified.

The full significance of society's shift to an epistemology of markets becomes apparent if one considers that for many neoliberals the current crises of ecology can only be resolved by markets.[82] Confronted with the Intergovernmental Panel on Climate Change's predictions regarding rising global average sea levels in the immediate future, neoliberal policy experts can only insist that the most rational response to the crisis is through more marketization.[83] In addition to the monopolistic commodification of nature (e.g., in the form of intellectual property rights and material transfer clause agreements), the now all-too-obvious fact of climate change is being administered by market evaluations.[84] Promulgated by neoliberal and libertarian think tanks such as the Heritage Foundation, Heartland, and the Cato Institute, and funded with significant support by oil conglomerates, a new brand of "climate capitalism" has emerged as the dominant response to the ecological crisis.[85] In addition to seeing climate change as an "opportunity for profit," the new climate capitalism advocates have responded to the crisis with carbon "cap-and-trade" markets and entrepreneurial geoengineering initiatives.[86] Through policies of deregulation, privatization, and carbon off-sets markets, neoliberals have largely succeeded in preempting efforts by regulators to reduce carbon emissions.[87]

Paradoxically, however, this victory reinstates the mythic, predetermined concept of nature that lies at the root of enlightenment. In trying to control nature through an economy of information, nature continues to control the subject who dominates. "There is a sense in which nature," Adorno suggests, "seems to keep receding from us."[88] The more "we take possession of nature, the more its real essence becomes alien to us."[89] By reducing nature to exchange-value, neoliberalism continues the compulsory domination of the civilizational process. In ratifying reason as an instrument of the market primarily, thinking imitates the very compulsion it attributes to nature. Such thinking is conditioned by the spell of the whole, that is, the "fetish character of commodities" that reflects the relations of society back to individuals inverted, as the natural and objective properties of things.[90] For Adorno, we "cannot eliminate from the dialectics of the extant what is experienced in consciousness as an alien thing," instead, the reconciled condition would "lie in the fact that the alien . . . remains what is distant and different, beyond the heterogeneous and beyond that which is one's own."[91] Reason today is submitting to the fated necessity it tried to overcome by suppressing the nonidentity of society and nature in exchange. This fated necessity can be seen in neoliberal theory's positivistic fetishism of prices, as well as in the overt denial by society's managers of the likely consequences of anthropogenic climate change. Neoliberalism therefore recreates the very subservience to a fated nature it must constantly disavow. The presumed inevitability and limitlessness of capitalist growth today indexes the irrationality of an untrue social whole, now captured by the spell of the economically arranged, second nature.

But Horkheimer and Adorno's critique of civilization is optimistic; its target is the false unity of reason and domination, which their argument exposes as socially necessary illusion.[92] The domination of nature, they argue, extends domination by prolonging the realm of necessity into the realm of freedom. True freedom would require a different relationship with nature. In capitalist modernity, reason could only be instrumentalized as a function in the socially constituted second nature. But rather than abandoning enlightenment's emancipatory promise in the name of a return to an unspoiled first nature, Horkheimer and Adorno's dialectic points to the growing anachronism of capital, and to a possible, post-work society. As Adorno later writes in *Negative Dialectics*, the "possible reduction of labor to a minimum could not but have a radical effect on the concept of practice."[93] Labor, freed from exchange, could become something more than mere self-preservation. All the "exertions rendered superfluous" by the state of the productive forces have become "objectively irrational."[94] The concept of an enlightened, non-dominating reason would "recognize the wounds which enlightenment has left behind as moments where enlightenment betrays its own imperfect character and reveals that it is actually not yet enlightened enough."[95] Once labor is reduced to a minimum and freed from the commodity-form, nature could be something other than a mere means, and reason could reflexively experience its own affinity with nature.

In bringing self-preservation to perfection through the advanced, techno-scientific knowledge of nature, Horkheimer and Adorno suggest that thought can begin to overcome domination: "Each advance of civilization has renewed not only mastery but also the prospect of its alleviation."[96] Substantive human freedom from compulsion would require the emancipation of human practice from mere preservation. In its total "dissociation" from the individuals who form it, the social totality threatens to undermine itself: "The straighter a society's course for the totality that is reproduced in the spellbound subjects, the deeper its tendency to disassociation. This threatens the life of the species as much as it disavows the spell cast over the whole, the false identity of subject and object."[97] The possibility of capitalism's collapse, however, is no guarantee that a truly reconciled world would replace it, because humanity has still not entered a truly human state.

The compulsory character of self-preservation, then, requires a critique of the cultural forms of identity that pervade neoliberal culture, and which mediate individuals according to specifiable types and classifications. Chapter 5 thus reinterprets Horkheimer and Adorno's notion of the "culture industry" to theorize contemporary forms of socialization. In what follows, I investigate the neoliberal culture of computationalism and argue that the "network" form of socialization today pervades the consumption sphere, connecting subjects to exchange through evermore diffuse mechanisms of commodification and control. The chapter asks how individuals today can resist the increasingly sophisticated social "web of blindness" that captures us in a now completely petrified, autonomous, negative totality.

Notes

1 Adorno, *Negative Dialectics*, 320.
2 Horkheimer and Adorno, *Dialectic of Enlightenment*, xiv.
3 Ibid., 2.
4 Stoetzler, "Needless Necessity," 55.
5 Horkheimer and Adorno, *Dialectic*, 11.
6 Ibid., xviii.
7 Ibid., 5.
8 Ibid., 1.
9 Ibid., 8.
10 Ibid.

11 Ibid., 6.
12 Ibid.
13 Ibid., 7.
14 Ibid., 40.
15 Ibid.
16 Ibid., 9.
17 Ibid., 43.
18 Stefan Breuer, "Adorno's Anthropology," 13.
19 Horkheimer and Adorno, *Dialectic*, 13.
20 Ibid., 23.
21 Theodor W. Adorno, "Sociology and Psychology (Part II)," trans. Irving N. Wohlfarth, *NLR*, 1/47 (1968): 84.
22 Horkheimer and Adorno, *Dialectic*, 168.
23 Ibid., 23.
24 Ibid.
25 Stoetzler, "Needless Necessity," 55.
26 Horkheimer and Adorno, *Dialectic*, 23.
27 Stoetzler, "Needless Necessity," 55.
28 Horkheimer and Adorno, *Dialectic*, 202.
29 Ibid., 11.
30 Ibid., 23.
31 Ibid.
32 Ibid.
33 Ibid., 25.
34 Adorno, *Minima Moralia*, 135.
35 Ibid., 129.
36 Adorno, "Late Capitalism," 117.
37 Adorno, *Minima Moralia*, 260.
38 See Breuer, "Adorno's Anthropology," 21.
39 Adorno, *Minima Moralia*, 229.
40 By the increasing "organic composition of capital" Marx meant the increasing ratio of "constant," or "fixed" capital to "variable capital." See Massimiliano Tomba, "Adorno's Account of the Anthropological Crisis and the New Type of Human," in *(Mis)Readings of Marx in Continental Philosophy*, ed. Jernej Habjan and Jessica Whyte (New York: Palgrave Macmillan, 2014), 38.
41 Adorno, *Minima Moralia*, 229.
42 Adorno, *Current of Music*, 462.
43 Tomba, "Adorno's Account," 43.
44 Ibid., 42.
45 Adorno, *Minima Moralia*, 229.

46　Ibid., 231.
47　Adorno, *Soziologische Schriften*, 68. Cited in Breuer, "Adorno's Anthropology," 21.
48　Ibid., 229.
49　Adorno, *Current Music*, 464.
50　Tomba, "Adorno's Account," 44.
51　Adorno, *Current of Music*, 463.
52　Ibid., 464.
53　See Breuer, "Adorno's Anthropology," 19.
54　As Jay Bernstein writes, "Adorno believes, like Weber, that for all intents and purposes it is the *same* conception of reason and rationality that governs scientific rationalism as governs societal rationalization. Adorno calls this conception of reason and reasoning 'identity thinking.'" See J. M. Bernstein, *Adorno: Disenchantment and Ethics* (Cambridge: Cambridge University Press, 2001), 10.
55　Adorno, *Negative Dialectics*, 305.
56　Adorno, *Soziologische Schriften*, 68. Cited in Breuer, "Adorno's Anthropology," 21.
57　Theodor W. Adorno, *Critical Models: Interventions and Catchwords*, trans. Henry W. Pickford (New York: Columbia University Press, 2005), 127–28.
58　In addition to other key developments, Alan Turing's theory of machine intelligence and John von Neumann's theory of automata were decisive innovations for the computationalist turn, as well as for its corresponding reverberation in the economics of information. See Mirowski's *Machine Dreams*, 94–136.
59　Jean-Pierre Dupuy, *On the Origins of Cognitive Science: The Mechanization of Mind*, trans. M. B. DeBevoise (Cambridge: Cambridge University Press, 2009), xi.
60　Ibid., 60.
61　Edwin Hutchins, *Cognition in the Wild* (Cambridge: The MIT Press, 1995), 363.
62　For an overview of machine functionalism, see Jaegwon Kim, *Philosophy of Mind* (Boulder: Westview Press, 2011), 129–65; John R. Searle, *Mind: A Brief Introduction* (Oxford: Oxford University Press, 2004), 64–82.
63　The computer model of mind can be seen in the Anglo-American tradition of academic philosophy, for example, in the machine functionalist approach of Hilary Putnam (at least for a time), as well as Jerry Fodor. See Golumbia, *The Cultural Logic of Computation*, 36.
64　Hubert Dreyfus, *What Computers Still Can't Do: A Critique of Artificial Reason* (Cambridge: The MIT Press, 1993), xi.
65　Adorno, *Negative Dialectics*, 206. Translation modified.
66　Adorno, *Critical Models*, 128.
67　Tomba, "Adorno's Account," 42.
68　Horkheimer and Adorno, *Dialectic*, 19.
69　Ibid., 18.
70　See Lotz, *The Capitalist Schema*, xiv.

71 Horkheimer and Adorno, *Dialectic*, 21.
72 Stoetzler, "Needless Necessity," 58.
73 See McNally, *Global Slump*, 100.
74 See Seb Franklin, *Control: Digitality as Cultural Logic* (Cambridge: The MIT Press, 2015), 70.
75 Adorno, "Society," 149.
76 Ibid.
77 Horkheimer and Adorno, *Dialectic*, 25.
78 See Stoetzler, "Needless Necessity," 56.
79 A, *Negative Dialectics*, 347.
80 Ibid., 355.
81 Ibid., 298. Translation modified.
82 For an account of this history, see Adrian Parr's *The Wrath of Capital: Neoliberalism and Climate Change Politics* (New York: Columbia University Press, 2013).
83 See Sharon Beder, "Neoliberal Think Tanks and Free Market Environmentalism," *Environmental Politics,* 10, no. 2 (Summer 2001): 128–33; Naomi Oreskes and Erik M. Conway, *Merchants of Doubt: How a Handful of Scientists Obscured the Truth on Issues from Tobacco Smoke to Global Warming* (London: Bloomsbury, 2001).
84 See Philip Mirowski, *Science Mart: Privatizing American Science* (Cambridge: Harvard University Press, 2011), 14, 140, 192.
85 Mirowski, *Never Let a Serious Crisis Go to Waste,* 337, 342.
86 Ibid., 340.
87 Ibid., 356–58.
88 Adorno, *Kant's Critique of Pure Reason*, 176.
89 Ibid.
90 Adorno, *Negative Dialectics*, 269.
91 Ibid., 191.
92 As Stoetzler suggests, the *Dialectic of Enlightenment* was equally a critique of the traditional labor movement, which for Horkheimer and Adorno resigned itself to the eternal character of "the economy," thereby prolonging the "prehistory" of humanity. See Stoetlzer, "Needless Necessity," 56.
93 Ibid., 244.
94 Ibid., 349.
95 Theodor W. Adorno, *An Introduction to Dialectics*, trans. Nicholas Walker (Cambridge: Polity Press, 2017), 188.
96 Horkheimer and Adorno, *Dialectic*, 32.
97 Adorno, *Negative Dialectics*, 346.

5

Neoliberal Culture

Neoliberal society is an abstractly veiled totality. Adorno's critical theory, we have seen, targets the socialization of individuals by exchange. Pervading the institutions of late capitalism, exchange is the "all-round mediator" that binds individuals to the antagonistic whole.[1] The exchange principle infiltrates every aspect of life, reducing difference to abstract identity. Neoliberalism, I have argued, perpetuates this form of mediation through new appearances. But how does contemporary culture contribute to this mediation? In addition to theory, economics, and the instrumentalization of reason, Adorno argues that commodity fetishism determines the sphere of culture. In the *Dialectic of Enlightenment*, Horkheimer and Adorno develop the concept of "the culture industry" to expand their critique of ideology. By consuming the products of the culture industry, they argue, individuals are socialized to internalize the standardized form of production. "Culture today," Horkheimer and Adorno begin, "is infecting everything with sameness."[2] The critique of the culture industry suggests that the mass industrial production and consumption of cultural goods play a fundamental role in the ideological reproduction of society. Moreover, by consuming the products of the culture industry, individuals are psychically constituted by the fetish character of the commodity.

Adorno and Horkheimer's concept of the culture industry, however, can easily be criticized for failing to anticipate the structure of cultural production that would characterize the virtual age of neoliberal capitalism, particularly the forms of popular culture that have come to define the "Web 2.0." The obsolescence of their approach, it is frequently said, is a necessary consequence of the technological innovations in electronic and digital media in the age of the computer.[3] Adorno and Horkheimer's critique of mass culture could hardly have predicted the hegemonic status of today's digital media. Reflecting on this development, Hullot-Kentor writes: "The concepts of 'net' and 'web' in which Adorno sought to capture self-consciously the totality of mediation, were instead themselves finally captured by the fact of all-encompassing electronic mediation in which their self-reflection was effaced."[4] And yet, in his effort to break out of the spell of exchange, Adorno's critique of the culture industry reverberates in the neoliberal age of total digital mediation. This is so because the reification of consciousness by the culture industry is not a function of the industrial structure of Fordist production, but rather the alienated form of cultural products. As Lotz puts it, "We misunderstand the thesis about the sameness of the products of the culture industry if we think of sameness as one of content; on the contrary, the sameness is an argument about the *form* of cultural products."[5] I argue that a return to Horkheimer and Adorno's critique of the culture industry can further illuminate the forms of cultural mediation that predominate in neoliberalism. Such an analysis, which does not reduce cultural productions to technological determinations, is grounded in the critique of the commodity-form and the law of exchange. As Horkheimer and Adorno suggest, the adverse effects of mass culture "should not be attributed to the internal laws of technology itself but to its function within the economy today."[6] This chapter engages forms of digital socialization in contemporary popular culture, as well as transformations within the neoliberal world of work. Moreover, the chapter explains how neoliberalism socializes individuals through the abstract and impersonal relations of networks, a process of integration that constitutes their psychic life by capitalist imperatives.

The Culture Industry: Mass Culture and the Commodity-Form

To briefly summarize, Horkheimer and Adorno's concept of the culture industry focuses on the ideological function of mass culture. "Film, radio, and magazines," they write, "form a system."[7] The integrated unanimity of mass culture constitutes a whole. Manufactured by the concentrated branches of monopoly capital, the products of the culture industry bear the imprint of abstract identity insofar as they reflect the fungibility of exchangeable commodities: "The conspicuous unity of the macrocosm and microcosm confronts human beings with a model of their culture: the false identity of universal and particular."[8] The systematic, planned, and standardized form of mass cultural production stamps the coercive form of monopoly capital on the foreheads of the consumers of mass culture, who are equally subsumed under the leveling effects of the industry's machinery. This integration compels individuals to reconcile themselves to the systematic alienation of society. Moreover, Adorno and Horkheimer's critique of the culture industry suggests that individuals who consume its products are, in effect, refashioned to incorporate the heteronomous structure of labor into experience itself. Such an analysis, it should be understood, is yet another iteration of Adorno's critique of the identity principle—the coercive reduction of the particular to the universality of exchange-value.

Horkheimer and Adorno's political economy of mass culture points to the entanglement of cultural production and commodification. As Shane Gunster indicates, "Culture is made specifically for the purpose of being sold; production is subordinated to distribution and the promise of art is thereby dissolved."[9] The mediation of culture by the commodity-form conditions the apparatus of production: "The dependence of the most powerful broadcasting company on the electrical industry, or film on the banks, characterizes the whole sphere, the individual sectors of which are themselves economically intertwined."[10] For Horkheimer and Adorno, there is something discernibly totalitarian about mass culture, which levels difference and integrates individuals to the administered form of industrial society. "The relentless unity of the culture industry," they argue, "bears witness to the emergent unity of politics."[11] In subordinating culture to profit, the culture industry must manufacture false needs to fuel consumption. The rise of the advertising and public relations industries is fundamental to standardizing tendencies of popular culture, which reflexively shape cultural products through branding and marketing.

The primacy of profit in cultural production manifests, according to Adorno, as a substitution of use-value for exchange-value. In the consumption of cultural commodities, individuals satisfy desire by realizing exchange-value. In the "Fetish-Character in Music and the Regression of Listening," for example, Adorno indicates that exchange-value "destroys use-values for human beings," and takes over the function of gratification as the primary "object of enjoyment."[12] Cultural commodities are now ruled by their function as the realization of exchange-value. According to Adorno, the culture industry openly admits to this phenomenon, and individuals willingly identify with this substitution: "Pure use-value, whose illusion the cultural goods must preserve in completely capitalist society, must be replaced by pure exchange-value, which precisely in its capacity as exchange-value deceptively takes over the function of use-value."[13] The deceptive replacement of use for exchange leads consumers to self-identify with the advertiser's brand names and status symbols. Although they may appear novel and unique, Horkheimer and Adorno's insist that the fetish character of cultural commodities only generates a kind of "pseudoindividuality."[14] Individuals who consume standardized products internalize standardization, but through the substitution of their gratification impulses, they experience consumption as a mode of self-authentication. The culture industry, therefore, is always in the business of "producing new wants," for consumers, who in turn find the consumption of exchange-value gratifying.[15]

Adorno and Horkheimer's analysis maintains that mass culture serves another key ideological function for the reproduction of capital—namely, the prolongation and extension of the structure of abstract labor into consciousness and private life. As Horkheimer and Adorno put it, "Even during their leisure time, consumers must orient themselves according to the unity of production."[16] Rather than providing individuals with an imaginative escape from the labor process, the consumption of mass culture merely extends the mass industrial structure of labor to the imaginations of consumers. "Entertainment," they write, "is the prolongation of work under late capitalism. It is sought by those who want to escape the mechanized labor process so that they can cope with it again."[17] Such a compensatory mechanism, however, which appears on the surface to be a flight from the mechanical, instrumental character of work, unfolds as an extension of the work process into consciousness. "At the same time," Adorno and Horkheimer continue, "mechanization has such power over leisure and its happiness, determines so thoroughly the fabrication of entertainment commodities, that the off-duty worker can experience nothing but after-images of the work process itself."[18] This prolongation of labor into leisure time expands reification. The cultural products of late capitalism pervade the circulation process, and with it, the reification of consciousness in cultural consumption: "The only escape from the work process in factory and office is through adaptation to it in leisure time."[19] The fundamental manipulation of individuals by mass culture does not result from the technological structure of cultural production, but belongs to the logic of negative socialization under late capitalism, where the boundaries of work and life are liquidated by the exchange principle.[20]

The Neoliberal Culture Industry

Anchored in the forms of mass cultural production that characterized the Fordist postwar boom and its specific media, Adorno and Horkheimer's critique of mass culture seems quaint if one considers the advanced technological state of the digital media revolution that would succeed it. But the widespread introduction of computers and digital media in the sphere of production in the 1970s and 1980s has reified consciousness in a manner that reflects the integrated character of neoliberal capitalism. In addition to the indirect forms of mediation on the internet, individuals today are socialized to relate to each other through increasingly integrated and abstract connections. The products of today's culture industries resemble the algorithms of production. "Auto-Tune" technologies, for example, mold popular music to fit the criteria of the industry's standards, removing elements of dissonance.[21] Individuals today interact through monopolistic platforms that "mine" users' private data, sell manufactured news cycles, while application of data analytics targets users with increasingly tailored advertisements.[22] The estrangement of individuals from the world they constitute is reflected back to them through the fragmentary contents of online chat rooms and message boards, which are often populated by the fixed opinions of authoritarian, racist, and sexist subcultures.[23] Observing the convergence of social estrangement and authoritarian attitudes, Adorno remarked, "Because the world is not our world, because it is heteronomous, it can express itself only distortedly in stubborn and inflexible opinions, and such delusions within opinions in turn ultimately tends to increase the predominance of alienation in totalitarian systems."[24]

The digital forms of networked mediation that have risen to prominence in the neoliberal period, I am suggesting, can be analyzed with reference to the concept of the culture industry, because they continue to be conditioned by the fetish character of the commodity. As Robert Kurz argues in his reconsideration of Horkheimer and Adorno's analysis, "The Culture Industry in the 21st Century" (2010), "The technology of the culture industry is immune neither to the fetishistic economic form of capital nor to the function of social control that is associated [with] that form."[25] Humanity today is classified as a network of consumers; the false unity of the system proceeds from the fetish form of the exchange abstraction. "In reality," Horkheimer and Adorno write, "a cycle of manipulation and retroactive need is unifying the system ever more tightly."[26] As an objective form of social synthesis, the rule of exchange binds individuals to accumulation; the circulation and consumption of cultural commodities by individuals represent an immanent moment in the social constitution of capitalist relations.

Adorno and Horkheimer's critique of mass culture targeted the integration of subjects into the standardized form of industrial production. Grounded in the historic productivity growth of the postwar boom (and with it, an unprecedented maturation of mass cultural consumption in the United States and Europe), the forms of cultural mediation that have characterized neoliberalism can be interpreted with reference to the objective crisis of capitalism I have delineated.

The expansion of financial markets in the neoliberal period, and with it, the pervasive immanence of exchange, mediates subjects increasingly according to a "network" structure, defined by the integration of individuals into the totalizing reproduction of capitalist relations. As we have seen in Chapter 2, the crises of overaccumulation in the 1970s led to the neoliberal assault against the welfare system. The succeeding period unfolded through credit-accumulation and privatization. In addition to submitting populations to the rule of money, neoliberalization instrumentalized developments in computing to manage risk. Moreover, the shift in economic activity to investment in computer technologies is a significant aspect of neoliberal culture, which is an increasingly "networked" form of mediation. As Kurz suggested, "The culturalist virtualization of the world of life corresponds to the economic virtualization of capital."[27] The objective but culturally produced context of neoliberal second nature has been reinforced by the active participation by subjects in the networked mediations of the web. Considered as a new form of mass cultural integration, the internet provides neoliberal society with a necessary form of mediation. This mediation, which assumes the appearance of a "virtual," "simulated" second reality, reflects the seeming unreality of financial capital. The virtualized interactions of financial capital appear to be entirely severed from its objective, social genesis.[28] As the site where subjects are mediated by the informational, networked relations of neoliberal socialization, the internet further reduces individuals to bearers of commodity exchange.

Flexible Standardization

If Adorno and Horkheimer's critique of the culture industry alighted upon the structural isomorphism between mass culture and the industrial structure of commodity production, the cultural logic of neoliberalism can only be deciphered with reference to the forms of digital mediation that have reinforced the financial capitalist relations. Understood as the most significant departure from the form of passive spectatorship, Adorno and Horkheimer identified in their critique of the culture industry, neoliberalism socializes individuals through active forms of participation. In the culture industry of Fordism, Adorno and Horkheimer stress, "No mechanism of reply has been developed"—spectators simply consume film, radio, and television as appendages to the system.[29] Neoliberal consumption, however, reproduces itself through a complex, indirect, and flexible "mechanism of reply" that induces subjects to objectify themselves through new technologies.

This process of digital mediation contains its own dialectic. In order to specify the cultural logic of neoliberalism, I refer to the social logic of "standardized flexibility." By "standardized flexibility," I mean that under financial capitalism, individuals who are socialized through virtual forms of technological mediation are compelled to associate their content with the digital forms of network-based interdependence that characterize the worlds of work and culture in the OECD north. Despite the active, flexible, and adaptational character of the individual's participation in digital media connections, this form of participation conforms to the structure of capitalist relations, as well as to the imperatives of capitalist accumulation.

Horkheimer and Adorno's critique of reification articulates the power of mass culture over consciousness. By consuming the products of popular culture, individuals consume capitalist imperatives in a manner that transforms the structure of experience. "The familiar experience of the moviegoer," Horkheimer and Adorno suggest, "who perceives the street outside as a continuation of the film he has just left, … has become the guideline of production."[30] The continuation in question does not simply identify the delusional aspect of popular spectatorship, but rather the extension of the estranged form of production in consciousness. This process of extension is only accelerated by participating on the internet. The dynamic ascendance of internet services, opportunities, and platforms for digital content creation buttresses the dominance of the advertising industry and its (primarily) distributional function in the reproduction of capital. The ubiquity of new electronic and cultural products mediates consciousness according to increasingly precise, instrumental methods of control. Smart phones, apps, video games and virtual reality devices headsets provide the user with a second social existence that is quickly replacing the first.[31]

The production of a virtual "mechanism of reply" for individuals reproduces neoliberal relations in the entwined worlds of work and free time. Through the pervasive integration, incorporation, and reproduction of subjects into the network of mediations that constitute financialized capitalist relations, subjects participate in their own reduction to mere "character masks" of capital. The semblance of digital interaction and communication between individuals on social media integrates subjects into the totality. Pointing to the capacity of capital to integrate subjects into the schematic reproduction of capitalist relations through cultural consumption, Adorno and Horkheimer suggest that in consumption, individuals assist capital in the "classification, organization, and identification of consumers."[32] Such practices have, of course, been revolutionized by innovations in data mining and sociometry. Today's social networks consume individuality through the pseudo-individualism of the network. The modern corporation has introduced a new age of digitally mediated systems of planning and control. In addition to market-pricing, credit-scoring software, and consumer emulation simulations, formalized business models allow IT managers to rationalize firms through the manipulation of simulated behavior.[33] As Hullot-Kentor writes, "Computerized systems of distribution have made corporations logistical devices for dominating consumption; single companies have installed themselves as the social appetite's sole gatekeeper at every turn and in all regions."[34] In addition to exporting manufacturing to the more easily exploitable labor markets of the developing South, the neoliberal corporation has harnessed the managerial class to financialization. As we have seen, the neoliberal corporation dismantled the "managerial" model of Fordism and its system of industrial relations, shifting to a "rentier" structure that prioritizes shareholder value.[35] In addition to the apparent virtuality of money capital, the computational instruments of rentier management further entrap empirical subjects into the labor abstraction—to financial managers, the digital spreadsheets of the firm are more real than concrete laborers on the factory floor.

Confronted with the substantial economic inequality that has defined neoliberalism, individuals have nevertheless adopted their roles as "character masks" of capital through the mediations of the network. The forms of virtual socialization that incorporate individuals into the interdependence of global financial capitalism protect the reproduction of a system in crisis. The virtual space of the internet does not merely represent a new phase in the general state of technology but also reflects the apparently "simulated" structure of finance, characterized by production of "fictitious" capital.[36] The virtual space of the network not only expands the scope of monetary relations but also functions as a constituent moment in the constitution of neoliberal subjects by the whole. This social constitution of subjectivity, I want to suggest, inverts the appearances of neoliberal society through the filter of the virtual space of the network. Specifically, within the world of work, the individual is socialized according to an apparently "entrepreneurial" logic, where every individual is both capitalist and employee.[37]

Exemplified best by the concept of "human capital" in the work of economists Gary Becker and Theodore Schultz, the neoliberal subject is induced to adopt an investment logic in every aspect of life.[38] The category of human capital expanded the grid of the neoclassical utility function to encompass a more diverse array of practices, relations, and skill sets within the model of market equilibrium. The concept of human capital refers to the economic agent's investments in knowledge, education, culture, and family. In addition to targeting public deficit spending on health care and education during the 1980s, human capital theorists like Becker and Schultz played a major role in reshaping the science of management.[39] Emphasizing time-saving techniques, professional connections, and the capacity to adapt to shifting and often unforeseeable working conditions, Becker and Schulz's human capital theory idealized an employee who was more flexible and self-disciplined than the intransigent union worker.

Often called "human capital management," the neoliberal firm not only has restructured the relations of management to ownership but also has crafted an entrepreneurial ethic that justifies de-unionization and labor discipline. The category of human capital represents the theoretical inversion of the objective heteronomy of neoliberal labor—by adopting an "entrepreneurial" identity that has been characterized by the exchange of employment security, protection, and benefits for stock ownership, the employee (now repackaged as entrepreneur) can assume new freedoms and responsibilities for self-creation.[40] The entrepreneur's activities are both flexible and self-defining. However, this flexibility is paid for in the disciplinary forms of labor precarity and insecurity, as well as the demands of mobility imposed by the networked structure of the firm. As sociologists Luc Boltanski and Eve Chiapello suggest, exploitation can be exported by extracting "surplus-value from the less mobile."[41] While the neoliberal subject's active investments in human capital may appear to have liberated the subject from the traditional division of labor, the category of human capital functions ideologically to invert the appearance of rising job insecurity, declining wage growth, and rising household debt as merely the negative outcome of irrational investments. The ascendance of the internet revolution has, indeed, provided the ideal outlet for neoliberal socialization. As Mirowski laments, "Chat rooms, online gaming, virtual social networks, and electronic financialization of household budgets have encouraged even the most intellectually challenged to experiment with the new neoliberal personhood."[42] Such personhood, as exemplified by the category human capital, represents the neoliberal inversion of the subject's objectification by abstract wealth—subjects in virtual space are encouraged to treat their poverty management as a new, entrepreneurial freedom.

This freedom, however, is in fact highly disciplined by the organization of work by the predominance of computer technologies, information processing, and management software. In addition to the direct surveillance of employees, computerized technologies function as crucial instruments of authority that increasingly liquidate the distinction between the subject's private and working life. The development of "Enterprise Resource Planning" software in the 1980s, for example, allowed business executives and managers to submit wider components of organization to computerized control (such as the automation of countless back-office functions).[43] The informational structure of the "lean," "flexible" firm imposes a structure of discipline, surveillance, and hierarchy. According to Alan Liu, the information culture in work represents a "migration" of the Taylorist methods of scientific management to white-collar work, developing in fields like industrial psychology and the utilization of computerized industrial mainframes. "The ideal organization," Liu suggests, "is one that has stripped out all intermediary levels of equipment, inventory, processes, organizational units, and people so that the information necessary to produce, for example, a new car flows laterally between customers, sales, design, plant, and suppliers with the speed of light."[44] Coordinated by software like "Enterprise Resource Planning," and "Customer Relationship Management," labor can now be rationalized by algorithms for corporate interests.[45] This form of instrumental standardization, which generates greater levels of heteronomous control over the conditions of work, nevertheless bears the semblance of "flexibility" by virtue of the seeming indirectness, informality, and fluidity of its connections. "Everyone and everything," Liu continues, "is part of an information network whose basic units are flexible team workers incessantly communicating with each other and with the larger organization."[46] The neoliberal subject, organized through networked points of contact, stands in a self-mediating relation. As the reified object of marketized connections, the subject is a constituent moment of the social object's determination. The subject, however, is socialized to participate in a form of "communicative exhibitionism," characterized by the externalization of the self as an identifiable unit.[47]

The integration of Taylorist strategies into new, labor-saving digital technologies in neoliberalism represents a double-sided form of coercive socialization imposed by management. This contradictory form of control has its historical antecedents. Elton Mayo, whose famous "Hawthorne investigation" of 1927–32, recommended to managers the incorporation of informal practices of spontaneous cooperation in the labor process. What Mayo called the "Hawthorne Effect" refers to the mere fact that workers under observation increase their productivity because they know they are being observed.[48] Echoing Taylor, Mayo argued that labor should be managed by creating new personal associations, as well as new emotional attachments through the total collapse of life into work. Adorno, observing the formation of a new technique of labor discipline in Mayo's findings, remarked in 1968: "This study showed that the productivity of work is increased by the cohesion between small groups which are 'informal,' that is, not organized. This revealed for the first time that, for rational reasons, irrational sectors . . . have become incorporated in socially rationalized work."[49] Mayo's report of the Hawthorne study concluded that the productivity of labor "does not simply rise with rationalization," but reaches a threshold in which, "beyond a certain level," the productivity of labor declines.[50] The inclusion of a certain "human factor," Adorno continues, can be instrumentalized for efficiency.[51]

The Mayo school generated a break within the discipline of management science by shifting to what would later be called the "human relations" branch of management.[52] Preferring a strategy of "spontaneous cooperation," "informality," and "communication" over isolation, Mayo's technique stressed the ideals of group cohesion, transparency, and well-being. The so-called "informal" organizational structure that Mayo championed (which also initiated the psychotherapeutic treatment of company employees) introduced a new form of interpersonal socialization in work. The human relations doctrine of industrial psychology broke with Taylorism—shifting from the priorities of efficiency and time-saving to the ideals of "adaptability" and "systemic balance." As William Whyte indicates in *The Organization Man* (1956), "Through the scientific application of human relations, these neutralist technicians will guide him into satisfying solidarity with the group so skillfully and unobtrusively that he will scarcely realize how the benefaction has been accomplished."[53]

But the coercive technique of manipulation Adorno identified in the Hawthorne studies represents a wider process of reification that extends social domination to the psychic life of individuals. In "Sociology and Psychology" (1967), Adorno details the manipulation of the psyche by the instrumental rationalization of labor. The application of industrial psychology methods to labor can be understood, as Adorno suggests, as the incorporation of an "irrational" element in the rationalization of labor. Identifying a form of conduct in work that requires economic individuals to adapt their behaviors to unforeseeable circumstances, Adorno claims that the individual who "wants to adjust himself to a competitive pattern of society has to pursue his own particularistic individual interests rather ruthlessly in order to find recognition—he has, so to speak, to adjust through non-adjustment."[54]

Adaptation to the societal process compels individuals to become "commensurable." Mediation, according to Adorno, does not merely refer to the objective integration of individuals into exchange relations, but is also reflected, subjectively, as a process of socialization that imposes a structure of "commensurability" on subjects. As Adorno argues, "The commensurability of individual's mode of behavior, the actual process of socialization, is based on the fact that as economic subjects they do not relate to one another at all immediately but act according to the dictates of exchange-value."[55] The commensurability of subjects to the commodity-form represents the competitive unsociability of a society dominated by exchange. Unless the individual adapts to the structure of value and its categories, such an individual cannot appear as an identifiable unit of potential exchange-value.

For Adorno, the commensuration of subjects to the abstract identity of exchange enables subjects to adapt to market conditions, and to internalize adaptation as a type of conduct that conforms to the social whole. Such a form of flexible, adaptational "adjustment" to reified relations has only been reinforced by the digital mediations of the neoliberal world of work. Subjects who revise their behavior according to the ideal of human capital must actively incorporate themselves into the network of monetized relations through techniques of self-branding. As Kurz remarks, the "objective forms of existence" are superimposed upon by a second virtual reality, characterized by a "mediated self-staging."[56] Through revisable practices and digitally mediated relations the subject performs a technique of self-externalization that objectifies identity, rendering the self available for market evaluation. The consumer of digitally mediated products assists capital in the classification of information for creditors. "Individuals," Kurz continues, "increasingly view themselves as their own actors in their own theater."[57] The virtual space of life and work—now so fully integrated that they have become indistinguishable—has served a crucial function in the social reproduction of neoliberalism—namely, it has supplied subjects with the "machinery of reply." Individuals today cannot "abandon their roles" as character masks of capital "even when they are alone."[58]

The convergence of human resources management and the restructuring of work by computers have extended the reification of subjects, reducing them to identifiable units in the network. The neoliberal subject is compelled to compete in market relations through practices of flexible commensuration. By disseminating information through the network of commercial relations, the subject is rendered available for market evaluation, review, and audit. This form of socialization, however, appears to be a conscious choice of the individual, rather than a manufactured differentiation. Insofar as the subject selects its own traits, subjectivity is objectified: "Character traits . . . are no longer the subject; rather, the subject responds to them as his internal object."[59] The digitally mediated culture of neoliberal society has rapidly expanded the purview regarding which individual attributes "count" as units of market value. As Wendy Espeland and Mitchell Stevens suggest, neoliberal practices of commensuration facilitate "comparative measurement" across vastly disparate categories and persons, such that it provides "an abstract form of unity that can potentially encompass any valued thing."[60] While it might appear that the neoliberal turn to the informal, fluid, and adaptational structure of network-based work has abolished the division of labor, such a structure only expands the law of society's autonomization those who form it.

The concentration of monopoly capital in narrow sectors subverts the neoliberal ideology of a decentralized, freely circulating, world of connections. The so-called "connexionist" world of private enterprise is conditioned by the hierarchical structure of monopoly capital. "The concept of connections," Adorno writes, "a category of mediation and circulation, never flourished best in the sphere of circulation proper, the market, but in closed and monopolistic hierarchies."[61] The concentration of capital in the current IT monopolies like Google, Facebook, and Amazon contradicts the neoliberal ideal of democratic decentralization. "Now that the whole of society is becoming hierarchical," Adorno continues, "these murky connections are proliferating wherever there used still to be an appearance of freedom."[62] Practices of commensuration enable subjects to quantify their knowledge, skill sets, and histories into identifiable packages of information. Increasingly regulated by the internet monopolies that have implemented computer models for "target marketing" and "data mining," the subject's digital information becomes an easily manipulable variable in the administrations of society.[63]

The proliferation of neoliberal techniques of evaluation, such as "performance metrics," "bench-marking," and "best practices," facilitates the rationalization of private information, as well as the formation of a fully "auditable subject." Niels van Doorn describes this dynamic: "The neoliberal construction of an 'auditable subject,' whose practices and self-management conform to the increasingly coinciding criteria of accountability, transparency, and efficiency, crucially depends on the establishment of quantified measures known as performance metrics."[64] Much as the neoliberal corporation—in striving to remove its redundancies—will submit every interaction to an algorithmic calculation, the neoliberal subject's performance is similarly rationalized as a function of the network. Mediated by the digital platforms and virtual relations on the Web 2.0, the neoliberal subject stages and broadcasts market information—a practice that recoils in the heteronomy of a culture of audit and surveillance.[65]

This form of digitally mediated control has equally unfolded as an assault on health care. In its neoliberal iteration, the very notion of "well-being" has been deployed as a punitive instrument against the precariously employed and impoverished. Obesity, sickness, and disability signify irresponsible self-management, while health, fitness, and well-being signify self-discipline. The masculinist idealization of strength and resilience in contemporary neoliberal culture reflects the rationalization of flexible labor; health is economized insofar as sickness represents a liability for management. As Kurz suggests, the "campaigns against . . . 'unhealthy' eating habits among the lower classes has nothing to do with a concern for their well-being." On the contrary, "What is taking place is that attention is being diverted from social inequalities, from poverty, from social abuses and from stressful working environments," as if sickness were merely the outcome of irresponsible habits.[66] The neoliberal culture of well-being, with its emphasis on freedom, self-responsibility, and discipline, is objectively contradicted in the United States by a private health insurance system that uses algorithms to target the most vulnerable.[67] Increasingly monitored by mood-tracking technologies of the "Health 2.0" industry, well-being is increasingly manufactured as a commodity.[68] In its rationalization by the health care industry, the ideal of health is functionalized—illness appears as the stigma of individuals who cannot be reduced to the exigencies of abstract labor. "All the prevalent movements of health," Adorno insists, "resemble the reflex-movements of beings whose hearts have stopped beating."[69] Health and beauty are commodities that signal adaptation to a system that profits from sickness.[70]

Simultaneously capitalist and employee, the neoliberal subject internalizes the identity principle, insofar as the subject's particularity is re-functioned according to abstract network of the totality. Interactions on social media perpetuate the deceptive replacement of use-value by exchange-value, as individuals who convey their status through the standardized criteria find gratification in their virtual, second life. As Kurz indicates, "The Internet . . . is becoming a kind of spiritual and cultural home that is, inversely, only occasionally abandoned for a visit to social and material reality."[71] By adopting the forms of flexible, mobile, and precarious labor that the modern "gig economy" has provided, subjects must modify their behavior through "pseudo-individual" practices of self-advertisement and public promotion. As Mirowski suggests, "The fundamental narcissism encouraged by neoliberalism demands that we participate in an active externalization of the experience of insecurity and vulnerability to revaluation."[72] This narcissism, as represented in the entrepreneurial logic of human capital, compels subjects to define themselves in terms of identifiably "unique," "specifiable," and "authentic" traits. This form of socialization is a ritual of neoliberal culture, where individuals freely exhibit their conformity to the system: "Existence in late capitalism," Adorno and Horkheimer suggest, "is a permanent rite of initiation. Everyone must show they identify wholeheartedly with the power that beats them."[73]

The cultural logic of neoliberal society liquidates individuality by expanding the "veil" of individualism. By defining the self as a unique, authentic, and therefore identifiable brand through the manipulation of signs in virtual space, the self becomes a constituent moment in the real abstraction of capital: "Amid the network of now wholly abstract relations" of mass culture, the incommensurable contents of the individual's experience are subsumed under the identity of exchange-value. "The estrangement of schemata and classifications from the data subsumed beneath them," Adorno writes, "indeed the sheer quantity of the material processed, which has become quite incommensurable with the horizons of individual experience, ceaselessly enforces an archaic retranslation into sensuous signs."[74] The ubiquity of online profiles and identities is modeled to fit classifying criteria; the individual's particularity is only identifiable as an object that has been formatted by the data-driven industries of advertising and marketing. In the digital representations of the subject in the network, "representation triumphs over what is represented."[75]

In the compulsory need to stand out in a cultural context of mass-produced sameness, the individual seizes upon particular attributes, and, by broadcasting them in virtual space, posits individuality as a function of society. This practice, which can best be described as the self-evident value of the individual's "authenticity," remains thoroughly entwined in the social totality. Despite the proliferation of techniques for digital externalization and self-authentication that are available today, the individual's specificity can only appear in its digitally encoded distribution. The neoliberal ideal of authenticity, however, is objectively prohibited from the outset by capitalism's form of socialization, which actively contributes to the contents of experience. The putative, "authentic" self posits uniqueness as a defensive reaction to impersonal grip of capitalist relations. The ideal of a unique individual can only sediment as the reflex of the systematic interchangeability of persons and things. "The more tightly the world is enclosed by the net of man-made things," the more stridently individuals proclaim their uniqueness.[76] The authentic individual would not have to assert itself so compulsively if society were not an autonomous, impersonal object.

The socially constituted context of second nature in neoliberalism allows the network form of interpersonal relations to appear emancipatory. "Freed" from the regimentation of Fordist and Taylorist production and the traditional division of labor, the neoliberal entrepreneur can embrace a future that appears open and liberated from traditional class structures. But the neoliberal subject is only free insofar as freedom means submission to the rule of exchange and its abstract, impersonal authority. The subject not only is objectively reduced to the imperatives of accumulation but learns to identify with the market system's authority. Freedom means learning to affirm what fate the markets have already determined. Adorno captures this well in his treatment of the astrology column in the *Los Angeles Times*:

> The idea that the freedom of the individual amounts to nothing more than making the best of what a given constellation of stars permits implies the very same idea of adjustment the affinity to which has been pointed out previously as one of the traits of astrology. According to this concept, freedom consists of the individual's taking upon himself what is inevitable anyway. If the individual acts according to given conjunctions, everything will go right, if he does not, everything will go wrong.[77]

The neoliberal norms of self-assertion, volunteerism, and risk define the concept of freedom, which becomes the mere freedom to adapt to the impersonal, and abstract, authority of markets. Divided from the outset by the commodity-form and its fetish character, the individual's particularity is preemptively functionalized by the universal. The apparent freedom of the neoliberal subject amounts to the freedom to accept the determinations of the market's fate. "The individual," Adorno writes in *Negative Dialectics*, "forms a moment of the commodity society; the pure spontaneity that is attributed to him is the spontaneity which society expropriates." The concepts of freedom and determinism are equally false. "In their inmost core," he continues, "the theses of determinism and freedom coincide. Both proclaim identity."[78] Freedom is wholly prefabricated by the coercive unity of the antagonistic whole.

Precarity and Crisis

The neoliberal reconfiguration of individualism, which has largely eroded the bourgeois ideals of the private sphere, perpetuates the reduction of individuals to character masks of capital. Individuals who participate in the virtual spaces of the net contribute, indirectly, to their financing. Through the pervasive extension of the network into every moment of life, the individual can reconstitute the structure of work into their private existence. The consumption of each digitally mediated cultural product reproduces the economic machinery, which in turn "keeps everyone on their toes, both at work and in the leisure time which resembles it."[79] The virtualization of culture drags private life into the reproduction of capitalist relations, eliminating the already precarious separation of work and life. Such participation, Kurz suggests, "is by no means indicative of any kind of emancipatory liberation of 'creativity,' but rather a kind of neoliberal 'privatization' of the mass production of the culture industry, normalized on an unprecedented scale."[80] Privacy under neoliberalism has been privatized; individuals in isolation connect on the net so that their virtual "friends" can keep the same watchful eye on their life as their employers do. As Adorno suggests, in *Minima Moralia*, "Private life asserts itself unduly, hectically, vampire-like, trying convulsively, because it really no longer exists, to prove it is alive. Public life is reduced to an unspoken oath of allegiance to the platform."[81] The neoliberal age of the network not only has perpetuated the commodification of labor but has also expanded the compulsory structure of labor within the privacy of consciousness.

Lamenting the loss of "free time," in late capitalism, Adorno writes, "Everybody must have projects all the time. The maximum must be extracted from leisure.... The whole of life must look like a job, and by this resemblance conceal what is not yet directly devoted to pecuniary gain."[82] The phenomena of free time, he suggests, "are organized for the sake of profit."[83] Notwithstanding the manufactured "lifestyles" that seem to be free from the strictures of work, the time free from work is "supposed to regenerate labor power," thereby reducing free time to an instrument of accumulation.[84] Today, as the injunctions to respond to the demands of labor expand (through email, texts, and alerts, for example), there is scarcely even time for the regeneration of labor power. The compulsory structure of work invades consciousness at the cost of leisure. "Organized free time," Adorno writes, "is compulsory." But this compulsion "is by no means only external. It is linked to the needs of human beings living under the functional system."[85] The impossibility of free time in neoliberalism reflects the wider social irrationality of capital accumulation as the objective social *a priori*. The priority of production for profit over need is reflected in the compulsory pursuit of what is insipidly branded in human resources management: "life-work balance."

Despite the elimination of living labor by technology, the introduction of automation has not emancipated life from alienated labor. The reduction of labor to a minimum, Adorno indicates, is possible, and would result in a changed conception of practice. The capitalistically arranged relations of society, however, requires the exploitation of labor, rendering a growing number of the population unnecessary: "To assert their positions people keep in motion an economy in which the extreme development of technology has made the masses in principle superfluous as producers in their own country."⁸⁶ Such automated technologies, however, have only expanded the fundamental unfreedom of domination, as surplus-value continues to be appropriated through the exploitation of labor. Rather than freeing time from the condition of abstract labor time, neoliberal capitalism has only modified the capital-labor relation to defend the system from its crisis tendencies.

To the consumers of digital content on the net, consumption is equally production. Paid for through the indirect mediations of advertising and data mining, the users of social media perpetuate the subsumption of life under capital. The functionalization of particular individuals by the universal mediations of virtual space is a constituent moment of what Adorno calls the "objective web of blindness" (*Verblendungszusammenhang*). The network of information that binds individuals to speculative chains of credit that stretch into the future provides a mechanism of integration that reproduces the law of society's independence. The organization of labor by information technologies has produced a systemic crisis of labor on a planetary scale. In addition to the displacement of living labor by microelectronic, automated technologies in the Global North, neoliberalization has subordinated flexible labor to the power of world money. In what Guy Standing describes as the new "precariat," today's emerging global class of underemployed populations is threatening to undermine the stability of capital accumulation on a global scale.[87] In addition to declines in real wages and regular employment in the Global North, the manufacturing sector has undergone a historic contraction through the rising superfluity of living labor. Despite steady output in the US manufacturing sector, jobs in manufacturing have declined as a result of automation.[88] The mutually reinforcing crises of labor and ecology belong to the form of the antagonistically divided totality that reduces individuals to roles and life to mere preservation.

Adorno and Horkheimer's critique of the culture industry revealed itself to be targeting a historical period of Fordism that was able to reproduce itself through the total administrations of the consumer class. Today the culture industry exists under the conditions of the planetary crises of the global capitalist system. The internet belongs to the very dynamic that is threatening to rationalize living labor out of existence. And yet the new technologies provide society with forms of antagonistic socialization that integrate subjects all the more completely. Notwithstanding the ubiquity, accessibility, and fluidity with which consumers participate in virtual productions, such practices also perpetuate the fetish form of the commodity, which inverts the appearances of society in a manner that transfigures the material relations between persons into social relations between things. Value, that immense "phantom objectivity" that appears to be a natural property of things, is being extended in the virtual spaces we inhabit. The unreality of neoliberalism's mediations reflects the objective falsity of capitalism, the most real thing of all. Disrupting the spell of this illusion would entail the subject's critical consciousness of how life could become something more than a response to the market's judgment.

Notes

1 Adorno, *Negative Dialectics*, 328.
2 Horkheimer and Adorno, *Dialectic of Enlightenment*, 94.
3 For an example of this critique, see Zygmunt Bauman's *Liquid Modernity* (Cambridge: Polity Press, 2011); Peter Uwe Hohendahl, "Frozen Imagination: Adorno's Theory of Mass Culture Revisited," *Thesis Eleven*, 34, no. 1 (1993): 17–41.
4 Hullot-Kentor, "The Exact Sense in Which the Culture Industry No Longer Exists," 140.
5 Christian Lotz, "The Culture Industry," in *The SAGE Handbook of Frankfurt School Critical Theory*, ed. Beverley Best, Werner Bonefeld, and Chris O'Kane (London: Sage, 2018), 980.
6 Horkheimer and Adorno, *Dialectic*, 95.
7 Ibid., 94.
8 Ibid., 95.
9 Shane Gunster, *Critical Theory for Cultural Studies* (Toronto: University of Toronto Press, 2004), 48.
10 Horkheimer and Adorno, *Dialectic*, 96.
11 Ibid.
12 Theodor W. Adorno, "On the Fetish-Character in Music and the Regression of Listening," trans. Maurice Goldbloom, *The Frankfurt School Reader*, 279.
13 Ibid., 279.
14 Horkheimer and Adorno, *Dialectic*, 125.
15 Ibid., 115.
16 Ibid., 98.
17 Ibid., 109.
18 Ibid.
19 Ibid.
20 Robert Kurz, "Kulturindustrie im 21 Jahrhundert. Zur Aktualität des Konzepts von Adorno under Horkheimer," *Exit! Krise und Kritik der Warengesellschaft*, no. 9 (March 2012): 12.
21 For background and discussion, see Simon Reynolds, "How Auto-Tune Revolutionized the Sound of Popular Music," *Pitchfork* (September 2018).

22 For background discussion on the neoliberal connection to the use of "bots" and "fake news," see Philip Mirowski, "Hell Is Truth Seen Too Late," *Boundary*, 2 (February 2019): 1–53.
23 For background regarding the use of chat rooms and message boards on the alt-right, consult the findings of the Southern Poverty Law Center's Intelligence Report, "Explaining the Alt-Right 'Deity' of Their 'Meme Magic,'" *Southern Poverty Law Center* (August 8, 2017). https://www.splcenter.org/fighting-hate/intelligence-report/2017/explaining-alt-right-%E2%80%98deity%E2%80%99-their-%E2%80%98meme-magic%E2%80%99.
24 Adorno, "Opinion Delusion Society," *Critical Models*, 110.
25 Kurz, "Kulturindustrie," 6.
26 Horkheimer and Adorno, *Dialectic of Enlightenment*, 95.
27 Ibid.
28 As Christian Lotz suggests, "The credit system and its temporal schema produces a specific emotional tie to money, as with financial operations that now only require a mouse click, money *seems* to be disconnected from any real transactions and labor." Lotz, *The Capitalist Schema*, 134.
29 Horkheimer and Adorno, *Dialectic of Enlightenment*, 96.
30 Ibid., 99.
31 As Lotz suggests, "Since these new digital systems keep track of virtually everything, and since they do not forget, they become more knowledgeable than their users. . . . Cultural products in digital and network form can be infinitely modified and placed virtually anywhere; in other words, the *entire* time span and the entire spatial world of individuals can now be occupied by these new cultural products." Lotz, "The Culture Industry," SAGE *Frankfurt School Reader*, 983.
32 Horkheimer and Adorno, *Dialectic*, 97.
33 See David Golumbia, *The Cultural Logic of Computation*, 164.
34 Hullot-Kentor, "The Exact Sense," 143.
35 See Gérard Duménil and Lévy: "Thus, neoliberalism biased managerial trends in favor of financial management. Managers are extensively active in financial mechanisms (maximizing shareholders' value, operations on derivative markets, conduct of mergers and acquisitions, and so on). Asset managers and traders are 'scientific' financial managers, with a broad use of mathematics. The hierarchy between the technical and financial segments of management was profoundly altered," *The Crisis of Neoliberalism*, 84.
36 See Kurz, "Kulturindustrie," 73–77.
37 Note that the shift to an entrepreneurial ethos of individual responsibility also developed in the United States through a key alliance between neoliberals and the "New Right" of the 1980s. Packaged as part of a wider culture war against the welfare state, the New Right promulgated an ideal known as "breadwinner conservatism," which was defined by the independence of the individual from any

social safety net. For historical details regarding this alliance, see Self's *All in the Family*, 399–425.

38 See, for example, Gary Becker, *Human Capital: A Theoretical and Empirical Analysis with Special Reference to Education* (Chicago: The University of Chicago Press, 1993). See also Gary Becker, "Irrational Action and Economic Theory," *Journal of Political Economy*, 70, no. 1 (1962): 153–68.

39 Human capital theory contributed to the disciplines of human resources management and business administration, which would play a key role in restructuring and service-sector labor in the neoliberal period. See Waseef Jamal and M. Iqbal Saif, "Impact of Human Capital Management on Organizational Performance," *European Journal of Economics, Finance and Administrative Sciences*, 34 (2011): 55–69. For details regarding how the human capital school made an important political alliance with the neoconservative "culture war" on public education, affirmative action, welfare in the 1980s, see Melinda Cooper's *Family Values: Between Neoliberalism and the New Social Conservatism* (New York: Zone Books, 2017), 215–57.

40 As Luc Boltanski and Eve Chiapello detail in their study, *The New Spirit of Capitalism* (1999), "The opportunistic networker endeavors instead to get other people—entrepreneurs or those in charge of institutions—to bear the risks attaching to the operations he conducts, while he concentrates on seeking to rake in the profits. . . . The transient, fluid character of the networker's activities prompts him to derive the maximum personal profit from each operation, without worrying unduly about the consequences for the institution from which he derives his resources. . . . Each of the operations that he transports himself through is thus an opportunity for the networker to aggrandize his self, to inflate it. He is 'his own entrepreneur.' For him, the value of the activity he participates in, of the 'mission' entrusted to him by a firm, will thus depend predominantly on how far it allows him to aggrandize himself by expanding and diversifying the universe of things and persons that can be associated with him" 358–60.

41 Ibid., 371.

42 Mirowski, *Never Let a Serious Crisis*, 59.

43 See Golumbia, *The Cultural Logic*, 164.

44 Alan Liu, *The Laws of Cool: Knowledge Work and the Culture of Information* (Chicago: The University of Chicago Press, 2004), 43.

45 See Golumbia, *The Cultural Logic*, 130.

46 Ibid., 43–44.

47 Kurz, "Kulturindustrie," 16.

48 Note that Elton Mayo's methodology and conclusions continue to be disputed. For an account of Mayo's influence on the integration of industrial psychology and business management, see Will Davies, *The Happiness Industry: How Government and Big Business Sold Us Well-Being* (London: Verso, 2015), 286–303.

49. Adorno, *Introduction to Sociology*, 56.
50. Ibid., 132.
51. Ibid.
52. See Braverman, *Labor and Monopoly Capital*, 100.
53. William H. Whyte, *The Organization Man* (New York: Simon and Shuster, 1956), 36.
54. Theodor W. Adorno, *The Stars Down to Earth and Other Essays on the Irrational in Culture* (London: Routledge, 1994), 106.
55. Adorno, "Sociology and Psychology," 74.
56. Kurz, "Kulturindustrie," 12.
57. Ibid.
58. Ibid.
59. Adorno, *Minima Moralia*, 230.
60. Wendy Espeland and Mitchell Stevens, "Commensuration as a Social Process," *Annual Review of Sociology*, 24 (1998): 324.
61. Adorno, *Minima Moralia*, 23.
62. Ibid.
63. See Golumbia, *The Cultural Logic*, 130–34.
64. Niels van Doorn, "The Neoliberal Subject of Value: Measuring Human Capital in Information Economies," *Cultural Politics*, 10 (2014): 362.
65. As Wendy Brown argues, "Whether through social media 'followers,' 'likes,' and 'retweets,' through rankings and ratings for every activity and domain, or through more directly monetized practices, the pursuit of education, training, leisure, reproduction, consumption, and more are increasingly configured as strategic decisions and practices related to enhancing the self's future value," *Undoing the Demos*, 34.
66. Kurz, "Kulturindustrie," 29.
67. See Golumbia, *The Cultural Logic*, 167. For historical details regarding the impact of neoliberal economists on private health care, see Cooper, *Family Values*, 176–80.
68. For details on this history, see Davies, *The Happiness Industry*: "'Mood Tracking' is now a particular wing of the larger quantified self movement, in which individuals seek to measure fluctuations in their own mood.... Apps such as Moodscope ... have been built to facilitate and standardize the tracking of one's own mood" (228).
69. Adorno, *Minima Moralia*, 59.
70. For an interesting analysis that connects Adorno's remarks on health and sickness to private medicine, see Adrian Daub's "'Half Necessity, Half Accident': Reading the Abolition of Good Health Through Adorno's Concept of 'Natural History,'" *Rethinking Marxism*, 18, no. 1 (2006): 141–51.
71. Kurz, "Kulturindustrie," 74.
72. Mirowski, *Never Let a Serious Crisis*, 133.
73. Horkheimer and Adorno, *Dialectic of Enlightenment*, 124.

74 Adorno, *Minima Moralia*, 140.
75 Ibid., 140.
76 Ibid.
77 Adorno, *The Stars Down to Earth*, 60.
78 Adorno, *Negative Dialectics*, 264. Translation modified.
79 Horkheimer and Adorno, *Dialectic of Enlightenment*, 100.
80 Kurz, "Kulturindustrie," 20.
81 Adorno, *Minima Moralia*, 33.
82 Ibid., 138–39.
83 Adorno, "Free Time," *Critical Models*, 169.
84 Ibid.
85 Ibid., 170.
86 Horkheimer and Adorno, *Dialectic*, 121.
87 Guy Standing: "Millions of people, in affluent and emerging market economies, entered the precariat, a new phenomenon even if it had shades of the past. The precariat was not part of the 'working class' or the 'proletariat.' The latter terms suggest a society consisting mostly of workers in long-term, stable, fixed-hour jobs with established routes of advancement, subject to unionization and collective agreements, with job titles their fathers and mothers would have understood, facing local employers whose names and features they were familiar with," *The Precariat: The New Dangerous Class* (London: Bloomsbury Publishers, 2011), 6.
88 See Martin Neil Baily and Barry P. Bosworth, "US Manufacturing: Its Past and Its Potential Future," *Journal of Economic Perspectives*, 28, no. 1 (Winter, 2014): 2–26.

Afterword

"Thought as such, before all particular contents, is an act of negation, of resistance to that which is forced upon it."[1] Adorno's thought is a struggle, written to disrupt "the course of the world."[2] This book, I hope, has shown how his thinking can help us understand forms of domination that exist today. Neoliberalism has unfolded through the antagonistic relations of capitalist society, and is now threatening to capture the globe in the net of exchange. The closure of the world by capitalism can be observed in the interlocking crises of labor, migration, and ecology. In the final analysis, the crises of neoliberalism belong to the capitalist totality in general, to its contradictory relations, and to its irrational subordination of needs to profit. Adorno's dialectical criticism is a "practice that fights barbarism."[3] His critical theory of society allows us to see the appearance of the self-moving economic forces that are, in fact, the result of our own practices. The constellation of concepts in his arsenal are tools of resistance that belong to the fundamental object of his critique—identity. The critiques of exchange, fetishism, reification, and instrumental reason form moments of his wider critique of identity, of the real abstractions in society that rule over individuals as an independent force. "Negative dialectics," Adorno remarks, "is the consistent sense of non-identity."[4] Critical theory is the awareness of nonidentity, of what cannot be subsumed under totality. Adorno's thought is optimistic. At every turn, his work points us to a possible world that is free from domination.

Today's new barbarism is the product of the global crises of neoliberalism. Following in the wake of the near-collapse of the world's financial system in 2008, the long waves of austerity and debt have produced an age of economic uncertainty. In the absence of any clear alternative to neoliberalism, the world has witnessed a catastrophic swing to right-wing, authoritarian, populist movements.[5] The brief (though significant) movements of resistance to neoliberal austerity that have punctuated the crisis (e.g., Occupy Wall Street and the election of Syriza in Greece) seem to have been overwhelmed by the political right. The election of Donald Trump in the United States, and Boris Johnson in the United Kingdom, are manifestations of this shift, not to mention the rise of the UK Independence Party and Brexit movements. Moreover, the emergence of far-right organizations, such as the Freedom Party of Austria, Golden Dawn, the Alternative für Deutschland, France's National Front, and the Alt-Right in the United States, all point to an unmistakable resurgence of fascism. This swing to the right has been characterized by anti-immigrant violence, Islamophobia, anti-Semitism, and the dissemination of all manner of xenophobic hate in its media channels.[6]

Understanding the global shift to ethnocentric nationalism and racism is, of course, a major task for critical theory today. The body of work developed by Adorno, Horkheimer, and other contributors to the Institute for Social Research can provide important resources for grasping forms of authoritarianism.[7] Through decades of declining wages, rising debt, and languishing job security, American workers proved susceptible to the manipulations of the right-wing populism that promises a return to a mythological, "Golden Age" of capitalism, captured best by the slogan "Make America Great Again!" Adopting the fantasy of a nation that has been cheated of its hegemony, the Trump administration scapegoats immigrants and Muslims to tap into the paranoia of a declining working class.[8] Efforts to build a "border-security" wall to protect America from immigrants fleeing decades of strangulation by neoliberal austerity reflect the antagonistic character of the present. Taken together, Trump's proposals regarding border security, the restoration of manufacturing jobs, and the termination of the Trans-Pacific Partnership Agreement (TPP) delineate his reactionary efforts to return the United States to the corporatist model of business, and to its corresponding ideal of the "white male breadwinner" family. Defended by his base as the putative victim of global, conspiratorial powers, Trump refers to himself as the only option for returning America to its rightful place as the global hegemon.

John Abromeit, in reflecting on these developments, referred to the manufacture by Trump of an American war between "producers and parasites."[9] This rhetoric, with its anti-Semitic connotations, preys on the insecurities attending a possibly jobless future. The Trump administration activates the latent authoritarianism of the American worker by naming putative enemies of the national community. Adorno's work in the *Authoritarian Personality* is apposite for grasping this paranoia, particularly his category, the "usurper complex."[10] This refers to the populist attitude, common in times of crisis, that the formal, democratic institutions of government have been captured by parasitic elites. Appealing to a pseudo-conservative attitude that is just as suspicious of government spending as it is of rent-seeking capital, the usurper complex casts the American worker against a sea of hostile forces: "Legitimate rulers are those who are actually in command of the machinery of production—not those who owe their ephemeral power to formal political processes."[11] To the disenfranchised, the usurpers appear in the form of government bureaucrats, cultural elites, or financiers. To the authoritarian type, the state requires an emergency rescue by the direct intervention of a productive member of business.

The failure of formal democracies to resolve the crises of capitalism has motivated populations to align themselves with an authoritarian leader. Because the system does not "fulfill what it promises," Adorno suggests, the population "regards it as a 'swindle' and [is] ready to exchange it for a system which sacrifices all claims to human dignity and justice" for "some kind of guarantee of their lives by better planning and organization."[12] By drawing on long-standing fantasies regarding the natural productivity of a white, male, patriarchal working class, the current administration has co-opted legitimate criticism of neoliberalism. The persistence of authoritarianism in America, with its racist scapegoating, signals the alarm of a possible return to fascism. As Adorno infamously stated, "I consider the survival of National Socialism *within* democracy to be potentially more menacing than the survival of fascist tendencies *against* democracy."[13] Faced with the dissatisfactions attending a global system that seems indifferent to the rising superfluity of human beings, individuals take refuge in the defense mechanisms of pathic projection, submitting themselves to personifications of capital.

The emergence of authoritarianism poses serious political challenges for resistance. In addition to the efflorescence of authoritarian political movements, the potential for a renewed economic crisis is still alive. This possibility can be observed, for example, in the ongoing crisis of the European currency union, which threatens the future of capital in the form of national bankruptcies. Moreover, the levels of private debt in the United States and EU continue to undermine the stability of the system, as does rising global inequality. The current levels of debt account for an unprecedented high of 225 percent of world GDP.[14] Despite a restoration of corporate profitability in the United States, the levels of private debt now exceed those prior to the collapse of the banking system.[15] The compensatory mechanism of credit-accumulation cannot defer the crisis indefinitely. Moreover, the ongoing autonomation of labor is likely to displace further waves of living labor in the future, as new populations will be expelled from the capital-labor relation.

The possibility of a systemic crisis of global capitalism does not, however, guarantee the supersession of the system by a better one. In the absence of any organized, international opposition to capitalism, a future crisis is more likely to be exploited by reactionary forces. Faced with the crises of labor, austerity, and climate change, the left has been significantly disempowered by a number of limited analyses of neoliberalism. The first (present to a degree in the Occupy Wall Street movements) emphasizes the inequalities of finance and banking, but leaves the antagonistic relations of production intact. In restricting analysis to circulation, the critique of financial capitalism identifies "guilty parties" such as speculators, bankers, and other prominent managers of capital, coming dangerously close to right-wing and anti-Semitic forms of anti-capitalism. Additionally, the demand to return to Keynesian management by the social democratic left (as seen in the campaigns of Bernie Sanders and Jeremy Corbyn's Labor Party), while necessary, is inadequate. Policies of redistribution, social protection, and a more equitable tax code are understandable in the context of neoliberal inequality. However, a sustainable form of political resistance to neoliberalism cannot merely push capitalism to its best self, but has to begin imagining a postcapitalist future.

The articulation of such a future is, indeed, a difficult task. There is no universal subject of history. Resistance to neoliberalism will require the forms of extra-parliamentary organization and activism that continue to oppose social domination. In its function as the institutional administrator of global system, the state will not be the mechanism for constructing a meaningful, lasting alternative. Such extra-parliamentary networks of activist resistance can take the form of organized campaigns for access to public health care, universal basic income, and debt forgiveness. Additionally, opposition to patriarchy and the naturalization of gendered identities, as well as the struggles over reproductive labor, will continue to be fundamental to overcoming exploitation. Opposition to privatization, austerity, and the commodification of nature is a necessary component of a long-term countermovement. In addition to large-scale international organizations and political parties, decentralized and informal associations of activists are needed to disrupt the course of the world on micro levels. The organized campaigns of resistance to racism, sexism, immigration policies, and police brutality in the United States have proven to be significant means of countering the authoritarian trends, as have the struggles for LGBTQ rights. Building an alternative to barbarism will require the sustained development of these movements, as well as an alternative to the private education system that is dramatically escalating private debt.

I have turned to Adorno's critical theory to illuminate forms of domination that continue to operate behind our backs. By developing the concepts of exchange, fetishism, natural-history, and totality, I have argued that capitalist society is a coercive object that rules over us as an autonomous power. However, this power is only the manifestation of our own doing. Economic nature is not an eternal, natural necessity, but is the manifestation of human beings under specific conditions. The essence of capitalist society, Adorno's theory shows, is the antagonistic relations of production. These relations, however, disappear in their form of appearance in commodities. Expanding Marx's critique of political economy, Adorno's critical theory is a form of conceptual practice that deciphers the abstractions that rule us, returning them to their genesis in social relations. But Adorno's concept of totality is immanently self-critical. By pushing identity against its own limit, this book has tried to render possible moments of negativity and resistance intelligible. The critical possibilities that still live in Adorno's thought consist in his utopian refusals of a closing world. Substantive freedom, as he indicated tirelessly, would not have to sacrifice life to any logic necessity, but would be a condition of a reconciled humanity, emancipated from the class-divided world of exploitation.

Notes

1 Adorno, *Negative Dialectics*, 19.
2 Ibid., 318.
3 Bonefeld, *Critical Theory*, 2.
4 Adorno, *Negative Dialectics*, 5.
5 For background and analysis, consult Enzo Traverso, *The New Faces of Fascism: Populism and the Far Right* (London: Verso, 2019); Seyla Benhabib, "The Return of Fascism," *The New Republic* (September 29, 2017). Retrieved from https://newrepublic.com/article/144954/return-fascism-germany-greece-far-right-nationalists-winning-elections.
6 As Bonefeld suggests, according to "Theodor Adorno and Max Horkheimer, this personalization of the movement of real economic abstractions entails the elements of antisemitism. The personalized critique of capitalism is not a critique of capitalism, it identifies the hated forms of capitalism in the guilty party." Bonefeld, *Critical Theory*, 198.
7 For a contemporary account that takes up Adorno's *Authoritarian Personality* to analyze Trump, see Peter Gordon, "The Authoritarian Personality Revisited: Reading Adorno in the Age of Trump," *Boundary2* (June 15, 2016). Retrieved from https://www.boundary2.org/2016/06/peter-gordon-the-authoritarian-personality-revisited-reading-adorno-in-the-age-of-trump/.
8 See Richard Seymour, "What's the Matter with the White Working Class?" *Salvage* (February 2, 2017). Retrieved from https://salvage.zone/online-exclusive/whats-the-matter-with-the-white-working-class/.

9 John Abromeit, "Critical Theory and the Persistence of Right-Wing Populism," *Logos*, 15 (2016). http://logosjournal.com/2016/abromeit/
10 Adorno, *The Authoritarian Personality*, 689.
11 Ibid., 686.
12 Ibid., 678.
13 Adorno, *Critical Models*, 90.
14 For details see the IMF's "Global Debt Database," 2018. Retrieved from https://www.imf.org/external/datamapper/datasets/GDD.
15 See Szu Ping Chan, "Global Debt Explodes at Eye-Watering Pace to Hit 170 Trillion," *The Daily Telegraph* (April 4, 2017). Retrieved from https://www.telegraph.co.uk/business/2017/04/04/global-debt-explodes-eye-watering-pace-hit-170-trillion/.

Bibliography

Works by Adorno (German and English)

Adorno, Theodor W. *Against Epistemology: A Metacritique*. Translated by Willis Domingo. Cambridge: Polity Press, 2003.

Adorno, Theodor W. *An Introduction to Dialectics*. Translated by Nicholas Walker. Cambridge: Polity Press, 2017.

Adorno, Theodor W. *Current of Music*. Edited by Robert Hullot-Kentor. Cambridge: Polity Press, 2009.

Adorno, Theodor W. "Gloss on Public Personality." In *Critical Models: Interventions and Catchwords*, 161–66. New York: Columbia University Press, 2005.

Adorno, Theodor W. "Graeculus. Notizen zu Philosophie und Gesellschaft." In *Frankfurter Adorno Blätter VIII*. Edited by Rolf Tiedemann, 9–41. Frankfurt: Edition Text und Kritik, 2003.

Adorno, Theodor W. *Hegel: Three Studies*. Translated by Shierry Weber Nicholsen. Cambridge: MIT Press, 1994.

Adorno, Theodor W. *History and Freedom: Lectures 1964–1965*. Edited by Rolf Tiedeman. Translated by Rodney Livingstone. Cambridge: Polity Press, 2001.

Adorno, Theodor W. "Individuum und Organisation." In *Soziologische Schriften I. Gesammelte Schriften*, Band 8. Frankfurt: Suhrkamp, 2018.

Adorno, Theodor W. "Introduction." In *The Positivist Dispute in German Sociology*. Translated by Glyn Adey and David Frisby, 1–67. London: Heinemann Educational Books, 1977.

Adorno, Theodor W. *Introduction to Sociology*. Translated by Edmund Jephcott. Stanford: Stanford University Press, 2002.

Adorno, T. W. and Arnold Gehlen. "Ist die Soziologie eine Wissenschaft vom Menschen? Ein Streitgespräch." In *Adornos Philosophie in Grundbegriffen. Auflösung einiger Deutungsprobleme*. Edited by Freidmann Grenz, 225–51. Frankfurt: Suhrkamp, 1975.

Adorno, T. W. *Kant's Critique of Pure Reason*. Translated by Rodney Livingstone. Stanford: Stanford University Press, 2001.

Adorno, T. W. "Late Capitalism or Industrial Society? The Fundamental Question of the Present Structure of Society." In *Can One Live after Auschwitz?* Edited by Rolf Tiedeman. Translated by Rodney Livingstone, 111–25. Stanford: Stanford University Press, 2003.

Adorno, T. W. *Lectures on Negative Dialectics*. Translated by Rodney Livingstone. Cambridge: Polity Press, 2008.

Adorno, T. W. "Marx and the Basic Concepts of Sociology." From a Seminar Transcript in the Summer Semester of 1962. Translated by Verena Erlenbusch-Anderson and Chris O'Kane. In *Historical Materialism*, 26:1 (2018): 1–11.

Adorno, T. W. *Minima Moralia: Reflections on a Damaged Life*. Translated by E. F. N. Jephcott. London and New York: Verso, 2005.

Adorno, T. W. *Negative Dialectics*. Translated by E. B. Ashton. New York and and London: Continuum, 2005.

Adorno, T. W. "Notes on Philosophical Thinking." In *Critical Models: Interventions and Catchwords*, 127–34. New York: Columbia University Press, 2005.

Adorno, T. W. "On the Fetish-Character in Music and the Regression of Listening." Translated by Maurice Goldbloom. In *The Frankfurt School Reader*. Edited by Andrew Arato and Eike Gebhardt. New York: Continuum, 1985.

Adorno, T. W. "On the Logic of the Social Sciences." In *The Positivist Dispute in German Sociology*. Edited by Theodor W. Adorno. Translated by Glyn Adey and David Frisby, 105–22. London: Heinemann Educational Books, 1994.

Adorno, T. W. *Philosophische Elemente einer Theorie der Gesellschaft*. In *Nachgelassene Schriften. Abteilung IV: Vorlesungen*. Band 12. Edited by Tobias ten Brink and Marc Phillip Nogueira. Frankfurt: Suhrkamp, 1964.

Adorno, T. W. *Philosophical Elements of a Theory of Society*. Translated by Wieland Hoband. Cambridge: Polity Press, 2019.

Adorno, T. W. *Philosophische Terminologie*. Band 2. Edited by Rudolf zur Lippe. Frankfurt: Suhrkamp. 1974.

Adorno, T. W. "Reflections on Class Theory." In *Can One Live after Auschwitz?* Edited by Rolf Tiedeman. Translated by Rodney Livingstone, 93–110. Stanford: Stanford University Press, 2003.

Adorno, T. W. "Society." Translated by Fredric Jameson. *Salmagundi* 3: 10–11 (1969–1970): 144–53.

Adorno, T. W. "Sociology and Empirical Research." In *The Positivist Dispute in German Sociology*. Translated by Glyn Adey and David Frisby, 68–86. London: Heinemann Educational Books, 1977.

Adorno, T. W. "Sociology and Psychology: (Parts I and II)." Translated by rving N. Wohlfarth. *New Left Review* 46 (1967): 63–97.

Adorno, T. W. "Static and 'Dynamic' as Sociological Categories." Translated by H. Kaal. *Diogenes* 9: 28 (1961): 28–49.

Adorno, T. W. "The Idea of Natural-History." Translated by Robert Hullot-Kentor. In *Things Beyond Resemblance: Collected Essays on Theodor W. Adorno*. 252–70. New York: Columbia University Press, 2006.

Adorno, T. W. *The Jargon of Authenticity*. Translated by Knut Tarnowski and Frederic Will. Evanston: Northwestern University Press, 1973.

Adorno, T. W. *The Stars Down to Earth and Other Essays on the Irrational in Culture*. London: Routledge, 2007.

Adorno, T. W., Else Frenkel-Brunswik, Daniel J. Levinson, and R. Nevitt Sanford, "Studies in the Authoritarian Personality." In *The Authoritarian Personality*, Vol.1 of *Studies in Prejudice*. Edited by Max Horkheimer and Samuel H. Flowerman. New York: Harper & Brothers, 1950.

Adorno, T. W. and Max Horkheimer. *Briefweschel*, vol. I. Edited by Hendi Lonitz and Christoph Gödde. Frankfurt: Suhrkamp, 2003.

Adorno, T. W. and Alfred Sohn-Rethel, *Theodor W. Adorno und Alfred Sohn-Rethel: Briefwechsel 1936–1969*, in *Dialektische Studien*. Edited by Christoph Gödde. München, 1991.

Horkheimer, Max and T. W. Adorno. *Dialectic of Enlightenment: Philosophical Fragments*. Translated by Edmund Jephcott. Stanford: Stanford University Press, 2002.

Horkheimer, Max and T. W. Adorno. *Dialektik der Aufklärung: Philisophische Fragmente*. In *Max Horkheimer: Gesammelte Schriften*, vol. 5. Edited by Alfred Schmidt and Gunzelin Schmid Noerr. Frankfurt am Main: Fischer Taschenbuch Verlag, 1997.

Further Sources

Abromeit, John. "Critical Theory and the Persistence of Right-Wing Populism." *Logos*, 15 (2016). http://logosjournal.com/2016/abromeit/.

Altvater, Elmar. "Postneoliberalism or Postcapitalism? The Failure of Neoliberalism in the Financial Market Crisis." *Development Dialogue*, 51: 7 (January, 2009): 73–86.

Anderson, Perry. *Considerations on Western Marxism*. London: New Left Review, 1979.

Aronowitz, Stanley and William DiFazio. *The Jobless Future: Second Edition*. Minneapolis: University of Minnesota Press, 2010.

Arzuaga, Fabian. "Socially Necessary Superfluity: Adorno and Marx on the Crises of Labor and the Individual." *Philosophy and Social Criticism*, 45 (2018): 1–25.

Backhaus, Hans-Georg. "Between Philosophy and Science: Marxian Social Economy as Critical Theory." In *Open Marxism*, vol. I. Edited by Werner Bonefeld, Richard Gunn, and Kosmas Psychopedis, 54–92. London: Pluto Press, 1992.

Baily, Martin Neil and Barry P. Bosworth. "US Manufacturing: Its Past and Its Potential Future." *Journal of Economic Perspectives*, 28: 1 (Winter, 2014): 2–26.

Bauman, Zygmunt. *Liquid Modernity*. Cambridge: Polity, 2011.

Becker, Gary S. *Human Capital: A Theoretical and Empirical Analysis, with Special Reference to Education*. 3rd ed. Chicago: The University of Chicago Press, 1993.

Becker, Gary S. "Irrational Behavior and Economic Theory." *The Journal of Political Economy*, 70 (1962): 1–13.

Beder, Sharon. "Neoliberal Think Tanks and Free Market Environmentalism." *Environmental Politics*, 10: 2 (2001): 128–33.

Bellofiore, Riccardo and Tommaso Redolfi Riva. "The New Marx-Lektüre: Putting the Critique of Political Economy Back into the Critique of Society." *Radical Philosophy*, 189 (January/February 2015). https://www.radicalphilosophy.com/article/the-neue-marx-lekture.

Benanav, Aaron and John Clegg, "Crisis and Immiseration Theory: Critical Theory Today." *The SAGE Handbook of Frankfurt School Critical Theory*. Edited by Beverley Best, Chris O'Kane, and Werner Bonefeld. London: Sage, 2018.

Benhabib, Seyla. "The Return of Fascism." *The New Republic*, September 29, 2017.

Benjamin, Jessica. "The End of Internalization: Adorno's Social Psychology." *Telos*, 32 (Summer 1977): 42–64.

Benzer, Matthias. *The Sociology of Theodor Adorno*. Cambridge: Cambridge University Press, 2011.

Berle, Adolf and Gardiner C. Means. *The Modern Corporation and Private Property*. London: Routledge, 1991.

Berlinski, Claire. *There Is No Alternative: Why Margaret Thatcher Matters*. New York: Basic Books, 2010.

Blyth, Mark. *Austerity: The History of a Dangerous Idea*. Oxford: Oxford University Press, 2015.

Boltanski, Luc and Ève Chiapello. *The New Spirit of Capitalism*. Translated by Gregory Elliot. London: Verso, 2007.

Bonefeld, Werner. "Authoritarian Liberalism: From Schmitt via Ordoliberalism to the Euro." *Critical Sociology*, 43 (2016): 1–29.

Bonefeld, Werner. *Critical Theory and the Critique of Political Economy: On Subversion and Negative Reason*. New York: Bloomsbury, 2016.

Bonefeld, Werner. "Monetarism and Crisis." In *Global Capital, National State, and the Politics of Money*. Edited by Werner Bonefeld and John Holloway. London: Macmillan Press, 1996.

Bonefeld, Werner. "Negative Dialectics and the Critique of Economic Objectivity." *History of the Human Sciences*, 29: 2 (2016): 60–76.

Bonefeld, Werner. *The Strong State and the Free Economy*. London: Rowman & Littlefield, 2017.

Braunstein, Dirk. *Adornos Kritik der politischen Ökonomie*. Bielefield: transcript Verlag, 2011.

Braverman, Harry. *Labor and Monopoly Capital: The Degradation of Work in the Twentieth Century*. New York: Monthly Review Press, 1998.

Brenner, Robert. *The Economics of Global Turbulence: The Advanced Capitalist Economies from Long Boom to Long Downturn, 1945–2005*. London: Verso, 2006.

Breuer, Stefan. "Adorno's Anthropology." *Telos*, 64 (1985): 15–31.

Brown, Wendy. *Undoing the Demos: Neoliberalism's Stealth Revolution*. New York: Zone Books, 2015.

Bruce, Kyle and Chris Nyland. "Elton Mayo and the Deification of Human Relations." *Organization Studies*, 32: 3 (2011): 383–405.

Buchanan, James and Gordon Tullock. *The Calculus of Consent: Logical Foundations of Constitutional Democracy*. Ann Arbor: University of Michigan Press, 1962.

Buck-Morss, Susan. *The Origin of Negative Dialectics: Theodor W. Adorno, Walter Benjamin, and the Frankfurt Institute*. New York: The Free Press, 1979.

Chan, Szu Ping. "Global Debt Explodes at Eye-Watering Pace to Hit 170 Trillion." The Daily Telegraph, April 4, 2017.

Chari, Anita. *A Political Economy of the Senses: Neoliberalism, Reification, Critique*. New York: Columbia University Press, 2015.

Clarke, Simon. "The Global Accumulation of Capital and the Periodisation of the Capitalist State Form." In *Open Marxism*, vol. 1. Edited by Werner Bonefeld, Richard Gunn, and Kosmas Psychopedis. London: Pluto Press, 1992.

Clarke, Simon. *Keynesianism, Monetarism, and the Crisis of the State*. Aldershot: Edward Elgar Publishing Company, 1988.

Clarke, Simon. *Marx, Marginalism, & Modern Sociology: From Adam Smith to Max Weber*. London: Macmillan. 1991.

Cohen, Lizabeth. *A Consumer's Republic: The Politics of Mass Consumption in Postwar America*. New York: Vintage Books, 2003.

Colander, David, Rie Holt, and J.B. Rosser. Editors. *The Changing Face of Economics*. Ann Arbor: University of Michigan Press, 2004.

Cook, Deborah. *Adorno, Foucault, and the Critique of the West*. London: Verso, 2018.

Cook, Deborah. "Adorno on Late Capitalism: Totalitarianism and the Welfare State." *Radical Philosophy*, 89 (1988): 16–26.

Cooper, Melinda. *Family Values: Between Neoliberalism and the New Social Conservatism*. New York: Zone Books, 2017.

Dardot, Pierre and Christian Laval. *The New Way of the World: On Neoliberal Society*. Translated by Gregory Elliott. London: Verso, 2013.

Daremas, Georgios. "The Social Constitution of Commodity Fetishism, Money Fetishism and Capital Fetishism." In *The Unfinished System of Karl Marx: Critically Reading Capital as a Challenge for Our Times*. Edited by Judith Dellheim and Frieder Otto Wolf, 219–49. New York: Palgrave Macmillan, 2018.

Davies, Will. *The Happiness Industry: How the Government and Big Business Sold Us Well- Being*. London: Verso, 2015.

Davies, Will. *The Limits of Neoliberalism: Authority, Sovereignty, and the Logic of Competition*. London: Sage, 2014.

Doorn, Niels van. "The Neoliberal Subject of Value: Measuring Human Capital in Information Economies." *Cultural Politics*, 10: 3 (2014): 354–75.

Duménil, Gérard and Dominique Lévy. *The Crisis of Neoliberalism*. Cambridge: Harvard University Press, 2013.

Dupuy, Jean-Pierre. *On the Origins of Cognitive Science: The Mechanization of the Mind*. Translated by M.B. DeBevoise. Cambridge: The MIT Press, 2009.

Dreyfus, Huber. *What Computers Still Can't Do: A Critique of Artificial Reason*. Cambridge: The MIT Press, 1993.

Engster, Frank. *Das Geld als Mass, Mittel, und Methode: Das Rechnen mit der Identität der Zeit*. Berlin: Neofelis Verlag, 2013.

Engster, Frank and Oliver Schlaudt. "Alfred Sohn-Rethel: Real Abstraction and the Unity of Commodity-Form and Thought Form." Translated by Jacob Blumenfeld. In *The SAGE Handbook of Frankfurt School Critical Theory*, vol. 2. Edited by Beverley Best, Chris O'Kane, and Werner Bonefeld, 284–301. London: Sage, 2018.

Espeland, Wendy Nelson and Mitchell L. Stevens. "Commensuration as a Social Process. Annual Review of Sociology 24." *Annual Review of Sociology*, 24 (1998): 313–48.

Federici, Silvia. *Revolution at Point Zero: Housework, Reproduction, and Feminist Struggle*. Oakland: PM Press, 2012.

Fischer, Karin. "The Influence of Neoliberals in Chile Before, During, and after Pinochet." In *The Road from Mont Pèlerin: The Making of the Neoliberal Thought

Collective, with a New Preface. Edited by Philip Mirowski and Dieter Plehwe. Cambridge: Harvard University Press, 2015.

Fong, Benjamin Y. *Death and Mastery: Psychoanalytic Drive Theory and the Subject of Late Capitalism*. New York: Columbia University Press, 2016.

Foucault, Michel. *The Birth of Biopolitics: Lectures at the Collège de France, 1978–79*. Edited by Michael Senellart. Translated by Graham Burchell. New York: Picador, 2010.

Franklin, Seb. *Control: Digitality as Cultural Logic*. Cambridge: The MIT Press, 2015.

Fraser, Nancy. "A Triple Movement? Parsing the Politics of Crisis after Polanyi." In *Beyond Neoliberalism: Approaches to Social Inequality and Difference*. Edited by M. Burchardt and G. Kirn, 29–43. London: Palgrave Macmillan, 2017.

Galbraith, John Kenneth. *The Affluent Society*. Boston: Houghton Mifflin Company, 1971.

George, Susan. *A Fate Worse than Debt: The World Financial Crisis and the World Poor*. New York: Grove Weidenfeld, 1990.

Golumbia, David. *The Cultural Logic of Computation*. Cambridge: Harvard University Press, 2009.

Gordon, Peter. "The Authoritarian Personality Revisited: Reading Adorno in the Age of Trump." *Boundary2*, June 15, 2016. Retrieved at https://www.boundary2.org/2016/06/peter-gordon-the-authoritarian-personality-revisited-reading-adorno-in-the-age-of-trump/.

Gunster, Shane. *Capitalizing On Culture: Critical Theory for Cultural Studies*. Toronto: University of Toronto Press, 2004.

Habermas, Jürgen. "Nachwort von Jürgen Habermas." Appendix to Max Horkheimer and Theodor W. Adorno, *Dialektik der Aufklärung*, 423–542. Frankfurt: Fischer, 1986.

Habermas, Jürgen. *The Philosophical Discourse of Modernity*. Translated by Frederick Lawrence. Cambridge: MIT Press, 2004.

Hardin, Garrett. *Nature and Man's Fate*. New York: Rinehart & Company, Inc., 1958.

Harvey, David. *A Brief History of Neoliberalism*. Oxford: Oxford University Press, 2007.

Harvey, David. *The Condition of Postmodernity*. Cambridge: Blackwell, 1990.

Hayek, Friedrich A. "Competition as a Discovery Procedure." Translated by Marcellus S. Snow. In *The Quarterly Journal of Austrian Economics*, 5: 3 (2002): 9–23.

Hayek, Friedrich A. *Denationalisation of Money: The Argument Refined*. London: The Institute of Economic Affairs, 1990.

Hayek, Friedrich A. *Law, Legislation and Liberty: A New Statement of the Liberal Principles of Justice and Political Economy*. London: Routledge, 2012.

Hayek, Friedrich A. *New Studies in Philosophy, Politics, Economics and the History of Ideas*. Chicago: University of Chicago Press, 1985.

Hayek, Friedrich A. *The Counter-Revolution of Science: Studies on the Abuse of Reason*. Glencoe: The Free Press, 1952.

Hayek, Friedrich A. *The Fatal Conceit: The Errors of Socialism*. In the Collected Works of Hayek, vol. 1. Edited by W.W. Bartley III. Chicago: University of Chicago Press, 1988.

Hayek, Friedrich A. "The Primacy of the Abstract." In *Beyond Reductionism: The Alpbach Symposium 1968*. Edited by Arthur Koestler and J. R. Smythies. New York: Macmillan, 1968.

Hayek, Friedrich A. *The Road to Serfdom: Text and Documents*. The Collected Works of F. A. Hayek, vol. 2. Chicago: University of Chicago Press, 2007.

Hayek, Friedrich A. *The Sensory Order: An Inquiry into the Foundations of Theoretical Psychology*. Chicago: University of Chicago Press, 2014.

Hayek, Friedrich A. "The Use of Knowledge in Society." *American Economic Review*, vol. XXXV: 4 (1945): 519–30.

Hayek, Friedrich A. "Wiemer-Hayek Discussion." In *Cognition and the Symbolic Processes. Volume 2*. Edited by Walter B. Weimer and David S. Palermo, 321–29. Hillsdale: Lawrence Erlbaum Associates. 1982.

Heims, Steve Joshua. *The Cybernetics Group*. Cambridge: The MIT Press, 1991.

Held, David. *Introduction to Critical theory: Horkheimer to Habermas*. Oxford: Polity Press, 2004.

Hobsbawm, Eric. *The Age of Extremes: A History of the World, 1914–1991*. New York: Vintage Books, 1996.

Hohendahl, Peter Uwe. "Frozen Imagination: Adorno's Theory of Mass Culture Revisited." *Thesis Eleven*, 34: 1 (1993): 17–41.

Holloway, John. "Global Capital and the National State." In *Global Capital, National State, and the Politics of Money*. Edited by Werner Bonefeld and John Holloway. London: Macmillan Press, 1996.

Houseman, Tom. "Social Constitution and Class." In *The SAGE Handbook of Frankfurt School Critical Theory*. Edited by Beverley Best, Chris O'Kane, and Werner Bonefeld. London: Sage, 2018.

Hulatt, Own. "Reason, Mimesis, and Self-Preservation in Adorno." *Journal of the History of Philosophy*, 54: 1 (2016): 135–51.

Hullot-Kentor, Robert. "The Exact Sense in Which the Culture Industry No Longer Exists." *Cultural Critique*, 70 (2008): 137–57.

Hullot-Kentor, Robert. *Things Beyond Resemblance: Collected Essays on Theodor W. Adorno*. New York: Columbia University Press, 2006.

Hutchins, Edwin, *Cognition in the Wild*. Cambridge: The MIT Press, 1995.

Jamal, Waseef and M. Iqbal Saif. "Impact of Human Capital Management on Organizational Performance." *European Journal of Economics, Finance and Administrative Sciences*, 34 (2011): 55–69.

Jameson, Fredric. *Late Marxism: Adorno, Or, The Persistence of the Dialectic*. London: Verso, 2007.

Jones, Daniel Steadman. *Masters of the Universe: Hayek, Friedman, and the Birth of Neoliberal Politics*. Princeton: Princeton University Press, 2012.

Kellner, Douglas. *Critical Theory, Marxism and Modernity*. Baltimore: The Johns Hopkins University Press, 1992.

Kim, Jaegwon. *Philosophy of Mind*. Boulder: Westview Press, 2011.

Kliman, Andrew. *The Failure of Capitalist Production: Underlying Causes of the Great Recession*. London: Pluto Press, 2012.

Kurz, Robert. "Kultureindustrie im 21. Jahrhundert. Zur Aktualität des Konzepts von Adorno under Horkheimer." *Exit! Krise und Kritik der Warengesellschaft*. 9 (March, 2012): 59–100.

Landes, David, S. *Revolution in Time: Clocks and the Making of the Modern World*. Cambridge: Harvard University Press, 1983.

Lavoie, Don. "A Critique of the Standard Account of the Socialist Calculation Debate." *The Journal of Libertarian Studies*, 5: 1 (1981): 41–87.

Lazonick, William. "Financial Commitment and Economic Performance: Ownership and Control in the American Industrial Corporation." *Business and Economic History*, 17 (1988): 115–28.

Lazonick, William. "The Financialization of the U.S. Corporation: What Has Been Lost, and How It Can Be Regained." *Seattle University Law Review*, 36 (2013): 857–909.

Lazonick, William and Mary O'Sullivan, "Maximizing Shareholder Value: A New Ideology for Corporate Governance." *Economy and Society*, 29: 1 (2000): 13–35.

LiPuma, Edward and Benjamin Lee. *Financial Derivatives and the Globalization of Risk*. Durham: Duke University Press, 2004.

Liu, Alan. *The Laws of Cool: Knowledge Work and the Culture of Information*. Chicago: The University of Chicago Press, 2004.

Lotz, Christian. *The Capitalist Schema: Time, Money, and the Culture of Abstraction*. London: Lexington Books, 2014.

Lotz, Christian. "The Culture Industry." In *The SAGE Frankfurt School Reader*. Edited by Beverley Best, Chris O'Kane, and Werner Bonefeld. London: Sage, 2018.

Lukács, Georg. *History and Class Consciousness: Studies in Marxist Dialectics*. Translated by Rodney Livingstone. Cambridge: MIT Press, 2013.

Lukács, Georg. *Ontology of Social Being, Vol. 2, Marx*. Translated by David Fernbach. London: Merlin Press, 1978.

Lukács, Georg. *The Theory of the Novel: A Historico-Philosophical Essay on the Forms of Great Epic Literature*. Translated by Anna Bostock. Cambridge: MIT Press, 1993.

Mandel, Ernest. *Late Capitalism*. Translated by Joris De Bres. London: Verso, 1999.

Marx, Karl. *Capital: Volume 1: A Critique of Political Economy*. Translated by Ben Fowkes. London: Penguin Books, 1981.

Marx, Karl. *Capital: Volume 3*. Translated by David Fernbach. London: Penguin Books, 1981.

Marx, Karl. *Grundrisse: Foundations of the Critique of Political Economy (Rough Draft)*. Translated by Martin Nicholaus. London: Penguin Books, 1993.

Mattick Jr., Paul. *Business as Usual: The Economic Crisis and the Failure of Capitalism*. London: Reaktion Books, 2011.

McNally, David. *Global Slump: The Economics and Politics of Crisis and Resistance*. Oakland: PM Press, 2011.

Mirowksi, Philip. "Hell Is Truth Seen Too Late." *Boundary* (February 2, 2019): 1–53.

Mirowksi, Philip. *Machine Dreams: Economics Becomes a Cyborg Science*. Cambridge: Cambridge University Press, 2002.

Mirowksi, Philip. *More Heat Than Light: Economics as Social Physics: Physics as Nature's Economics*. Cambridge: Cambridge University Press, 1999.

Mirowksi, Philip. *Never Let a Serious Crisis Go to Waste: How Neoliberalism Survived the Financial Meltdown*. London: Verso, 2014.

Mirowksi, Philip. *Science Mart: Privatizing American Science*. Cambridge: Harvard University Press, 2011.

Mirowski, Philip and Dieter Plewhe. *The Road from Mont Pèlerin: The Making of the Neoliberal Thought Collective, with a New Preface*. Cambridge: Harvard University Press, 2015.

Mirowski, Philip and Edward Nik-Khah. *The Knowledge We Have Lost in Information: The History of Information in Modern Economics*. Oxford: Oxford University Press, 2017.

Mishel, Lawrence, Josh Bivens, Elise Gould, and Heidi Shierholz, *The State of Working America*. Ithaca: Cornell University Press, 2012.

Müller-Doohm, Stefan. *Adorno: A Biography*. Translated by Rodney Livingstone. Cambridge: Polity Press, 2005.

Nelson, Wendy and Mitchell L. Stevens. "Commensuration as a Social Process." *Annual Review of Sociology*, 24 (1998): 313–43.

O'Kane, Chris. "Fetishism and Social Domination in Marx, Lukács, Adorno, and Lefebvre." PhD diss., University of Sussex, 2013.

O'Kane, Chris. "Introduction to 'Theodor W. Adorno on Marx and the Basic Concepts of Sociological Theory: From a Seminar Transcript in the Summer Semester of 1962." *Historical Materialism*, 26: 1 (2018): 1–17.

O'Kane, Chris. "Society Maintains Itself Despite All the Catastrophes That May Eventuate": Critical Theory, Negative Totality, and Crisis." *Constellations*, 25 (2018): 287–301.

Oliva, Gabriel. "The Road to Servomechanisms: The Influence of Cybernetics on Hayek from *The Sensory Order* to the Social Order." *The Center for the History of Political Economy Working Paper Series*, No. 2015-11 (2015): 1–41.

Oreskes, Naomi and Erik M. Conway. *Merchants of Doubt: How a Handful of Scientists Obscured the Truth on Issues from Tobacco Smoke to Global Warming*. New York: Bloomsbury Press, 2011.

Parr, Adrian. *The Wrath of Capital: Neoliberalism and Climate Change Politics*. New York: Columbia University Press, 2013.

Peck, Jamie. *Constructions of Neoliberal Reason*. Oxford: Oxford University Press, 2012.

Piketty, Thomas. *Capital in the 21st Century*. Translated by Arthur Goldhammer. Cambridge: Belknap Press, 2014.

Pollock, Friedrich. "State Capitalism: Its Possibilities and Limitations." In *The Essential Frankfurt School Reader*. Edited by Andrew Arato and Eike Gebhardt, 71–94. New York: Continuum, 1990.

Postone, Moishe. "Anti-Semitism and National Socialism: Notes on the German Reaction to the Holocaust." *New German Critique*, 19 (1980): 97–115.

Postone, Moishe. "Critique and Historical Transformation." *Historical Materialism*, 12: 3 (2004): 53–72.

Postone, Moishe. *Time, Labor, and Social Domination: A Reinterpretation of Marx's Critical Theory*. Cambridge: Cambridge University Press, 2003.

Robbins, Lionel. *An Essay on the Nature and Significance of Economic Science*. Cambridge: Cambridge University Press, 1932.

Rose, Gilliam. *Hegel Contra Sociology*. London: Verso, 2009.

Rose, Gilliam. *The Melancholy Science: An Introduction to the Thought of Theodor W. Adorno*. London: Verso, 2014.

Sandel, Michael. *What Money Can't Buy: The Moral Limits of Markets*. New York: Farrar, Straus and Giroux, 2012.

Schmidt, Alfred. *The Concept of Nature in Marx*. Translated by Ben Fowkes. London: NLB, 1971.

Searle, John R. *Mind: A Brief Introduction*. Oxford: Oxford University Press, 2004.

Self, Robert O. *All in the Family: The Realignment of American Democracy since the 1960s*. New York: Hill Wang, 2012.

Seymour, Richard. "What's the Matter with the White Working Class?" *Salvage*, February 2, 2017. Retrieved at https://salvage.zone/online-exclusive/whats-the-matter-with-the-white-working-class/.

Shaikh, Anwar. *Capitalism: Competition, Conflict, Crises*. Oxford: Oxford University Press, 2016.

Slobodian, Quinn. *Globalists: The End of Empire and the Birth of Neoliberalism*. Cambridge: Harvard University Press, 2018.

Smith, Adam. *The Wealth of Nations*. New York: Bantam Dell, 2003.

Sohn-Rethel, Alfred. *Intellectual Manual Labor: A Critique of Epistemology*. Translated by Martin Sohn-Rethel. Atlantic Highlands: Humanities Press, 1978.

Sohn-Rethel, Alfred. *Warenform und Denkform*. Frankfurt: Suhrkamp, 1978.

Solomon, Lewis D. "The Microelectronics Revolution, Job Displacement, and the Future of Work: A Policy Commentary." *Chicago-Kent Law Review*, 65 (1987): 65–95.

Standing, Guy. *The Precariat: The New Dangerous Class*. London: Bloomsbury Publishers, 2011.

Stoetzler, Marcel. "Needless Necessity: Sameness and Dynamic in Capitalist Society." *Fast Capitalism*, 12 (2015): 51–64.

Strange, Susan. *Casino Capitalism*, 15–17. Manchester: Manchester University Press, 1997.

Traverso, Enzo. *The New Faces of Fascism: Populism and the Far Right*. London: Verso, 2019.

Tomba, Massimiliano. "Adorno's Account of the Anthropological Crisis and the New Type of Human." In *(Mis)Readings of Marx in Continental Philosophy*. Edited by J. Habjan and J. Whyte, 34–50. London: Palgrave Macmillan, 2014.

Veneberghe, Frederic. *A Philosophical History of German Sociology*. London: Routledge, 2009.

Van der Wee, Herman. *Prosperity and Upheaval: The World Economy 1945–1980*. Harmondsworth, 1987.

Van Doorn, Niels. "The Neoliberal Subject of Value: Measuring Human Capital in Information Economies." *Cultural Politics*, 10 (2014): 354–75.

Veblen, Thorstein. *The Place of Science in Modern Civilization and Other Essays*. New York: B.W. Huebsch, 1919.

Walras, Leon. *Elements of Pure Economics: Or, the Pure Theory of Wealth*. Translated by William Jaffee. Evanston: Northwestern University Press, 1954.

Whyte, William H. *The Organization Man*. New York: Simon and Shuster, 1956.

Wiggershaus, Rolf. *The Frankfurt School: Its History, Theories, and Political Significance*. Translated by Michael Robertson. Cambridge: Polity Press, 2007.

Wiener, Norbert. *Cybernetics: Or Control and Communication in the Animal and the Machine*. Cambridge: The MIT Press, 1985.

Index

Note: Page numbers followed by "n" refer to notes.

Abromeit, John   79 n.4, 166
abstraction   106–7, 108, 123
abstract labor   13, 14, 16, 31, 65, 126, 144, 154, 158
abstract labour time   106
Adorno, Theodor W.   2–3. *See also individual entries*
   critical theory   1
   critique of fetishism   42–3 n.43
   critique of late capitalism   72
   critique of the Kantian subject   45 n.103
   critique of transcendental idealism   29
   dialectical conceptualization of natural-history   4–5
   dialectical criticism   1–3, 29, 30, 32, 33, 39, 40, 165
   ego formation, psychoanalytic interpretation of   44 n.79
   socially necessary illusion of capitalist society   17, 34, 72, 107, 135
AfD   78
AFL–CFO   81 n.39
alienation   73, 74, 103, 111 n.16, 142, 145
Alternative für Deutschland   166
Alt-Right   166
Altvater, Elmar   77
Amazon   153
American Enterprise Institute   116 n.98
anthropological approach   2
Aronowitz, Stanley   69, 83 n.97
asset-price inflationism   108
authoritarianism   55, 79 n.4, 166, 167
Authoritarian Personality (Adorno)   166
automation   157–8
autonomization   105, 116 n.108

Backhaus, Hans-Georg   3, 15, 87
Becker, Gary   148, 149

Bellofiore, Riccardo   10
Benanav, Aaron   73
Bernstein, J. M.   138 n.54
Birth of Biopolitics (Foucault)   2
Bloomberg Terminal   133
Boltanski, Luc   161 n.40
Bonefeld, Werner   1, 11, 19, 37, 39, 57, 69, 70–1, 109, 111 n.25, 116 n.108, 169 n.6
bourgeois society   15–16, 21, 29, 56, 93
Braunstein, Dirk   3
Bretton Woods System   39, 52, 66, 67
Breuer, Stefan   123–4
Brown, Wendy   85 n.128, 162 n.65

Capital (Marx)   11, 13, 15, 43 n.46
capitalism
   climate   134
   crony-capitalism   74
   financial   106, 147, 148, 168
   globalized   2, 32, 38, 50, 51, 74, 78
   Golden Age of   57–67, 166
   late   10, 24, 28, 30, 34, 36–8, 44 n.79, 57–63, 72, 74, 119, 126–9, 141, 144, 154, 157
   neoliberal   6, 51, 130, 141, 145, 158
   state   4, 54–6, 72, 75
capitalist mode of production   6, 11–16, 54, 55, 61, 63, 67, 91, 106, 124–5, 133–4
capitalist society   21, 31
   late   10, 11, 16, 22–4, 26, 28, 32, 51, 63, 64, 82 n.70, 106, 129, 130
   socially necessary illusion of   17, 34, 72, 107, 135
capitalist totality   6, 20, 49, 51, 53, 56, 62–5, 73, 90, 93, 103, 165
catallaxy   115 n.97
Cato Institute   134
Chiapello, Eve   161 n.40

Chile, neoliberal revolution   71
Clarke, Simon   70, 73, 74, 96, 112 n.34
class antagonism   4, 19–22, 32, 34, 37, 38, 49–86
   Golden Age of capitalism   57–67
   neoliberal revolution   68–78
   state capitalism   53–7
Clegg, John   73
climate capitalism   134
cognition   5, 24, 25, 27–9, 51, 96, 97, 99, 100, 109, 125–8, 130–3
cognitive science   131–2
Cohen, Lizabeth   80 n.37
commodity fetishism   3–5, 9–24, 30, 37, 38, 41 n.2, 51, 87, 90, 141
commodity-form   3, 11–14, 16, 24, 25, 27, 28, 31, 39, 51, 61, 90, 93, 106, 115 n.89, 134, 135, 142–4, 152
computationalist theory of mind   130
computational theory of mind   5
computer model of mind   131, 138 n.63
concrete labor   13, 148
contradiction   2, 18, 21, 29, 37, 39, 51, 55, 62–4, 82 n.70, 121
Cook, Deborah   35
Corbyn, Jeremy   168
Cowles Commission   115 n.84
credit-sustained accumulation   52, 67, 69–72, 74, 133
critical theory   1–4, 9, 11, 17, 24, 27, 31, 36–8, 40, 41 n.2, 46 n.135, 51, 53, 55, 62, 63, 73, 87, 109, 119, 141, 165, 166, 168, 169
crony-capitalism   74
culture
   industry   5, 136, 141–6
   mass   5, 141–7, 155
   neoliberal   5–6, 141–63
"The Culture Industry in the 21st Century" (Horkheimer and Adorno)   145
"Customer Relationship Management" software   150
cybernetics   99–101

data-mining   153
deindustrialization   68, 73
dialectical criticism   1–3, 29, 30, 32, 33, 39, 40, 165
dialectical materialism   41 n.13

dialectical theory of society   107
Dialectic of Enlightenment (Horkheimer and Adorno)   5, 110, 119–25, 129, 139 n.92, 141
DiFazio, William   69, 83 n.97
domination of nature   133–6
Doorn, Niels van   153
Dreyfus, Hubert   131
dual character of commodities   12
dual character of labor   13
Dupuy, Jean-Pierre   130–1

economics, definition of   92
economics of information   130, 133
   neoliberal theory and   95–103
Edgeworth, Francis   92
ego formation, psychoanalytic interpretation of   44 n.79
enlightenment   119–27
"Enterprise Resource Planning" software   149–50
epistemology   4, 24–6, 28, 29, 44 n.87, 46 n.139, 95–7, 99, 100, 102, 103, 106, 130, 134
Espeland, Wendy   152–3
exchange society (*Tauschgesellschaft*)   1, 3, 4, 9–47, 57, 62, 74, 76, 125
   commodity Fetishism   11–24
   negative totality   32–40
   real abstraction   24–32
exchange-value   4, 12, 13, 17, 21, 22, 26, 31, 39, 42 n.43, 51, 61, 64, 77, 90, 93, 105, 108, 120, 132, 134, 143, 144, 152, 154, 155
exploitation
   of living labor   20–1
   theory of   18–19

Facebook   153
false consciousness   23, 90, 104
fascism   53, 55, 59, 166, 167
The Fatal Conceit: The Errors of Socialism (Hayek)   102
The Fatal Conceit (Hayek)   102
fictitious commodities   2
financial capitalism   106, 147, 148, 168
financial crisis of 2007–08, 9, 39
financialization   9, 38, 39, 49–51, 67, 68, 70, 72, 75, 148, 149

first nature   89–95, 103, 106, 107, 111 n.16, 135
flexible standardization   146–56
Fodor, Jerry   138 n.63
Fordism   56, 58, 65, 69, 73, 146, 148, 158
Foucault, Michel   2, 79 n.2, 85 n.128, 86 n.132
Freedom Party of Austria   166
free market   2, 3, 5, 6 n.4, 57, 70, 72, 88, 95, 96, 99, 100, 103–6, 119
free time   157
Friedman, Milton   69, 85 n.129

globalization   49
Global North   158
Global South   59
Golden Age of capitalism   57–63, 166
   end of   63–7
Golden Dawn   78, 166
Google   153
government bureaucracy   70, 74
Great Depression   54
Great Recession   1
Grundrisse (Marx)   21, 44 n.86, 104–5

Hardin, Garrett   101, 115 n.89
Hawthorne Effect   150, 151
Hayek, Friedrich von   5, 95–108, 116 n.102
Heartland   116 n.98, 134
Heidegger, Martin   88
Heritage Foundation   134
Homer   124
homo economicus   100, 115 n.84
homo oeconomicus   92, 93, 124
homo regularis   100
Horkheimer, Max   3, 5, 44–5 n.90, 53, 55, 78, 119–26, 129, 132, 133, 135, 136, 139 n.92, 141–7, 154–5, 158, 166
Hullot-Kentor, Robert   2, 89, 141–2, 148
human capital   148–9, 152, 154, 161 n.39
Hutchins, Edwin   131

"The Idea of Natural-History" (Adorno)   88
identity principle   4, 123
identity thinking   28–32, 37, 51, 90, 93, 109, 129, 138 n.54
IMF. *See* International Monetary Fund
immanence principle   121, 122, 126, 133

information   95–103, 107
   theory   114 n.80
Institute of Social Research   3, 4, 53, 55, 166
instrumental reason   5, 110, 119, 120, 130, 132, 133, 165
Intellectual and Manual Labor: A Critique of Epistemology (Sohn-Rethel)   25
Intergovernmental Panel on Climate Change   134
International Monetary Fund (IMF)   59, 67
irrationality   39, 62, 63, 65, 108, 133, 135, 157. *See also* rationality/rationalization

Japan, neoliberal revolution   68
Jevons, William Stanley   92
Johnson, Boris   165

Kant, Immanuel
   Copernican revolution   28
   transcendental subject   27, 29
Kellner, Douglas   56
Keynesian-Fordist system   4, 38, 50, 53, 57, 60, 63, 67, 68
Keynesianism   62, 68
   military   58, 80 n.38
Kurz, Robert   145, 146, 152, 154, 157

labor theory of value   91
Lange, Oscar   95
late capitalism   10, 24, 28, 30, 34, 36–8, 44 n.79, 57–63, 72, 74, 119, 126–9, 141, 144, 154, 157
"Late Capitalism or Industrial Society?" (Adorno)   57
late capitalist society   10, 11, 16, 22–4, 26, 28, 32, 51, 63, 64, 82 n.70, 106, 129, 130
lawfulness   29, 41 n.13, 90
"law of value," theory of   10, 34
Lazonick, William   86 n.133
liberalism   91–5
liberty   103, 106, 107
liquidation   21, 34, 60, 123, 126, 129, 131, 144, 149, 155
Liu, Alan   150
Lotz, Christian   17–18, 32, 142, 160 n.31
Lukács, Georg   41 n.2, 88, 89, 111 n.16

McCulloch, Warren   131
Machine Dreams (Mirowski)   99
machine functionalist theory of mind   131
McNally, David   68, 71
Macy Conferences (1941)   99
Mandel, Ernest   66, 80–1 n.38
Mannheim, Karl   1
Marcuse, Herbert   3
Marginalist Revolution of the 1870s   92, 95, 112 n.38
marginal utility theory   93
market fundamentalism   6, 57, 69, 70, 76
Marshall Plans   84 n.112
"Marx and the Basic Concepts of Sociological Theory" (Backhaus)   15
Marxism   28, 57
Marxists
    critique of fetishism   24
    view of neoliberalism   2
Marx, Karl. *See also individual entries*
    critique of commodity fetishism   14–16, 51
    critique of economic self-interest   104–5
    critique of political economy   3, 4, 9–11, 17, 24, 55, 56, 91, 92, 112 n.34, 169
    critique of the classical theory of liberalism   90
    dual character of commodities   12
    dual character of labor   13
    and Golden Age of capitalism   58, 62
    organic composition of capital   127, 137 n.40
    on real abstraction   44 n.86
    on surplus-value   18
    theory of exploitation   18–19
    theory of pauperization   63
    theory of the "law of value"   10, 34
mass culture   5, 141–7, 155
mathematical theory   114 n.80
Mattick Jr., Paul   85 n.131
Mayo, Elton   150–1, 161 n.48
Menger, Carl   95
military Keynesianism   58, 80 n.38
mimesis   46 n.135
mind, theory of   97

Minima Moralia (Adorno)   50, 127, 157
Mirowski, Philip   92, 99–103, 116 n.98, 149, 154
monetarism   69–71
monopoly capitalism   4, 38, 51, 53, 57, 60, 61, 75, 76, 107, 108, 142, 153
Mont Pelerin Society   6, 116 n.98
Mood Tracking   162 n.68
mythic nature   89, 93, 102
myths   121–7

National Front   78
National Front (France)   166
natural-history (*Naturgeschichte*)   4–5, 87–117
    idea of   88–91
negative dialectics   3, 11, 24, 28, 30–2, 37, 109, 165
Negative Dialectics (Adorno)   20, 28, 90, 134, 135, 156
negative feedback   100
negative totality   4, 9, 32–40, 51
neoclassical economic theory   87–8, 93, 95–103, 110 n.6, 119
neo-Kantianism   88, 89
neoliberal capitalism   6, 51, 130, 141, 145, 158
neoliberal culture   5–6, 141–63
    flexible standardization   146–56
    industry   144–6
    precarity and crisis   156–9
neoliberal governmentality   50
neoliberal individualism   39
neoliberal reason   5, 50, 119–39
    computation   129–33
    Dialectic of Enlightenment   120–2
    domination of nature   133–6
    mechanization   129–33
    organic composition of humanity   127–9
    sacrifice   122–7
neoliberal revolution   68–78
neoliberal theory, critique of   87–117
Neoliberal Thought Collective   116 n.98
neo-ontology   88, 89
New Right   68–71, 73, 74, 160–1 n.37

objectification   13, 22, 23, 34, 132, 149

"objective web of blindness" (*Verblendungszusammenhang*) 158
Occupy Wall Street 165, 168
O'Connor, Brian 30
Odyssey (Homer) 124
OECD 39, 52, 76, 147
offshoring 69
"On the Fetish-Character in Music and the Regression of Listening" (Adorno) 143
OPEC oil embargo of 1973, 66
order 100, 106
organic composition of humanity 127–9
The Organization Man (Whyte) 151
O'Sullivan, Mary 86 n.133
outsourcing 68–9
overproduction 65

Pareto, Vilfredo 92, 94
pauperization 57, 59, 62, 63
Peck, Jamie 103
Pinochet, Augusto 71, 84 n.115
Pitts, Walter 131
Polanyi, Karl 2
Polanyi, Michael 97
Pollock, Friedrich 3, 53–5, 72, 79 n.19
Popper, Karl 94
populism 79 n.4, 166
positivism 5, 88, 94–5, 107, 125, 126
The Positivist Dispute 82 n.70, 94
"post-Fordist" model of lean production 68
Postone, Moishe 3, 115 n.89
"The Primacy of the Abstract" (Hayek) 98
privacy 157
privatization 2, 39, 49, 50, 68–70, 134, 146, 157, 168
property rights 102
Putnam, Hilary 138 n.63

rationality/rationalization 32, 39, 62, 65, 92–3, 94, 97, 99, 102, 107, 122, 126, 138 n.54. *See also* irrationality
  abstract 30
  political 2
  scientific 122

Reagan, Ronald 68, 70, 76
real abstraction 4, 13, 24–32, 44 n.86, 51, 67
"Reflections on Class Theory" (Adorno) 57
Reichelt, Helmut 3
reification 2, 4, 24, 29, 31, 35, 37–8, 41 n.2, 42–3 n.43, 51, 58, 59, 73, 94, 95, 125–9, 131–2, 142, 144, 147, 151, 162, 165
"The Results of Human Action but not of Human Design" 115 n.97
Ricardo, David 91
Riva, Tommaso Redolfi 10
The Road to Serfdom (Hayek) 97
Robbins, Lionel 92
Ryle, Gilbert 97

sacrifice 122–7
Sanders, Bernie 168
Schmidt, Alfred 110 n.13
Schultz, Theodore 148, 149
second nature 3, 5, 11, 22, 30, 39, 87–90, 94–5, 103–10, 111 n.16, 119, 130, 135, 146, 155
self-preservation 5, 34, 35, 46 n.135, 102, 120–4, 126–8, 130, 132–6
self-regulation 100, 103, 107
The Sensory Order (Hayek) 97, 98
Shannon, Claude 114 n.80
shareholder primacy 75
Smith, Adam 91
social Darwinism 101
social domination 1, 5, 20, 22, 33, 38, 40, 55, 59, 63, 67, 73, 74, 76, 119, 120, 132, 151, 168
Socialist Calculation Debate 95
socialization 10, 50, 51, 73, 93, 104, 105, 109, 124, 136, 141, 151–2, 154, 155
  antagonistic 34, 158
  capitalist 23
  coercive 150
  digital 142
  by exchange 35
  interpersonal 151
  negative 37, 144
  neoliberal 5, 146, 149
  virtual 148
social labor 14, 17, 52, 106

socially necessary illusion of capitalist society   17, 34, 72, 107, 135
society   3, 46 n.139
   appearance of   35
   bourgeois   15–16, 21, 29, 56, 93
   commercial   91
   dialectical theory of   107
   essence of   35
   exchange (*Tauschgesellschaft*)   1, 3, 4, 9–47, 57, 62, 74, 76, 125
   as negative totality   4, 32
"Sociology and Psychology" (Adorno)   151
Sohn-Rethel, Alfred   4, 24–8, 44 n.86, 44–5 n.90
Soviet Union, 53, 54
   Golden Age of capitalism   58
spontaneity   23, 29, 103, 107, 129, 156
spontaneous order   98, 99, 101–3
Standing, Guy   158, 163 n.87
state capitalism   4, 53–7, 72, 75
Stevens, Mitchell   152–3
Stoetzler, Marcel   56, 121, 132, 139 n.92
Strange, Susan   71
subjective economics   93–4
surplus-value   18–20, 22, 32, 51, 61, 64, 65, 69, 74, 77, 149, 158

tacit knowledge, theory of   97
target marketing   153
Thatcher, Margaret   68, 70, 76
The Theory of the Novel (Lukács)   111 n.16
third technological revolution   68
Third World debt crisis   71
Tomba, Massimiliano   128, 132
totality   2
   antagonistic   22, 52
   capitalist   6, 20, 49, 51, 53, 56, 62–5, 73, 90, 93, 103, 165
   negative   4, 9, 32–40
   reproduction of   56
   social   6

subjective-objective   3
TPP. *See* Trans-Pacific Partnership Agreement
transcendental idealism   27–9
Trans-Pacific Partnership Agreement (TPP)   166
Trump, Donald   165, 166
Turing, Alan   138 n.58

UKIP   78
United Kingdom   80 n.36
   Brexit movement   165
   Independence Party   165
   neoliberal revolution   68
United States (US)   80 n.36
   Alt-Right   166
   cybernetics   99
   Federal Reserve   77
   Golden Age of capitalism   58, 60, 66
   mass cultural consumption   145
   neoliberal culture   158
   neoliberal revolution   68–70, 75–7
   New Right   68–71, 73, 74, 160–1 n.37
   private debt   167
   shareholder orthodoxy   75
"The Use of Knowledge in Society" (Hayek)   96
use-value   12, 13, 16, 26, 28, 143, 154
utility   92, 93

Veblen, Thorstein   91
Volker, Paul   68
Volker Shock   68
von Mises, Ludwig   95
von Neumann, John   138 n.58

wage-labor   19, 20, 31, 32
Walras, Leon   92
Whyte, William   151
Wiener, Norbert   99
World Bank   59, 67

www.ingramcontent.com/pod-product-compliance
Lightning Source LLC
Chambersburg PA
CBHW070638300426
44111CB00013B/2158